WHO WAS JESUS?

FINGERPRINTS OF THE CHRIST

D.M. MURDOCK

Foreword by Dr. Robert M. Price

Stellar House Publishing
www.stellarhousepublishing.com

ALSO BY D.M. MURDOCK a.k.a. ACHARYA S

The Christ Conspiracy: The Greatest Story Ever Sold
Suns of God: Krishna, Buddha and Christ Unveiled

Library of Congress Cataloging in Publication Data
Murdock, D.M./Acharya S
 Who was Jesus? Fingerprints of the Christ.
 1. Jesus Christ—Historicity 2. Christianity—Origin
Includes bibliographical references and index
ISBN: 0-9799631-0-9
ISBN13: 978-0-9799631-0-0

Design and layout by D.M. Murdock

"Dedicated to all the wonderful and inspiring people in life."

Table of Contents

Table of Contents

First Century Palestine

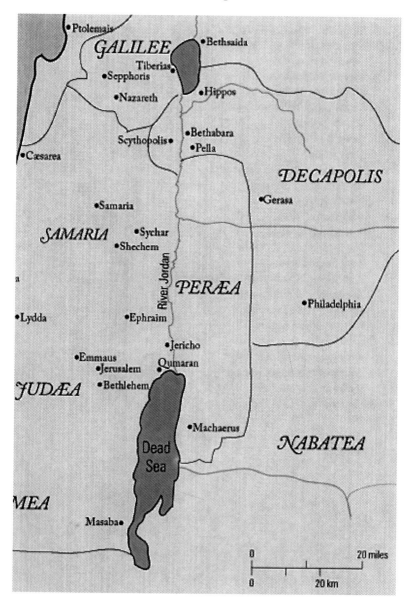

"The entire area in which the gospel story takes place is only 90 miles long."

Foreword

"The men of old, unlike in their simplicity to young philosophy, deemed that if they heard the truth even from 'oak or rock,' it was enough for them; whereas *you* seem to consider not whether a thing is or is not true, but who the speaker is and from what country the tale comes."

Socrates, *Plato's Phaedrus*

D.M. Murdock, familiarly known to admirers and friends as "Acharya," the Teacher, depends as much upon conservative writers, both Catholic and Protestant, this time around as she did on radical scholars in her first book, *The Christ Conspiracy*. I do not mean to suggest an unduly polemical goal or tone (indeed, she is everywhere moderate and restrained), but the effect is to take the fight right into the opposite camp. It can be a friendly debate, and it is good sport. Without rancor, differences of opinion are quite instructive. This time, she scrutinizes what might at first seem unexceptionable observations by evangelical scholars and apologists (usually the same thing) and Catholic scholars and encyclopedists, and then goes on to show how even their reassurances to the flock contain the seeds of serious doubt that Jesus was divine—or even human! Did he exist at all?

Ms. Murdock spends some time on textual criticism, "Lower Criticism," which has long served as a "safe" subdiscipline for sophisticated but conservative Christian scholars. Though textual criticism takes its starting point from the element of doubt, many or even most evangelicals see the need for it. Some of the first text critics were Plymouth Brethren and conservative Anglicans, and their concern was a natural extension of their doctrine of the verbal inspiration of the Bible. If the very words of the text were inspired, then, isn't it logical to get as close as we can to the authentic text? It may be tedious, but it is a holy task. How interesting, as Murdock's quotations suggest, that while wearing the cap of the text critic, an evangelical scholar stresses the complexity of the issue, the huge number of textual variants, i.e., errors of transmission; but when donning the hat of the apologist, the evangelical minimizes their importance! Oh, don't worry: most of the errors are unimportant bits of grammatical inaccuracy or of a wandering eye, the scribe writing what he expected to be next on the page, not what was actually there. So the Lower Critic wants to keep himself in business, but as an apologist, and lest Lower Criticism open the forbidden door to the Higher Criticism (questions of author-attribution, historical accuracy, etc.), he maintains that his labors were basically for nothing, since the New Testament is close enough to a perfect original. No important theological point hinges on a textual decision. Oh no? How about the all-important Trinity doctrine? If only 1 John 5:8b ("For there are three that bear witness in heaven: the Father, the Word, and the Holy Spirit, and these three are one.") had not been revealed as a cheat smuggled into the text by a pal of Erasmus, theologians would have firm "proof" of the Trinity.

Perhaps even worse is the fundamentalist retreat to the "original autographs" (the biblical writings as they came fresh from the pens of their authors). It is a true *pharmakon* such as the French philosopher Jacques Derrida discussed: a ventured remedy that turns out instead to be a poison. Benjamin B. Warfield, one of the chief architects of the modern notion of biblical inerrancy, demanded that, before one pronounced the Bible to be in error at any point, one must demonstrate that the original autographs contained the same text we are reading at that point. And that, as Warfield knew well, is impossible, the autographs having long since perished. How did Warfield (and his legions of followers) not see the terrible implication? Could we not propose that the Bible is as full of errors as Tom Paine and Colonel Ingersoll said it was, but then posit that once upon a time there existed a miraculous error-free Bible? Sure we could, and it would do us no good at all. That is a case of destroying the village in order to save it.

Ms. Murdock makes much of the neglected issue of a scripture the composition of which was ostensibly inspired, but whose preservation was apparently left to the shifting winds of fortune. If one were to claim only that the Bible had been infallibly inspired, we could not readily verify or falsify the claim, because the believer could always retreat to the autographs, or, failing that, he might appeal to an imaginary vindication in some "Bible Contradictions Seminar" to be offered one day in heaven. But if one were to claim the scripture has been infallibly *preserved* through the many centuries of copying, well, we can falsify that claim, and it's been done. So why believe in infallible inspiration either? Actually, there are "scriptural preservationists," but they are no better off in practical terms, since all they can claim is that God has seen to it that the true reading of every line has survived *somewhere* in vast manuscript tradition, like a needle in a haystack. And it is the textual critic's job to find it. And once you've honed the claim for providential preservation of inerrant scripture in this peculiar manner, where do you differ from mainstream text critics? They, too, hope the true text is back there somewhere. Neither side claims to have it.

Are the four gospels a quartet of independent witnesses? Murdock shows what first appears to be, again, non-controversial: that even Catholics and evangelicals are by and large disposed to accept source criticism, that Matthew and Luke used Mark, etc. But they do not seem to realize, as Murdock does, that this admission is doubly fatal. First, it means that at least some of the gospels are not based on eyewitness testimony. Luke and Mark never claim to be. Matthew and John share names with two characters who appear in the gospel story, but that does not even hint that they are supposed to be the disciples Matthew and John. If Matthew the evangelist were Matthew the eyewitness disciple, how is it possible he would base his gospel on the account of Mark, who was not? But if sophisticated evangelicals understand and accept basic source criticism, why do they continue to harmonize the gospels with the rationalization that different witnesses to the same event may include, exclude, or stress different elements, resulting in accounts that differ but are all accurate as far as they go? That analogy is simply impossible once you realize that source criticism entails redaction criticism: If author A uses source B yet differs at some point from B, then A has modified B. They are not independent.

Worse yet for the enterprise of apologists is that the very presupposition of source criticism disallows the appeal they make to verbal accuracy in the transmission of oral accounts of Jesus and his adventures (i.e., before they were recorded in the gospels). Leaving aside the doctrine of inerrancy (actually only pretending to do so), apologists claim that the unknown individuals who repeated and repeated the Jesus traditions did so with such remarkable fidelity that we may trust any given gospel passage to be an accurate report. But if that is true, then the whole basis for positing interdependence between written gospels is out the window! Source criticism is based on the axiom that no one passes down material with the verbal fidelity it would take for the gospels to be independent records of Jesus' words and yet so nearly identical.

Just as scholastic commentators on the Koran invented a special grammar to apply to the sacred text so it would say what they wanted it to say, so do Christian apologists have a set of rules, not for weighing evidence, but for twisting it toward a desired outcome. "Acharya" Murdock helpfully lists some of these for us. And she shows how the criterion for "plausibility" for such "eel wrigglers" (as the Buddha called them) is not whether such stratagems make good sense of the text the way we would read any other text, but rather if the rationalization would result in a reading more compatible with inerrantist dogma. We are not playing the same game as inerrantist apologists. Or, more to the point, they are not playing the game they claim they are playing, the historian's game. They have a different goal and play by different rules. No wonder they seem always to win as long as you don't realize what they are really doing. But now you will. Thanks, Acharya!

Robert M. Price, PhD
Author, *The Pre-Nicene New Testament*
August 30, 2007

Introduction

"Everyone—Hindus, Muslims, liberals, conservatives—wants to claim Jesus as their own. Why? Because He casts a shadow across world history, and no one wants to acknowledge being aligned against His ideas."

Dr. J.P. Moreland, "What Would Jesus Think or Do?"

"We are a Jesus-haunted culture that is so historically illiterate that anything can now pass for knowledge of Jesus."

Dr. Ben Witherington, III, "Tomb of the (Still) Unknown Ancients"

In the nearly two millennia since the story of Jesus Christ began to be circulated, millions of people have wondered, "Who is Jesus Christ?" Much ink has been spilled, and many thousands of books have been written about this grandest of gods and men, in the quest to portray the "real Jesus." Practically every personality type and special interest group has been able to find a reflection of itself in Jesus, and countless people have looked to Christ as their example, inspiration and champion. Many millions, in fact, are quite convinced that Christ is indeed *the* God of the universe who came to Earth in a human body 2,000 years ago. Still others have settled into a comfortable position that Jesus was a "nice guy" and a "great leader" or a "political rebel" who fought for the underdog. These individuals often believe that Jesus was simply a human being, not God, but that his enthusiastic followers added a series of fairytales to his biography after his death. A minority of others have looked at the gospel story with a jaundiced eye and found little evidence to be convinced of either of these two perspectives.

It has been remarked that, because of a lack of material outside of the New Testament, previous efforts at determining who Jesus was have relied heavily on "wishful thinking" on the part of numerous authors, who ultimately have found a Jesus who resembled their ideal man. Concerning this development, in specific as regards the Christ of the controversial Jesus Seminar, Christian apologist Dr. Gregory Boyd remarked, "Basically, they've discovered what they set out to find. Some think he was a political revolutionary, some a religious fanatic, some a wonder worker, some a feminist, some an egalitarian, some a subversive—there's a lot of diversity."[1] Christian apologist Dr. J.P. Moreland concurs: "In other words, the Jesus Seminar's methods for deciding what Jesus said and believed created a Jesus that looks exactly like the members of the Jesus Seminar."[2] The problem of discovering the "true Jesus" or the "historical Jesus," in fact, has been so acute that not a few observers have felt the same as Dr. Boyd when he also stated, "Jesus is not a symbol of anything unless he's rooted in history."[3] Indeed, this subject is important enough to warrant a serious examination that may yield some shocking and unexpected results in our scientific inquiry as to who Jesus was.

The life of Jesus Christ is principally drawn in four "gospels" or books found in the New Testament section of the Holy Bible. During the second century of the common era (CE), there were many other gospels, numbering around 50 and written by a variety of people, but these four were deemed "canonical," or authorized, and placed into the Bible. Along with the canonical letters or epistles, as well as the books of Acts and Revelation, these four gospels—the word "gospel" meaning, among other definitions, "good tidings"— are asserted to be the only truly inspired Christian texts out of hundreds. In other words, the faithful believe these books were written at the behest of God himself, with the guidance of the Holy Spirit. In the exploration here to discover Jesus, the analysis will be confined mainly to these four books, the Gospels according to Matthew, Mark, Luke and John, as well as certain other biblical and Christian texts. In determining the task at hand, the latest and best "forensic" methodology must be applied, to conduct an investigation that leaves no major stone unturned and does

---

[1] Strobel, 153.
[2] Moreland, "WWJTD."
[3] Strobel, 166-167.

not exclude the important details. Therefore, without shirking uncomfortable questions, unpopular positions and unpredicted conclusions, this scientific analysis of who Jesus was will attempt to identify the "fingerprints of the Christ."

The Gospel According to Matthew

"If His words were not accurately recorded in the Gospels, how can anyone know what He really taught? The truth is, we couldn't know. Further, if the remainder of the New Testament cannot be established to be historically reliable, then little if anything can be known about what true Christianity really is, teaches, or means."

Dr. John Ankerberg and Dr. John Weldon
"The Historical Reliability of the New Testament Text"

"If we want to read the gospels as eye witness accounts, historical records and so on, then not only are we in for some tough going, I think there's evidence within the material itself that it's not intended to be read that way."

Dr. Allen D. Callahan, "From Jesus to Christ: The Story of the Storytellers"

The gospel of Matthew is traditionally placed at the beginning of the New Testament canon, but there have been many debates over the centuries as to which book was written first, with arguments for practically every order. It is generally agreed that Matthew is placed first because it was done so in the most ancient traditions, and because it presents a satisfactory synopsis of Christ's life. In reality, over the centuries, every possible order for the gospels has been proposed, with a variety of reasons.

The Nativity of Jesus Christ

The story begins with a genealogy of Christ's ancestors, including the Jewish King David, which makes Christ the "son of David," as was asserted in the Old Testament that the coming messiah would be. Jesus's miraculous conception and birth are depicted as having been of the "virgin" from the Old Testament scripture Isaiah 7:14.[1] The nativity is accompanied by the tale of King Herod, the star and the wise men. Because Herod orders all male children under the age of two to be killed, so that the "king of the Jews" could not live to adulthood, Jesus's parents, Joseph and Mary, take Jesus into Egypt to escape Herod's wrath. They return after Herod has died, to live in Nazareth, so that the Old Testament scripture can be fulfilled that the savior was to be a "Nazarene."

The Baptism and Temptation

The next scene in Matthew cuts to Jesus's adulthood, when John the Baptist, preaching in the Judean wilderness, predicts Christ's coming and then baptizes him in the Jordan. During this event, the heavens open up to Jesus, the Holy Ghost descends on him in the shape of a dove, and a heavenly voice says, "This is my beloved Son, with whom I am well pleased." (Mt 3:16-17) Jesus next spends 40 days in the desert, being tempted by Satan, who offers him "all the kingdoms of the world." Christ resists the devil and emerges from the desert unscathed, but discovers that John the Baptist has been arrested, so he goes to Galilee, where he passes through Nazareth and onto Capernaum. Most of the rest of Matthew depicts Jesus as moving about in this northern part of Palestine.[2]

The Calling of the Disciples

At this point, Jesus begins to pick up his first followers, including the fishermen Peter and his brother Andrew, as well as the fishermen James and John, sons of Zebedee,

---

[1] Note on biblical translations: While the King James Version (KJV) of the Bible is currently the most popular in the United States, a fact that might warrant usage here, its language is so archaic as to make it difficult to read by both native and non-native English speakers alike. For that reason, unless otherwise noted the biblical passages presented here are from the Revised Standard Version (RSV), copyright © 1946, 1952, and 1971 National Council of the Churches of Christ in the United States of America. Used by permission. All rights reserved. (A fuller discussion of the differences between and problems with the various bible versions occurs below.)

[2] It is useful to keep in mind that the area in which this biblical drama allegedly occurred was a mere 90 miles in length.

leaving their father behind on the boat. With them, Jesus proceeds all over Galilee, preaching and teaching, as well as healing "every disease and every infirmity among the people." (Mt 4:23) According to this gospel, Jesus now begins to become very famous "throughout all Syria," with "great crowds" following him throughout Palestine "and from beyond the Jordan."

The Sermon on the Mount

With the throng in tow, Jesus climbs up a mountain and delivers the famous Sermon on the Mount, including the Beatitudes and the Lord's Prayer. In the Beatitudes, Jesus says that the "poor in spirit" are blessed, as are those who are in mourning, as well as the meek and those who are reviled and persecuted. Those who "hunger and thirst after righteousness," the merciful, the "pure in heart" and the peacemakers are also blessed. Christ further tells his followers that they are the "salt of the earth" and the "light of the world," adding: "Let your light so shine before men, that they may see your good works and give glory to your Father who is in heaven." (Mt 5:16)

In speaking of the commandment not to kill, which brings with it judgment, Jesus remarks that someone who becomes "angry with his brother" will also "be liable to judgment," and "whoever insults his brother shall be liable to council." Christ further admonishes that whoever says, "You fool!" will be "liable to the hell of fire." (Mt 5:22)

In discussing adultery, Jesus asserts that someone merely looking at a woman with lust "has already committed adultery with her in his heart." He then advises his followers to pluck out their eyes and throw them away if they cause them to sin. Christ's followers are also to cut off their hands for the same reason. At Matthew 5:32, Jesus further states that divorcing a woman for any reason other than infidelity or unchastity "makes her an adulteress" and that "whoever marries a divorced woman commits adultery."

Christ next cautions, "Do not swear at all," and then states, "Let what you say be simply 'Yes' or 'No'; anything more than this comes from evil." (Mt 5:34, 37) Jesus also advises, "Do not resist one who is evil. But if any one strikes you on the right cheek, turn to him the other also..." He commands us to give our cloak to anyone who sues for our coat and to go an extra mile with someone who forces us to go one mile. Christ exhorts his followers, "Give to him who begs from you, and do not refuse him who would borrow from you." (Mt. 5:39-42)

During the Sermon, Jesus utters the immortal words: "Love your enemies and pray for those who persecute you..." Christ says that this kind of behavior will make his followers "sons of the Father" in heaven. He also states, "You, therefore, must be perfect, as your heavenly Father is perfect." (Mt 5:44-48)

Next, Jesus asserts that if we practice our piety in front of others, we will receive no reward from our Father in heaven. Later (Mt 6:3-4), Christ admonishes not to pray in public or expose our alms-giving. He also warns not to "let your left hand know what your right hand is doing, so that your alms may be in secret; and your Father who sees in secret will reward you."

The Lord's Prayer

At Matthew 6:9-13, Christ teaches the proper way to pray, which is in a room with the door shut, seen by our Father in secret. Subsequently, Jesus teaches his followers the Lord's Prayer:

> "Our Father who art in heaven,
> Hallowed be thy name.
> Thy kingdom come,
> Thy will be done,
> On earth as it is in heaven.
> Give us this day our daily bread;
> And forgive us our debts,
> As we also have forgiven our debtors;
> And lead us not into temptation,
> But deliver us from evil."

Christ promises a reward also for fasting in secret, advising his followers to anoint their heads and wash their faces first. (Mt 6:17-18)

After teaching the Lord's Prayer and how to pray, Christ further advises his followers to "lay up" treasures for themselves not on Earth "but in heaven." Moreover, Jesus states, "You cannot serve God and mammon," the last word being translated as "treasure" or "riches." Jesus comments, "Take no thought for your life..." and do not be "anxious about your life, what you shall eat or what you shall drink, or what you shall put on." He points to the birds as being well taken care of by God—how much more valuable are we? Those who are concerned with what they eat, drink or wear possess little faith, since God knows we need them. Instead, we are to seek after righteousness and not be anxious about tomorrow, "for tomorrow will be anxious for itself." (Mt 6:19-34)

One of the most important passages in Jesus's Sermon is "Judge not, that you be not judged." (Mt 7:1) Following that exhortation, Christ tells his followers, "Do not give dogs what is holy; and do not throw your pearls before swine..." In his saying about knocking and having the door open, Jesus also says, "If you then, who are evil, know how to give good gifts to your children, how much more will your Father who is in heaven give good things to those who ask him!" He next recites what is known as the "Golden Rule," paraphrased as: "Do unto others as you would have them do unto you." But, he declares that "this is the law and the prophets." (Mt 7:12)

Next, Jesus advises his followers to "enter by the narrow gate," which refers to the sin-free way of living, because the wide path—full of sin and temptation—leads to destruction. The sinless path to heaven is difficult and for the few. Christ also warns to beware of false prophets, who are wolves in sheep's clothing and who will be known "by their fruits." Jesus declares that not everyone who calls him Lord will enter into the kingdom of heaven "but he who does the will of my Father who is in heaven." Lastly, Jesus tells the parable of the wise man who builds upon a rock, rather than the foolish who construct upon sand. (Mt 7:13-27)

Healing of the Sick and Casting out Demons

After Jesus finishes his sermon, the multitudes are "astonished by his teaching," and when he comes down the mountain he is followed by "great crowds." Surrounded by the sick, Christ heals a leper and then instructs him to "tell no man" about his healing. When he enters Capernaum again, a centurion approaches him about his paralyzed servant, whom Jesus also heals. (Mt 8:5-13) Jesus then heals Peter's mother-in-law and many demoniacs, in fulfillment of scripture in the OT book of Isaiah. Continuing to attract great crowds around him, Christ gets into a boat with his disciples. Jesus is asleep in the boat when a sudden storm arises, and he rebukes his disciples when they wake him out of fear. He next famously calms the sea.

Proceeding to the "country of the Gadarenes," Jesus casts the demons out of a couple of people, sending them into a herd of swine, which promptly drown themselves. At this point, "all the city came out to meet Jesus," begging him to leave the area. (Mt 8:34) Christ returns to the boat and to Nazareth, where he heals another paralyzed man and then finally meets Matthew. Jesus is approached by "a ruler" whose daughter has just died. Christ raises her from the dead, heals a bleeding woman and two blind men, but charges the latter not to tell anyone about the healing. Nevertheless, the two go out and "spread his fame though all that district." (Mt 9:31) The Pharisees at this point are starting to become agitated and claim Jesus is casting out demons "by the prince of demons."

The Mission of the Twelve

Next, Jesus is depicted as going "about all the cities and villages," again teaching, preaching and healing. He gathers his 12 disciples and gives them their mission and authority, and the disciples are named at this point in the gospel (Mt 10:2-4):

> Simon, who is called Peter, and Andrew his brother; James the son of Zebedee, and John his brother; Philip and Bartholomew; Thomas and Matthew the tax collector; James the son of Alphaeus, and Thaddaeus; Simon the Cananaean, and Judas Iscariot, who betrayed him.

Jesus specifically tells his disciples not to go to the Gentiles or Samaritans but only to the "lost sheep of the house of Israel." He also instructs them that they will be able to heal the sick, raise the dead and cast out demons, and that they should take no money or any extra belongings. Jesus then informs his disciples that any town which does not welcome them will be harshly judged by God, describing a fierce martyrdom scene:

> Brother will deliver up brother to death, and the father his child, and children their parents and have them put to death; and you will be hated by all for my name's sake. But he who endures to the end will be saved. When they persecute you in one town, flee to the next; for truly, I say to you, you will not have gone through all the towns of Israel, before the Son of man comes.... (Mt 10:21-23)

Christ next says:

> Do not think that I have come to bring peace on earth; I have not come to bring peace, but a sword. For I have come to set a man against his father, and a daughter against her mother, and a daughter-in-law against her mother-in-law; and a man's foes will be those of his own household. He who loves his father or mother more than me is not worthy of me; and he who loves son or daughter more than me is not worthy of me; and he who does not take his cross and follow me is not worthy of me. He who finds his life will lose it, and he who loses his life for my sake will find it. (Mt 10:34-39)

After giving this speech, Jesus goes about preaching in the cities. The imprisoned Baptist hears about Christ's work and sends word to ask him if he is the messiah. Jesus replies in the affirmative. He then castigates various cities, such as Chorazin and Capernaum.

Working on the Sabbath

Christ and his disciples proceed to pick grain to eat on the sabbath, for which they are excoriated by the Pharisees for defiling the sabbath. Jesus replies that he is the "lord of the sabbath" and therefore cannot defile it. He continues on to their synagogue, where he heals a man with a withered hand. Again, Jesus is assailed for working on the sabbath, but he responds by pointing out that the Jews themselves would pull a sheep out of a pit but would not lift a finger to help a man on the sabbath. At this point, the Pharisees begin to plot to destroy Jesus.

Although Christ is aware of the plot against him, he nevertheless keeps healing people, in fulfillment of another of Isaiah's prophecies. The Pharisees continue to harass Jesus, again saying he is working by the prince of demons. Christ replies with the famous line "a house divided against itself cannot stand." (Mt 12:25) Jesus also says that those who speak against him will be forgiven but not those who blaspheme the Holy Spirit. He then calls the Pharisees and other Jews present a "brood of vipers." (Mt 12:34) Jesus is asked for a sign, but he responds that the only sign will be that of Jonah, meaning that he will be "three days and three nights in the heart of the earth." (Mt 12:40) When Christ is informed that his mother and brothers are outside, he asks, "Who is my mother, and who are my brothers?"

John the Baptist Beheaded

Jesus proceeds to go outside near the sea, where he is surrounded by great multitudes. He begins telling the crowds various parables, which the disciples question him about. Returning inside the house, he explains some of these parables further to his disciples. Afterwards, Christ goes back to Nazareth, where the people are astonished to see what the carpenter's son has become. Eventually, Herod hears about Jesus's presence, and nervously believes that he is John the Baptist raised from the dead, as Herod has had John beheaded at the behest of his wife's daughter. When Christ discovers this gruesome fact, he goes off in a boat alone, but he is followed again by great crowds. The throng becomes hungry, so Jesus takes the little food present, five loaves of bread and two fish, and miraculously multiplies them to distribute to the hungry horde, feeding about 5,000 people. (Mt 14:21)

Walking on Water

After this feast, Jesus sends the disciples into the boat to the other side of the sea, while he retires to pray by himself in the hills. After a time, Christ walks across the water to reach the boat, which is "many furlongs distant from the land." (Mt 14:24) His disciples become terrified by the sight, thinking he is a ghost, but he assures them otherwise. Jesus then leads Peter out of the boat to walk on the water as well. These miracles cause the disciples to fall down and pronounce Christ the "Son of God." Across the sea in Genesaret, once again Jesus heals the crowd and is approached by the Pharisees, who castigate him for not compelling his disciples to wash their hands before they eat. Christ then tells the people it is not what goes into a man's mouth but what comes out of a man's mouth that defiles him. (Mt 15:11)

The Canaanite Woman

Jesus next goes to Tyre and Sidon, where a "Canaanite" woman approaches him, begging for his help. He ignores her and tells his disciples that he came only for the lost sheep of Israel. He then compares the woman with a "dog," but she responds that even a dog needs crumbs, so he heals her because of her faith in him. As Jesus continues along the Sea of Galilee, he is pursued by great crowds once again who beseech him to heal them. Once more Christ multiplies a few fishes and seven loaves in order to feed the hungry throng of about 4,000 people. (Mt 15:37-38)

Jesus returns to the boat and heads off to another region, where again he is confronted by the Pharisees and Sadducees, who want to test him with a "sign from heaven." Christ responds that "an evil and adulterous generation seeks for a sign, but no sign shall be given except the sign of Jonah." (Mt 16:4) When the disciples forget the miracle of the multiplying of the loaves, Jesus blames the Pharisees and Sadducees.

Peter the "Rock"

Later, when Jesus is in Caesarea, he tells Peter that the apostle is Jesus's "rock" and that Christ's church will be built upon Peter. Jesus then instructs his disciples not to tell anyone that he is the Christ and informs them that he will be taken away and killed, but will rise again on the third day. Peter, upset by this news, objects to anything bad happening to Jesus, to which Christ replies, "Get behind me, Satan!" (Mt 16:23) Jesus then tells his disciples to take up the cross and follow him, stating, "Truly, I say to you, there are some standing here who will not taste death before they see the Son of man coming in his kingdom." (Mt 16:28)

The Transfiguration

Jesus next takes Peter, James and his brother John up to a mountain, where Christ is transfigured in front of them, his face shining like the sun and his garments becoming "white as light." Moses and Elijah appear on either side of Jesus, and begin speaking with him. A voice comes out of a cloud, saying, "This is my beloved Son, with whom I am well pleased; listen to him." (Mt 17:5) Jesus then appears by himself and, as the group proceeds down the mountain, instructs the others not to say anything about this event until he is risen from the dead. Christ also informs them that John the Baptist was Elijah, for whose return the scribes had been waiting. As the four come down the mountain, the crowd comes back and asks for more healings. Christ lectures the throng and his disciples about their lack of faith. Once more, while in Galilee Jesus states that he will be taken, killed and will rise again after three days.

Becoming like Children

In Capernaum, the disciples are asked if their master pays taxes, to which they respond "yes." Next comes Jesus's famous pronouncement, "Truly, I say to you, unless you turn and become like children, you will never enter the kingdom of heaven. Whoever humbles himself like this child, he is the greatest in the kingdom of heaven." (Mt 18:3-4) Jesus then instructs the people that they should cut off their hand or foot, and pluck out their eye, if these cause them to sin. He reiterates that children should not be led astray, and then instructs the disciples in forgiveness.

Christ also says that if someone's brother sins against him, he should confront him, with witnesses if necessary. If the brother doesn't repent, the offended person should confide in the church, but if the offender still doesn't listen, declares Jesus, "let him be to you as a Gentile and a tax collector," which are bad things to be avoided. Still, when Peter asks Jesus how many times he should forgive his brother's sins against him, Christ replies that it should be not seven times but "seventy times seven." (Mt. 18:22) He then tells a story about a king who was owed money by a servant but who forgave him the debt, until the servant attacked another servant who owed *him* money and then had him put in prison. Commenting on this parable, Jesus tells his followers that his heavenly Father would imprison them in the same manner, if they did not forgive their brothers "from their hearts."

Eunuchs for the Kingdom of Heaven

Afterwards, Jesus leaves Galilee and goes to Judea, again followed by large crowds who are healed by him. In response to a question regarding divorce, Christ strictly forbids it and says that a person who marries after an improper divorce is guilty of adultery. Jesus then instructs men to become eunuchs if they can, by being castrated:

> "For there are eunuchs who have been so from birth, and there are eunuchs who have been made eunuchs by men, and there are eunuchs who have made themselves eunuchs for the kingdom of heaven. He who is able to receive this, let him receive it." (Mt 19:12)

Jesus further teaches the crowd about the kingdom of heaven and eternal life, exhorting the people to follow the commandments, saying, "Honor your father and mother."

The Rich Young Man

A young man in the crowd asks Jesus what good he should do to attain to eternal life. Christ wonders why the man is asking this question, but replies that he should keep the commandments: "You shall not kill, you shall not commit adultery. You shall not steal, You shall not bear false witness, Honor your father and mother, and, You shall love your neighbor as yourself." (Mt. 19:18-19) The youth replies that he had already kept all those commandments and then asks what he is still lacking. Jesus answers that if he "would be perfect," he would have to sell his possessions and "give to the poor." He should thus lay up his treasures in heaven and follow Christ. As this fellow is rich, he leaves feeling despondent.

Jesus next makes his famous pronouncement that it is easier for a "camel" to pass through the eye of a needle than for a rich man to enter heaven. After that, Christ tells his followers, "And every one who has left houses or brothers or sisters or father or mother or children or lands, for my name's sake, will receive a hundredfold, and inherit eternal life." (Mt 19:29)

Jesus and the 12 disciples begin to make their way to Jerusalem, with Christ informing them that he would be taken and killed, and delivered up to the Gentiles, "to be mocked and scourged and crucified, and he will be raised on the third day." (Mt 20:18) At this point, the mother of the brothers Zebedee, James and John, asks Jesus to appoint them at his left and right hands in heaven. Christ responds that it is not *his* decision but that of his Father. The other disciples are angered by the brothers' audacity.

Entry into Jerusalem

As the group is leaving Jericho, they are followed by great crowds once again. Two blind men beg Jesus to have mercy on them, and he restores their sight. Finally, Jesus and his disciples reach the Mount of Olives, near Jerusalem, where Christ sends two of the disciples to fetch an ass and her colt, which he would ride into Jerusalem. He instructs the disciples just to take the animals and to tell anyone who might object that the "Lord has need of them." (Mt 21:3) This event occurs in fulfillment of an Old Testament prophecy. In this manner, Jesus enters the city of Jerusalem, amid shouts of "Hosanna to the Son of David!"

Driving out the Moneychangers

Once in Jerusalem, Jesus enters the temple and overturns the tables of the moneychangers, saying that they have converted the holy place into a "den of robbers." Christ then heals those who come to him in the temple, but his behavior angers the chief priests and scribes, who object to the crowd saying, "Hosanna to the Son of David." Jesus responds with his famous line, "Out of the mouth of babes and sucklings thou hast brought forth perfect praise?" (Mt 21:16)

Cursing the Fig Tree

Jesus then proceeds to Bethany, where, hungry, he curses a fig tree because it has no fruit for him to eat. The tree promptly withers, leaving his disciples marveling, to whom he responds that by faith they themselves can move a mountain.

Next, Jesus enters the temple and is challenged by the chief priests and elders. He refuses to answer their questions about his authority and instead tells some parables. He then identifies himself with the "very stone which the builders rejected" (Mt 21:42), a reference to a scripture in Psalms. Christ's authority disturbs the chief priests and Pharisees, who feel the crowd might consider him a prophet. Jesus tells more parables and then, when the Pharisees try to trap him by questions about paying taxes to Caesar, he asks them whose likeness is on a coin he shows them, to which they respond, "Caesar." At this point, Jesus says, "Render therefore to Caesar the things that are Caesar's, and to God the things that are God's." (Mt 22:21) The priests and Pharisees are astounded and go away. Christ is next challenged by the Sadducees about the resurrection, and again the Pharisees come back to ask him more questions. Jesus publicly castigates the scribes and Pharisees, calling them "hypocrites" and "blind fools." Says he:

> "Woe to you, scribes and Pharisees, hypocrites! For you are like white-washed tombs, which outwardly appear beautiful, but within they are full of dead men's bones and all uncleanness. So you also outwardly appear righteous to men, but within you are full of hypocrisy and iniquity." (Mt 23:27-28)

Jesus again calls the scribes and Pharisees "serpents" and a "brood of vipers," asking how they have escaped "being sentenced to hell." He further castigates Jerusalem for killing its prophets. Leaving the temple, Jesus remarks that every last stone of it will be thrown to the ground.

Signs of the Times/Second Coming

While sitting on the Mount of Olives, Jesus answers his disciples' questions about the sign of his "coming and the close of the age." Replying that many false Christs will come to lead them astray, Jesus then states:

> "For nation will rise against nation, and kingdom against kingdom, and there will be famines and earthquakes in various places; all this is but the beginning of the sufferings." (Mt 24:7-8)

Christ next reiterates that his disciples will be hated for his name's sake and that they too will suffer being put to death. He further explains that there will be false prophets and that Judea will be laid waste as prophesied in the Old Testament book of Daniel. Next, he speaks of the coming tribulation, when the sun and moon will be darkened, and "the stars will fall from heaven," after which the "sign of the Son of man" will appear in heaven. As the people of Earth mourn, they will see the "Son of man coming on the clouds of heaven." Jesus then says, "Truly, I say to you, this generation will not pass away till all these things take place." He next exhorts his followers to be watchful of this day and tells them more parables. When Jesus is done speaking about these things, he tells his disciples that he will be taken away in two days' time, at the Passover, when he will be crucified. As Jesus is talking, the chief priests and elders are gathering in the house of the high priest, Caiaphas, where they plot to arrest Jesus and kill him.

Jesus's Anointment with Oil

While Jesus is staying at Bethany, a woman with an alabaster jar approaches him and pours costly ointment over his head. This act incenses the disciples, who think it is a waste of money, which could have been given to the poor. Christ responds that the woman has done a "beautiful thing" by preparing him for his burial. "For," says Jesus, "you always have the poor with you, but you will not always have me." (Mt 26:11) At this point, Judas approaches the priests and agrees to deliver Jesus to them for the sum of 30 pieces of silver.

The Last Supper

On the first day of the Passover, Jesus and his disciples sit for their last supper together, at which time Christ tells the 12 that someone among them will shortly betray him. Judas singles himself out, and Christ affirms that he knows it is Judas who will betray him. Jesus next picks up the bread, breaks it and passes it around, saying, "Take, eat; this is my body." He also lifts up his cup of wine and gives it to them, saying, "Drink of it, all of you; for this is my blood of the covenant, which is poured out for many for the forgiveness of sins." (Mt 26:28)

After singing a hymn, the group continues to the Mount of Olives, where Jesus tells them he will be "struck down" but will rise and go ahead of them to Galilee. He says that as he, their shepherd, is struck down, so the sheep will flee, but Peter objects that he will never "fall away" from Jesus. Christ assures Peter that he will indeed deny him.

The Garden of Gethsemane

Jesus and the disciples then proceed to Gethsemane, where Christ exhorts them to sit while he goes to pray, taking with him Peter, James and John. Jesus expresses regret at what is about to transpire, asking his Father in heaven to "let this cup pass" from him. (Mt. 26:39) Christ then approaches the disciples, hoping they will stay awake with him, but they cannot, so he goes and prays again, twice more asking his Father to absolve him from his coming duty. After these private moments, Jesus wakens the disciples and tells them that Judas is near with the authorities, who have come to arrest him. Judas informs the priests and elders that he will identify Christ by giving him a kiss.

The Betrayal by Judas

When Judas arrives, Jesus asks him, "Friend, why are you here?" After Judas kisses Christ, someone next to him takes out his sword and cuts off the ear of a priest's slave. Christ tells this armed person, "Put your sword back into its place; for all who take the sword will perish by the sword." (Mt 26:52) Jesus further exhorts his followers to understand that what is about to happen was prophesied and must be fulfilled. At this point, the disciples run away.

Christ's Trial

After he is seized, Jesus is led to the high priest Caiaphas, who castigates him and tears his robe, accusing him of blasphemy when Jesus affirms his question of whether or not he is the Christ. The scribes and elders present insist that Jesus must be killed for blasphemy. Outside, Peter has followed Jesus, but, just as Christ predicted, when Peter is identified, he denies that he ever knew Jesus, no less than three times.

In the morning, Jesus is bound and brought before the Roman governor Pilate. At this point, Judas becomes remorseful and tries to return the 30 silver pieces of "blood money." When the priests won't take back the money, Judas throws it to the ground, and then goes out and hangs himself. The money is used to buy a "potter's field" in which to bury "strangers," including Judas.

Meanwhile, Pilate is grilling Jesus over the latter being called "King of the Jews." Because it is a custom during Passover to release a prisoner, Pilate asks the crowd outside whom to let go. The crowd shouts that they want the infamous criminal Barabbas released and Christ crucified. Pilate then takes some water and symbolically washes his hands of the blood of an innocent person. In response to his action, the crowd shouts, "His blood be on us and on our children!" (Mt 27:25) Barabbas is released, while Jesus is scourged and prepared for crucifixion.

The Passion and Crucifixion

The soldiers remove Jesus's robe and put a scarlet one on him, as well as a crown of thorns on his head and a reed in his hand to serve as a scepter. Then they make fun of him, calling him, "King of the Jews," while they spit on him and beat him. Finally, they put Christ's clothes back on him and take him to be crucified.

While they are proceeding to Golgotha, the soldiers compel a man called Simon of Cyrene to carry Jesus's cross. They then give Christ wine mixed with gall to drink, which he refuses. After they crucify him, they divide up his clothes and place a sign above his head reading, "This is Jesus the King of the Jews." (Mt 27:37) Two robbers are crucified on either side of him, they too joining in the abuse being heaped upon Jesus. The passersby also taunt Christ that he claimed he could tear down the temple and rebuild it in three days, but he cannot save himself. From the sixth to ninth hours after Jesus is crucified, the land becomes dark, and Jesus utters the words, "My God, my God, why hast thou forsaken me?" (Mt 27:46) Christ is given vinegar to drink, but shortly after, he dies.

The Resurrection of the Dead

At the point of Jesus's death, the following occurs, according to Matthew:

> "And behold, the curtain of the temple was torn in two, from top to bottom; and the earth shook, and the rocks were split; the tombs were also opened, and many bodies of the saints who had fallen asleep were raised, and coming out of the tombs after his resurrection they went into the holy city and appeared to many."

These supernatural events make many believers of the people present, including some of the soldiers who were persecuting Christ. Eventually, a rich man named Joseph of Arimathea approaches Pilate and begs for Jesus's body, which he receives and lays to rest in his own tomb, rolling a rock in front of it. Mary Magdalene and Mary the mother of the Zebedee brothers, James and John, remain close to Jesus and outside his tomb. The Pharisees, remembering that Christ had proclaimed he would rise again after three days, post a guard at the tomb and make sure the rock is sealed, so that Christ's followers can't steal his body and pretend that he has risen.

The Empty Tomb

The next day, the two Marys approach the sepulcher, but an earthquake occurs, and an angel is found sitting on the rock he has rolled away from the tomb. The angel advises the women that Jesus has risen from the dead, at which point they run off in great joy. Jesus encounters them on the way and says, "Hail!" (Mt 28:9) The Marys fall to Christ's feet, and he instructs them to go tell all his disciples that he has risen and that they will see him in Galilee. The priests, having discovered that the tomb is empty, pay soldiers to spread the rumor that the disciples have stolen the body, "and this story," says Matthew, "has been spread among the Jews to this day." (Mt 28:15)

The remaining disciples, minus Judas, journey to Galilee, where they find Jesus on the mountain, but are doubtful and afraid. Christ tells them that he now has "all authority in heaven and on earth" and that they should preach the gospel all over the world. He then says that he will be with them "to the close of the age."

Conclusion

Thus ends the book of Matthew, with no mention of the ascension of Christ into heaven, as recorded in Mark and Luke. Like the ascension, there are many other events, themes or selections—called "pericopes"—present in the other gospels, including John, but lacking in Matthew. In Matthew's gospel, however, there appear over 300 verses not included in the other evangelists. Concerning the parts or pericopes "peculiar" to Matthew and not found in the other gospels, the authoritative Christian source the *Catholic Encyclopedia* ("CE") states:

> These are numerous, as Matthew has 330 verses that are distinctly his own. Sometimes long passages occur, such as those recording the Nativity and early Childhood (i, ii), the cure of the two blind men and one dumb man (ix, 27-34), the death of Judas (xxvii, 3-10), the guard placed at the Sepulchre (xxvii, 62-66), the imposture of the chief priests (xxviii, 11-15), the apparition of Jesus in Galilee (xxviii, 16-20), a great portion of the Sermon on the Mount (v, 17-37; vi, 1-8; vii, 12-23), parables (xiii, 24-30; 35-53; xxv, 1-13), the Last Judgment (xxv, 31-46), etc., and sometimes detached sentences, as in xxiii, 3, 28, 33; xxvii, 25, etc.... Those passages in which Matthew reminds us that facts in the life of Jesus are the fulfilment of the prophecies, are likewise noted as peculiar to him.... ("Gospel of St. Matthew")

The pericopes found in Matthew and not elsewhere include the following:

- Joseph's vision (Mt 1:20-24)
- The visit by the wise men (Mt 2:1-12)
- The flight of Joseph, Mary and the babe into Egypt (Mt 2:13-15)
- Herod's massacre of the infants (Mt 2:16)
- Judas's death (Mt 27:13)
- The saints rising out of their graves at the crucifixion (Mt 27:52)
- The "baptismal commission" (Mt 28:19-20)

Despite the differences, a detailed comparison of the gospels of Matthew, Mark and Luke reveals that these three are not independent of each other, which is why they are grouped together as "synoptics." The term "synoptic" means "to see together," although in reality the discrepancies even among these three gospels are significant. The study of this subject is called the "Synoptic Problem" and is defined by conservative evangelical Christian scholar, professor of theological studies and dean of the Graduate school of Theology at Wheaton College Merrill C. Tenney in *New Testament Survey*:

> ...If the three Synoptic Gospels are totally independent of each other in origin and development, why do they resemble each other so closely, even to exact verbal agreement in many places? If, on the other hand, they have a literary relationship to each other, how can they be three independent witnesses to the deeds and teachings of the Lord Jesus Christ?[1]

This latter point is an important one, as it is asserted that the historicity of the gospel story is enhanced by the existence of more than one "eyewitness account." Moreover, it should be kept in mind that two of three synoptics, Mark and Luke, were not even eyewitnesses but based their accounts on those of others.

Regarding the Gospel of Matthew, Dr. Tenney—who was one of the translators of the NASB and NIV editions of the Bible—evinces that it was based on "notes that Matthew took

---

[1] Tenney, 139.

on Jesus' teaching," with a narrative that "closely...resembles Mark." He then states that this resemblance between the two gospels "could be explained on the basis of common tradition and living contact, as well as by appropriation of written work."[1] In reality, centuries-long New Testament scholarship has demonstrated the complexity of the issues surrounding the authorship of the gospels, including their value as "eyewitness" documents. In this regard, the phrase "appropriation of written work" is important to note, as it affirms that the authors were copying either each other or other sources, not simply relating their own memories as alleged eyewitnesses (Matthew and John) or companions to eyewitnesses (Mark and Luke). As we shall see, when it comes to who wrote the gospels and what they based their accounts on, there is more to the mystery than meets the eye.

---

[1] Tenney, 144.

The Gospel According to Mark

"The Gospels are neither histories nor biographies, even within the ancient tolerances for those genres."

Dr. John Dominic Crossan, *The Historical Jesus*

The general order of all three of the synoptic gospels, Matthew, Mark and Luke, proceeds through Jesus's life from "his birth, baptism, temptation, ministry, passion, death and then resurrection." Between the gospels of Matthew and Mark appear "many points of resemblance in the construction of sentences," as well as similarities in "their mode of expression, often unusual, and in short phrases," while in certain pericopes "the greater part of the terms are identical."[1] For a variety of reasons, including the fact that nearly the entirety of Mark's gospel appears within Matthew, as well as these various germane similarities between the texts, many scholars have concluded that Mark was the first gospel and that Matthew and Luke based theirs upon his. Because Mark contains verses not found in the other synoptics, among other reasons, other scholars aver that Mark is founded upon another document, "Ur-Markus," which is the basis also of Matthew and Luke.

Was Mark First?

In reality, there are a number of instances in Mark which indicate that in order to follow the tale the reader would need to have been familiar with details of the gospel story that are not presented in that text. For example, neither Mark nor John mention the virgin birth—if Mark's gospel was the first, which means he may have thought it would stand alone, how could he leave out such a significant event? Another such instance appears in Mark's reportage of what happened to John the Baptist (Mk 1:14): The phrase "[a]fter John was arrested" presumes the reader already knew what had happened, indicating that Mark expected his readers to have previously read *another preceding gospel*. These

---

[1] *Catholic Encyclopedia*, "Gospel of Matthew."

examples are among several such reasons why Matthew's gospel has been placed first.

Indeed, it has even been suggested that Mark was written *in response to* criticisms of Matthew's gospel. One example used to craft the case that Mark was composed in order to answer commentary about Matthew occurs in the story of Jesus calling James and John from their boat, after which the two run off and leave their father alone. Perhaps this behavior caused Jesus to look like someone who led children away from their parents, directly contravening Jewish customs that make disobeying one's parents a capital offense, punishable by stoning. In Mark (1:20), at the end of the verse where James and John leave their father in the boat, we find the phrase "with hired servants" appended to the sentence, softening the impression of abandonment.

In discussing the possible order of the gospels, however, the Catholic Encyclopedia comments that Mark "makes no reference to the adoration, nor to the striking confession of the disciples that Jesus was [the] Son of God." CE then asks, "how can we account for this, if he had Matthew's report before him?... It would seem, therefore, that the view which makes the Second Gospel dependent upon the First is not satisfactory."[1]

Moreover, even though it also appears to have been built upon Matthew in order to answer questions raised by that gospel, the beginning of Mark seems to have been written to follow directly the last Old Testament book of Malachi, since, instead of the birth narrative, Mark begins his gospel with an account of John the Baptist, the "voice crying in the wilderness" and "the messenger" as prophesied "in the prophets," e.g., Malachi.

Comparison of Matthew and Mark

Furthermore, although there are many striking similarities that demonstrate common source texts, there are also details in each gospel that differ significantly in some places, with serious chronological discrepancies and other difficulties as well. Much shorter than Matthew's, the gospel of Mark contains several important differences, including in the

---

[1] *CE*, "Gospel of St. Mark."

language, story details and chronology of events. The differences between Mark and Matthew include the omission in Matthew of 31 verses found in Mark, as at 1:23-28; 4:26-29; 7:32-36; 8:22-26; 9:39, 40; and 12:41-44. The pericopes present in Mark but not in Matthew include the risen Jesus appearing to the disciples in Jerusalem, and the ascension. Yet another difference can be seen at Matthew 5:15, with a passage from the Sermon on the Mount, which Mark (4:21) places in a different setting. In another instance of disparity between the texts, three of Jesus's miracles appear together at Matthew 8:1-5 but are set apart in Mark (1:40-44; 3:12, 5:43, 7:36, 8:30, 9:9). Also, in the pericope of the demoniac's exorcism, in Matthew (8:28) there are two possessed men, while in Mark (5:2) there is only one. At Matthew 26:34, Peter is depicted as denying Christ three times before the cock crows; whereas, in Mark (14:68), the apostle only manages two denials prior to the rooster crowing.

The chronological order between Matthew and Mark diverges in several places as well, such as at Matthew 8:23-9:9, depicting events that are given a different arrangement at Mark 4:36-41, 5:1-17 and 2:1-12. In Matthew, Jesus climbs into in a boat, calms the storm, heals the demoniac, goes back to Galilee and heals the paralytic. Mark parallels Matthew up to the point of the healing of the paralytic, which he puts much earlier in the narrative at 2:1-12, long before Jesus gets into the boat.

Another serious chronological discrepancy occurs in the story of Jesus raising Jairus's daughter from the dead (Mt 9:18-26; Mk 5:21-43; Lk 8:40-56). As evangelical Christian Tom Dixon relates:

> Mark and Luke assert that Jairus approached Jesus when he and the disciples got out of the boat near Capernaum, as crowds came rushing up to him. Matthew, on the other hand, states that it was while John the Baptist's disciples were talking with Jesus at Matthew's house.

Yet another disparity occurs with the story of Jesus overturning the tables of the moneychangers in the temple. In Matthew, Christ enters Jerusalem, cleanses the temple, spends the night in Bethany and the next day curses the fig tree, which immediately withers. (Mt 21:12) In Mark, however, Jesus enters Jerusalem, spends the night in Bethany, curses the fig tree, cleanses the temple, and then the next day the disciples notice the fig tree is withered. (Mk 11:11-21) Moreover, all the synoptists place the cleansing of the temple at the *end* of their gospels, while John puts it at the *beginning* of the story.

In addition, while Matthew records more of Jesus's sayings and speeches, Mark is more detailed about the events or narrative of the story, adding more or less vague references to time and place. Matthew, however, is more precise about other facts, and it is generally agreed that Matthew's Greek is more elegant and refined than Mark's. Furthermore, it appears that Matthew was concerned with painting Jesus and the disciples in a more favorable light, omitting Christ's displays of anger (Mk 3:5) and other overwrought emotionality (Mk 3:21), as well as the evident dimwittedness, hardheartedness and trepidation of the disciples (Mk 6:52; 8:17-21; 9:32). Matthew seems more aware of the (Jewish) readers' sensibilities concerning religious customs, excluding, for instance, the "Saying of the Lord" at Mark 2:27: "And he said to them: 'The sabbath was made for man, not man for the sabbath.'" Regarding these differences between Matthew and Mark, the Catholic Encyclopedia states, "Omissions or alterations of this kind are very numerous."[1]

The Missing Scriptures

One of the most noticeable omissions in the gospels appears in the last verses of Mark, 16:9-20, which are absent in several versions of the Bible, including the Revised Standard Version (RSV), which appends them in a footnote. This omitted pericope concerns the appearance of the risen Christ to Mary Magdalene and others. The RSV also excludes some sentences at the end of Mark 16:8, referring to Jesus sending out "the sacred and imperishable proclamation of eternal life." Also absent in the RSV is the ascension, which is included in the King James Version (KJV). The RSV further

---

[1] *CE,* "Gospel of St. Matthew."

places Mark 11:26 in a footnote, while the KJV puts it in the text. The King James Bible was translated using preceding English translations and Greek texts dating to the 12th to 15th centuries—the "Textus Receptus"—as well as "some influence from the Latin Vulgate." The RSV utilized the most ancient Greek manuscripts currently extant, along with preceding English translations such as the KJV and others. Certain Fundamentalist Protestant Christians believe that the KJV is "inspired" and "inerrant," regardless of the fact that the texts upon which it was based differ in many places from the earliest Greek manuscripts, which were not available during the translation of the King James Bible. The original Textus Receptus (TR) compiled by Dutch theologian Erasmus (1516) was hurriedly put together and contained "thousands of typographical errors," as well as scribal commentary that was not in the original Greek. In 1550, the TR was eventually reissued by Stephanus/Stephens, whose edition was the basis of the KJV, with a significant amount of the same problems intact. The fact that various versions of the Bible differ from each other is very significant and needs to be kept in mind, as does the realization of the flawed nature of the Textus Receptus.

The Catholic Bible, the Douay-Rheims, based on St. Jerome's Latin Vulgate translation of the 5th century, contains all of the controversial verses in Mark, about which the Catholic Encyclopedia remarks:

> ...the great textual problem of the Gospel concerns the genuineness of the last twelve verses. Three conclusions of the Gospel are known: the long conclusion, as in our [Catholic] Bibles, containing verses 9-20, the short one ending with the verse 8...and an intermediate form...[1]

The CE relates one argument that these verses were present in the original text but became lost at some point, proposing a "defective copy" missing the scriptures that "fell into the hands of ignorant scribes" who spread the error. This suggestion indicates that Christian scholars agree there are *mistakes* in the transmission of the gospel texts, which would in turn imply that the Holy Spirit was *not* infallibly

---

[1] *CE*, "Gospel of St. Mark."

overseeing the all-important composition and *copying* of the gospels, as has been asserted by certain Christian fundamentalists in regard to various manuscripts, including the Textus Receptus.

Concerning the last verses of Mark, in *What Critics Ask*, Christian apologist Dr. Norman Geisler provides several cogent arguments against their authenticity:

> (1) These verses are lacking in many of the oldest and most reliable Greek manuscripts as well as in important Old Latin, Syriac, Armenian, and Ethiopic manuscripts. (2) Many of the ancient church fathers reveal no knowledge of these verses, including Clement, Origen, and Eusebius. Jerome admitted that almost all Greek copies do not have it. (3) Many manuscripts that do have this section place a mark by it indicating it is a spurious addition to the text. (4) There is another (shorter) ending to Mark that is found in some manuscripts. (5) Others point to the fact that the style and vocabulary are not the same as the rest of the Gospel of Mark.[1]

Regardless of these important facts, Dr. Geisler attempts to salvage the suspect passage by reasoning, "Whether or not this piece of *text* belongs in the original, the *truth* it contains certainly accords with it." He then states it makes no difference whether or not this text belongs in the original gospel. In this manner, Christ's ascension—a stunning, miraculous and supernatural improbability—is accepted on mere faith without a verifiably genuine account of it in Mark, as relayed by the apostle Peter, who would have been an eyewitness to this astounding event but who apparently felt no interest in having Mark record it. One would think that if the ascension really happened, Mark would have jumped at the chance to depict it! The ascension, in fact, would constitute one of the major "fingerprints of the Christ," demonstrating his divinity, so its absence is rather inexplicable.

The fifth argument against the genuineness of the verses at 16:9-20 includes that they were written by a different hand, using language peculiar to them and not found

---

[1] Geisler, *WCA*, 378.

elsewhere in Mark. Concerning this thesis, CE remarks that "the cumulative force of the evidence against the Marcan origin of the passage is considerable." Although it later indicates confidence in the Markan authority of these passages, CE advises that "Catholics are not bound to hold that the verses were written by St. Mark." This fact is important to note, as it demonstrates that even in the most fervently believing sector the authorship of at least parts of the gospels is not adhered to as dogma. The CE is quick to admonish, however, that, no matter who wrote them, these verses are canonical and inspired, so they "must be received as such by every Catholic." CE, therefore, is claiming canonicity and inspiration for verses not necessarily included in the autograph or written by the original evangelist—another important clue to note, as this claim of "inerrancy" for scribal additions/copyists' notes has played a significant role in New Testament history as well.

Moreover, it seems odd that the Catholic authorities would not know who wrote these passages, especially since the Catholic Church has been in possession of certain early Christian texts for centuries, and since the New Testament books are claimed to have emanated from, or been inspired by, the Holy Spirit. Logic would suggest that the Holy Spirit could therefore validate the authenticity of these verses and texts, especially in response to queries from Christian authorities themselves. In consideration of its prominent role within Christianity for almost 2,000 years, it is surprising that the Catholic Church has not been in possession of many more of the most ancient Christian texts, including the precious originals written by the evangelists themselves.

The Three Synoptics Juxtaposed

A comparison of all three synoptic gospels reveals that Mark is also missing the first two chapters in Matthew and the first chapter of Luke. Regarding the material found in these three evangelists, the Catholic Encyclopedia ("Gospel of St. Mark") states:

> In the arrangement of the common matter the three Gospels differ very considerably up to the point where Herod Antipas is said to have heard of the fame of Jesus (Matthew 13:58; Mark 4:13; Luke 9:6)....

After this point, the synoptics are "practically the same." The most glaring exceptions appear in the order of the triumphal entry into Jerusalem, the clearing of the temple and the cursing of the fig tree. Luke and Mark differ in their placement of Christ's announcement of Judas's betrayal. (Mk 14:18-24; Lk 22:19-23) Regarding this development, CE also admits that "in many passages, some of considerable length, there is such coincidence of words and phrases that it is impossible to believe the accounts to be wholly independent. On the other hand, side by side with this coincidence, there is strange and frequently recurring divergence."

Raising the question of priority again, CE further states:

Literary dependence or connexion of some kind must be admitted, and the question is, what is the nature of that dependence or connexion? Does Mark depend upon Matthew, or upon both Matthew and Luke, or was it prior to and utilized in both, or are all three, perhaps, connected through their common dependence upon earlier documents or through a combination of some of these causes?[1]

In concluding its entry on the Gospel of Mark, CE remarks:

There is no reason, therefore, why Catholics should be timid about admitting, if necessary, the dependence of the inspired evangelists upon earlier documents, and, in view of the difficulties against the other theories, it is well to bear this possibility in mind in attempting to account for the puzzling relations of Mark to the other two synoptists.

Here we see that even the synoptic gospels differ from each other substantially in several important aspects, yet also contain such similarities as to indicate one or more common source. The reliance of the evangelists upon earlier documents, rather than the gospels serving as memorialization of the experiences of important eyewitnesses, constitutes a

---

[1] *CE*, "Gospel of St. Mark." (Emph. added.)

highly salient factor that needs to be emphasized in our analysis. As Tenney notes, if these texts rely on common source documents, how can we possibly claim they represent the views of three separate eyewitnesses?

The Gospel According to Luke

"The gospels are not primarily works of history in the modern sense of the word."

Dr. John Meier, *A Marginal Jew* (I, 41)

As a reflection of the important fact that the evangelists relied upon earlier documents as source texts for their gospels, the gospel of Luke makes mention of a number of narratives that preceded it. These sources may have included Matthew and Mark, which possess many similarities to Luke's gospel, or, more probably, a core text used by all three. The most well known material common to all three synoptics and missing in the gospel of John includes:

- The temptation
- The calming of the storm
- The healing of Jairus's daughter
- The plucking of the grain on the sabbath
- The healing of the man with the withered hand
- The naming of the disciples
- The parable of the sower
- The parable of the mustard seed
- The transfiguration
- The "second" cleansing of the temple
- The foretelling of Christ's second coming
- Judas's betraying overture to the priests
- The appearance of Christ before the Sanhedrin
- The darkness descending upon Christ's crucifixion

While this list forms the nucleus of similarities between the synoptic gospels, there are also disparities, some significant and others less so. For instance, the lists of the disciples differ from one another and vary in diverse manuscripts as well. The major difference between these lists is that "Lebbaeus Thaddaeus" (Mt 10:3) or just "Thaddaeus" (Mk 3:18) is recorded in the first two, while

Luke-Acts[1] names this disciple "Judas son of James." The KJV translates this phrase as "Judas *brother* of James." In any event, in order to reconcile these lists, we must simply accept that "Judas of James" is the same as Lebbaeus Thaddaeus. There is no biblical authority asserting this connection, however. Nor is there any external evidence of even the *existence* of the apostles, much less their specifics. We are left to take this connection on faith, based on the circular reasoning that the lists differ and must be reconciled. Although the lists do not seem to diverge significantly, the discrepancies do raise the question of whether they are historically accurate, or one or more of the evangelists made a mistake.

There are still other discrepancies between the synoptic gospels, including in the genealogies and the birth accounts, entirely absent in Mark, and in Luke diverging in several details from Matthew. In addition, Luke does not record the flight into Egypt, while Matthew does. Furthermore, Luke, the longest of the gospels, includes some 520 verses not found in the other evangelists,[2] comprising several important pericopes such as:

- The birth of John the Baptist (Lk 1:57-80)
- The annunciation of Jesus's birth (Lk 1:26-38)
- The shepherds in the field (Lk 2:8-20)
- Jesus's circumcision (Lk 2:21)
- Christ being presented in the temple (Lk 2:22-38)
- Jesus teaching in the temple as a youth (Lk 2:40-52)
- The woman with the alabaster jar washing Jesus's feet with her tears, etc. (Lk 7:36-50)
- The disciples James and John threatening to destroy a Samaritan village by bringing down fire from heaven (Lk 9:54)
- The story of the Good Samaritan (Lk 10:25-37)
- The healing of the 10 lepers (Lk 17:11-19)

As an example of other disparities between the gospels, not only does Luke place Jesus's Sermon on a *plain*, rather

---

[1] "Luke-Acts" designates the gospel of Luke and the New Testament book the "Acts of the Apostles," both widely considered to have been written by the same person.
[2] Geisler, *CA*, 312.

than the *mount* of Matthew, but he also recounts only *four* beatitudes (Lk 6:20-25), whereas Matthew gives *eight* (Mt 5:3-12), and even these are significantly different from each other "in general form and conceptions." Moreover, the Lord's Prayer in Luke (11:2-4) differs from that in Matthew, suggesting that one or the other version does not reflect Jesus's actual words. Also, Matthew often arranges Christ's speeches and sayings thematically or topically, while in Luke they appear scattered about.

Chronological Discrepancies

When discussing the differences between the gospels, it is useful to consider the beginning paragraph of Luke:

> Inasmuch as many have undertaken to compile a narrative of the things which have been accomplished among us, just as they were delivered to us by those who from the beginning were eyewitnesses and ministers of the word, it seemed good to me also, having followed all things closely, for some time past, to write an orderly account for you, most excellent Theophilus, that you may know the truth concerning the things of which you have been informed. (Luke 1:1-4)

Luke thus states that "many" had compiled narratives of Christ's life before him. The verbiage here for "an orderly account" indicates the evangelist was aware of the chronological difficulties of the other narratives, including not only canonical gospels but also apocryphal gospels and other texts.

In reality, the chronology of events differs widely in some places between Luke and the other gospels. For instance, in addition to the problem of Jairus's daughter, previously mentioned, another pericope in which the chronology between Luke and Matthew is not reconcilable occurs at Luke 2:4 and Matthew 2:21-23, concerning the story of Joseph and Mary arriving in Bethlehem so Jesus's birth would "fulfill prophecy." Matthew states that the Holy Family lived in Nazareth only *after* Jesus's birth, while Luke depicts Joseph and Mary as possessing a home in Nazareth *before* Jesus's birth, portraying them as compelled to go to Bethlehem in order to participate in the census of Quirinius or Cyrenius, as he is called by Josephus.

In addition, Mark (1:16-45) and Luke (4:31-44; 5:1-16) differ in the order of the sequence of pericopes in which Christ calls his disciples; the ministry in Capernaum; the casting out of a demon in the synagogue; and, the healing of Peter's mother-in-law. Also, the story of the centurion's servant being healed by Jesus appears in Matthew (8:5-13) *before* the sabbath-breaking grain plucking and the healing of the man's withered hand, while in Luke (7:1-10) the servant is healed *after* these other two occurrences. Furthermore, in his account of Jesus's transfiguration (9:28-36), Luke claims it took place *eight* days after "these sayings," whereas Matthew and Mark put it *six* days after. In general, Luke has a similar chronology as that of Mark, although disagreeing in a number of details, but nevertheless suggesting that Luke followed Mark rather than Matthew. At the same time, Matthew and Luke possess in common some 250 verses that are not found in Mark. As in Mark, the one brief mention of Christ's ascension in Luke (24:51) is lacking in the earliest texts and is omitted in the RSV among other translations.

Luke's Tenor

One pericope in Matthew repeated by Luke is that of Jesus addressing the "great multitudes," preceding the parable of the prodigal son. In this pericope, Luke portrays Christ as stating:

> "If any one comes to me and does not hate his own father and mother and wife and children and brothers and sisters, yes, and even his own life, he cannot be my disciple. Whoever does not bear his own cross and come after me, cannot be my disciple.... So therefore, whoever of you does not renounce all that he has cannot be my disciple." (Lk 14:26-33)

This disturbing commentary appears also at Matthew 10:37-38, with different terminology omitting the word "hate." The original Greek of Luke specifically uses the verb μισεω—*miseo*—which means "**to hate**," despite the recent trend to soften the word by mistranslating it.

Another troubling passage occurs at Luke 19:27, part of a parable that Jesus tells in regard to his disciples' concern about the coming Kingdom of God. Within this parable about a king—widely interpreted as referring to Jesus himself—appears the following scripture:

"But as for these enemies of mine, who did not want me to reign over them, bring them here and slay them before me."

This dark and violent remark ends the parable, with the impression of a serious threat to anyone who obstructs Jesus and the Kingdom of God lording over them. This entire parable is extremely odd, as it emphasizes severity, power, brutality and money-mongering. Over the centuries many commentators on this particular passage with its menacing "lesson," such as conservative Christian Matthew Henry, have agreed that the king in this parable refers to Christ himself.

Luke, of course, is not alone in his portrayal of a berserkers Christ, as Mark too depicts Jesus in a less-than-stellar light. As New Testament scholar, theologian, former Catholic priest and Professor Emeritus of Religious Studies at DePaul University, Dr. John Dominic Crossan, says, "You have a Jesus out of control almost in Mark, a Jesus totally in control in John. Both gospel. Neither of them are historical."[1]

Startling Conclusions

Regarding the disparities between the synoptic gospels, Dr. Crossan concludes:

...when Matthew or Luke are using Mark as a source for what Jesus said or did or what others said or did to Jesus, they are unnervingly free about omission and addition, about change, correction, or creation in their own individual accounts.[2]

As noted, New Testament scholarship has revealed common source material used by the evangelists, indicating their reliance upon these earlier texts rather than recounting their own memories as witnesses to the events described. All

---

[1] Crossan, *THJ*, xxx.
[2] Crossan, *THJ*, xxx.

of this copying makes little sense, if these gospels in fact constitute the eyewitness accounts of the historical Jesus. If Matthew is describing actual experiences he had, why does he need to copy Mark? Since Luke is clearly not an eyewitness but is working from the earlier narratives of others, how can his account be considered that of a "separate eyewitness?" Moreover, if all of the gospels were inspired by the Holy Spirit, as Christian doctrine professes, why would they need to copy each other? Could there not be another more rational, logical and scientific explanation, such as that the gospels are manmade accounts written by fallible human beings who were not eyewitnesses? And what about the gospel of John, which sits squarely apart from the others—why is John's gospel so different from the rest?

The Gospel According to John

"John, the apostle whom Jesus most loved, the son of Zebedee and brother of James, the apostle whom Herod, after our Lord's passion, beheaded, most recently of all the evangelists wrote a Gospel, at the request of the bishops of Asia, against Cerinthus and other heretics."

St. Jerome, *De Viris Illustribus* (ch. 9)

"John, the disciple of the Lord, preaches this faith, and seeks, by the proclamation of the Gospel, to remove that error which by Cerinthus had been disseminated among men, and a long time previously by those termed Nicolaitans, who are an offset of that 'knowledge' falsely so called..."

Irenaeus, Bishop of Lyons, *Against Heresies* (III, 11.3)

The Gospel of John is located last in the canon but in early times was also placed directly after Matthew. The tone and structure of John's gospel diverge significantly from the other three, which is why the latter are categorized together as synoptics, while John is not included in this group. The most noticeable difference between John and the other evangelists is that his gospel takes place mainly in Jerusalem and Judea, whereas the others focus on Christ's advent in the north of Palestine. John also appears to be more concerned with Jesus's sayings and speeches rather than his deeds and miracles, concentrating particularly on Christ's interactions with the Jewish authorities, and displaying a more pronounced anti-Jewish tone and sentiment than the other gospels. John's gospel is frequently out of sync with the synoptics, so the tendency is to view it not as a strict history or biography but mainly as a theological text. In fact, John is considered the most theological of the gospels, specifically highlighting Christ's divinity, and evidently serving as a response to those who denied Jesus was God. There is a longstanding debate as to the true authorship of the gospel of John called the "Johannine problem," which includes not only denials beginning in antiquity that the apostle John wrote the gospel but also the fact that John speaks of "the Jews" as if he is not one himself.

The differences between John and the other gospels include a number of important pericopes present in John but not in Matthew, Mark and Luke:

- Jesus as God's Word or "Logos" (Jn 1:1-4)
- The wedding feast and water-to-wine miracle in Cana (Jn 2:1-11)
- The "first" cleansing of the temple (Jn 2:12-25)
- The healing pool of Bethesda (Jn 5:2-15)
- The raising from the dead of Lazarus (Jn 11:1-44)
- Jesus's mother, Mary, appearing at the cross (Jn 19:25-27)
- The side piercing (Jn 19:31-37)

There are many other pericopes in John that do not appear in the others. Some of the Johannine pericopes—such as the raising of Lazarus from the dead—are so significant it is difficult to believe that the other evangelists would not record them, if they had been aware of them. It is logical to ask whether or not these episodes were added later to the story for specific purposes.

Moreover, John does not mention the transfiguration, even though he was purportedly a witness to it! In his quest to demonstrate the divinity of Jesus, it would be highly logical for John to have reported the transfiguration, if it really happened. Nor does John mention the ascension, which is equally curious in light of his desire to reveal Christ's divinity.

As concerns chronological discrepancies, John's gospel presents the clearing of the temple at the beginning, while the others place it at the end. The solution to this problem has been to suggest that there was more than one cleansing, but many critics find this proposal unsatisfactory.

Another disparity between the synoptics and John appears in Jesus's arrest: The former states he was "taken away" to the high priest (Mt 26:57; Mk 14:53; Lk 22:54), while the latter depicts Jesus first being brought to the high priest's father-in-law, Annas, and sometime later to the high priest (Jn 18:13-24).

Continuing with the discrepancies, the accounts of the resurrection differ between gospels as well. In Matthew, Mary Magdalene and "the other Mary" find Jesus's tomb empty, while in Mark it is Mary Magdalene, Mary the mother of James and someone named Salome. In Luke, Mary Magdalene, Mary the mother of James and a woman called Joanna are present, with the suggestion at Lk 24:10 that others were present as well. Meanwhile, John depicts the empty tomb as being discovered by Mary Magdalene alone, who runs off to retrieve Peter and another, unnamed disciple!

Next, we have four different accounts of whom these individuals found at the scene. First, Matthew states that the stone in front of the tomb rolled away following an earthquake after the women arrived on the scene. Mark, Luke and John report the stone was rolled away *before* the witnesses arrived, although Luke and John do not record any earthquake. Matthew depicts an angel sitting on the rock; Mark, a young man in a brilliant robe; Luke, two men in "dazzling apparel" somewhere inside or outside of the tomb; and, in John, Mary and company find no one at all, until after Peter and the disciple leave, at which point Mary sees two angels inside.

We also possess four separate descriptions of what happened afterwards concerning whom the discoverers told about the empty tomb: Was it the disciples, as at Matthew 28:8; no one, as at Mark 16:8; "the eleven and...all the rest," as at Luke 24:9; or Mary telling the disciples not about the empty tomb but about her seeing the risen Lord, as at John 20:18? These are only a few of the problems with the gospel accounts of this most auspicious of events in the life, death and resurrection of Jesus Christ. As another example, the time and day when the resurrection occurred are also not agreed upon; nor is when and where the risen Jesus first appeared to his followers.

Authentic or Adulterated?

As is the case with the synoptics, there is doubt as to the authenticity of several verses in John. For example, at John

5:3-4, regarding the pool of Bethsaida/Bethesda, the last half of the first sentence and the entire fourth verse are missing from the three oldest extant manuscripts of the New Testament and are therefore omitted in several translations, including the RSV, which appends them in a footnote. For the same reason, the authenticity of the story of the "woman caught in the act of adultery" found at John 7:53-8:11 is called into question, not being found in the oldest manuscripts and likewise omitted in some translations such as the RSV. If this episode really occurred, why would some authorities and translations omit it? Did the Holy Spirit inspire some writers and scribes to include it and some to omit it?

In *When Critics Ask*, apologist Geisler gives reasons for questioning the genuineness of this pericope of the adulterous woman:

(1) The passage does not appear in the oldest and most reliable Greek manuscripts. (2) It is not found in the best manuscripts of the earliest translations of the Bible into Old Syriac, Coptic, Gothic, and Old Latin. (3) No Greek writer commented on this passage for the first 11 centuries of Christianity. (4) It is not cited by most of the great early church fathers, including Clement, Tertullian, Origen, Cyprian, Cyril, and others. (5) Its style does not fit that of the rest of the Gospel of John. (6) It interrupts the flow of thought in John. John reads better if one goes right from John 7:52 to 8:12. (7) The story has been found in several different places in Bible manuscripts—after John 7:36; after John 21:24; after John 7:44; and after Luke 21:38. (8) Many manuscripts that include it in John 7:53-8:11 have marked it with an obelus, indicating they believe it is doubtful.[1]

In spite of all these reasonable and scientific facts, Geisler further relates that "many Bible scholars believe this story is authentic," reflecting more about the tenacity of religious faith than about the authenticity of the passage in John.

Other scholars possessed with less fervor for upholding the text's inspiration do not hesitate to call this suspect

---

[1] Geisler, *WCA*, 415.

pericope an interpolation by a later scribe. As noted theologian and professor Dr. Bart Ehrman, author of *Misquoting Jesus*, comments:

> Despite the brilliance of the story, its captivating quality, and its inherent intrigue, there is one other enormous problem that it poses. As it turns out, it was not originally in the Gospel of John. In fact, it was not originally part of any of the Gospels. It was added by later scribes.... Scholars who work on the manuscript tradition have no doubts about this particular case.[1]

Ehrman also recounts the logical and scientific reasons for the conclusion that these verses in John are interpolations, i.e., forgeries, including that they do not appear in the earliest manuscripts and that their terminology is different from the rest of John. As also noted, this pericope was likewise interpolated into different chapters or even different gospels in various manuscripts, likely for a "political" purpose.

The authenticity of the entire 21st chapter of John has also been questioned, as it appears from the text itself that the 30th verse of the 20th chapter was meant to be the ending. The gospel of John currently ends with the following verse (Jn 21:25):

> But there are also many other things which Jesus did; were every one of them to be written, I suppose that the world itself could not contain the books that would be written.

At John 20:30, however, the evangelist had already written a similar statement:

> Now Jesus did many other signs in the presence of his disciples, which are not written in this book....

By all appearances, the 21st chapter seems to have been appended, with its author trying to wrap it all up with much the same ending as at John 20, as the fact that this passage constitutes the chosen ending at John 21:25 is a strong

---

[1] Ehrman, *MJ*, 63-64.

indication that the person who wrote John 20:30 *also* meant *that* scripture as the ending of his book.

In discussing the various strata of early Christian texts, Dr. Crossan posits a "Gospel of John II" and remarks:

> A second addition of the Gospel of John is indicated most clearly by the appended John 21... Many other additions, such as 1:1-18; 6:51b-58; 15-17 and the Beloved Disciple passages, may also have been added as this late stage.[1]

If this 21st chapter is in fact an interpolation, it would seem to have been added in order to establish the writer, John, as "immortal," since traditionally he has been identified as the "beloved disciple" specifically discussed at the end of the gospel as "remaining until Jesus comes." It is possible that this passage extending John's age was added because the gospel itself emerged so late as to cast doubt on the claim that it was written by the apostle. Biblical inerrantists, however, deny that there is anything unusual about this chapter being added after the seeming ending in the 20th chapter. The Catholic Encyclopedia ("Gospel of Saint John") concludes that the 21st chapter is indeed an addition, but asserts that there remains no reason to believe John himself did not write it.

Another disparity between the synoptic gospels and the gospel of John is in their presentation of Jesus as either exorcising or baptizing. The synoptics depict Christ as performing exorcisms from the initial stages of his ministry but do not portray him ever as baptizing anyone. John, on the other hand, has Jesus baptizing from the beginning onward but never exorcising anyone.[2]

One more difficulty arises in examining the language used to recount the speeches of Jesus and other gospel characters, rendered in John's gospel in the "peculiar Johannine style," which differs considerably from that of the synoptic gospels. The solution proposed is that these speeches were originally given in Aramaic and thus the translations would be different, depending on the author. Furthermore, as may be expected of the evangelist with the

---

[1] Crossan, *THJ*, 432.
[2] Meier, II, 125.

most Christological orientation, in his discussion of the eucharist (6:52-57), John's language is more explicit and disturbing than the others in describing the consumption of Christ's flesh and blood:

> The Jews then disputed among themselves, saying, "How can this man give us his flesh to eat?" So Jesus said to them, "Truly, truly, I say to you, unless you eat the flesh of the Son of man and drink his blood, you have no life in you; he who eats my flesh and drinks my blood has eternal life, and I will raise him up at the last day. For my flesh is food indeed, and my blood is drink indeed. He who eats my flesh and drinks my blood abides in me, and I in him. As the living Father sent me, and I live because of the Father, so he who eats me will live because of me."

Needless to say, a civilized person in a non-cannibalistic society may look with revulsion upon such peculiar and repulsive concepts, regardless of whether or not they are meant literally.

In addition, John's hostility towards Jewish authorities eclipses any similar sentiment found in the other gospels. At John 8:44, Jesus declares to the Jewish priests, the Pharisees:

> "You are of your father the devil, and your will is to do your father's desires. He was a murderer from the beginning, and has nothing to do with the truth, because there is no truth in him. When he lies, he speaks according to his own nature, for he is a liar and the father of lies."

Unfortunately, over the centuries since this scripture was written, such sentiment towards Jewish people has not been confined to the gospels but took root in many places the gospel story was spread, with often dire consequences.

Who Killed Jesus?

The issues of textual reconciliation and the hostility towards Jews come to a head in the discussion of Christ's death. The alleged circumstances of Jesus's demise are extremely important, because over the centuries this subject has led to the deaths of many thousands of Jews, who have been attacked and murdered as "Christ-killers." In examining the earliest Christian texts relating Jesus's death, it becomes obvious that the story was altered at various points to place the onus upon either the Romans or the Jews, depending on which faction was portraying the tale. Concerning this issue, Dr. Ehrman remarks:

> Whereas in the oldest available form of the text, Pilate hands Jesus over to his Roman guard for crucifixion, in some of our early manuscripts, after hearing the Jewish crowd accept responsibility for Jesus' death, Pilate "delivered Jesus over to *them*, so that *they* might crucify him." In these manuscripts, the Jews are *fully* responsible for Jesus' death.[1]

If the gospel story is true, how can it be changed at will in this manner? Which of these depictions is historically accurate? In reality, this point illustrates the fact that the history of the Christian church has been rife with political infighting, dissension and splitting off, first in dozens, then hundreds, and eventually thousands of different branches. Every one of these branches has believed it has possessed the best interpretation of the truth. In the early days as Christianity began to develop, dozens of these sects had their own books, including the non-canonical gospels, and each one was convinced that theirs was sacred, holy and inspired. Each canonical gospel, in fact, has its own target audience.

These examples are some of the more obvious disparities and difficulties found in and between the four canonical gospels. When all is said and done and the evidence is examined, in order for us to accept the gospel story as "factual history," we remain with the overwhelming need for a concerted effort to reconcile these numerous discrepancies and differences between the texts. The reconciliation of these problems is complex and has been the focus of much New Testament scholarship, as we shall soon see in our quest to solve this "spiritual whodunnit."

---

[1] Ehrman, "Text and Tradition 2."

Textual Harmonization

"The Bible, at the end of the day, is a very human book."

Dr. Bart Ehrman, *Misquoting Jesus* (12)

"With all of the differences between Matthew, Mark, Luke, and John and with numerous other gospels existing, we have an obvious problem. Each gospel has a particular way of seeing Jesus. How close to the historical facts are they?"

Dr. John Dominic Crossan, *Who Is Jesus?* (4)

Many of the problems, disparities and differences in the canonical gospels have been known for centuries, as even several of the early Church fathers attempted to explain them. As a result, over the centuries of New Testament scholarship a complex process called "harmonization" has been developed within Christian apologetics by which these numerous issues may be reconciled, typically using five "principles of harmonization." The five principles of harmonization are as follows:

1. Ancient writers were not particularly interested in chronological and geographical accuracy.
2. The material was arranged topically or thematically.
3. Jesus moved about preaching, thus repeating his actions and sayings.
4. The evangelists were selective about what they included, and they compressed their accounts.
5. Jesus's deeds and words needed to be interpreted, translated and condensed.[1]

The difficulty of harmonization is profound, particularly when the thousands of manuscripts of the New Testament are factored into the puzzle, with upwards of 150,000 "variant readings," including not only differences in wording but also *errors*. Many of these "variant readings" were

---

[1] See McCallum and DeLashmutt.

composed by those whom modern translators term "ancient authorities," i.e., the writers, editors, scribes and copyists of a wide variety of Bible editions, including and especially the earliest extant manuscripts. As books aged, they were copied by hand—frequently with mistakes and deliberate alterations. The NT is no different, as the evidence abundantly shows. Under such circumstances, the logical question is, can we really consider the gospels to represent accurate renderings of the real life and career of a historical Jesus, as they are claimed to be?

Regarding these "variant readings" in the New Testament, one conservative Christian authority, *The Interpreter's Dictionary of the Bible*, remarks:

> The NT [New Testament] is now known, in whole or in part, in nearly five thousand Greek MSS [manuscripts] alone. Every one of these handwritten copies differs from every other one. In addition to these Greek MSS, the NT has been preserved in more than ten thousand MSS of the early versions...and in thousands of quotations of the Church Fathers. These MSS of the versions and quotations of the Church Fathers differ from one another just as widely as do the Greek MSS. Only a fraction of this great mass of material has been fully collated and carefully studied. Until this task is completed, the uncertainty regarding the text of the NT will remain.

> *It has been estimated that these MSS and quotations differ among themselves between 150,000 and 250,000 times. The actual figure is, perhaps, much higher. A study of 150 Greek MSS of the Gospel of Luke has revealed more than 30,000 different readings... It is safe to say that **there is not one sentence in the NT in which the MS tradition is wholly uniform**.*

> *Many thousands of the variants which are found in the MSS of the NT were put there deliberately. They are not merely the result of error or of careless handling of the text. Many were created for theological or dogmatic reasons... It is because the books of the NT are religious books, sacred books,*

canonical books, that they were changed to conform to what the copyist believed to be the true reading.[1]

The Interpreter's Dictionary continues with a discussion of the more significant of the 64 papyrus fragments of New Testament manuscripts now known, one small fragment speculatively dated to the middle of the second century (Rylands/P52) with the rest from the beginning of third to the eighth centuries. All of these pieces, which constitute about 40 percent of the New Testament, were found in Egypt "and undoubtedly were written there." Concerning these fragments, the Interpreter's Dictionary states:

> Many of them are too small to be of much value textually. Their cumulative evidence, however, is of value. They prove conclusively that in Egypt, particularly in the second, third, and fourth centuries, no one type of NT text was dominant. In those early centuries many types of text flourished side by side.[2]

Thus, even in early times there was no uniformity of the New Testament manuscripts.

The editors of *The Anchor Bible Dictionary* are likewise explicit in their pronouncements concerning the many "imperfections," "alterations" and "divergent nature" of New Testament texts and copies:

> Among our earliest manuscripts, some show signs of being copied with workmanlike care...while others appear to have been copied by rather careless scribes... Scribal habits, including errors and alterations, need to be analyzed carefully. Commonly they are divided into two categories: unintentional and intentional alterations.[3]

Hence, as we can see, the quest for a pristine copy of the New Testament, from which we can be sure to possess the true story and words of Jesus Christ, remains a complex and seemingly impossible quest.

---

[1] *IDT*, "Text, NT," v. 4; 594-595. (Emph. added.)
[2] *IDT*, 596.
[3] *AB*, v. VI; 416.

Inspired Originals?

These facts make abundantly clear that the manuscripts we possess are full of variations and mistakes, such that believers in the inerrancy of the Bible have asserted that it is only the originals or *autographs* that represent the inerrant Word of God, infallibly inspired by the Holy Spirit. For example, in "Discovering and Classifying New Testament Manuscripts," fundamentalist writer James Arlandson remarks:

> The original authors were inspired, but we do not have their very originals... The original New Testament documents were transmitted by scribes, who were not inspired.

This more recent claim regarding only the originals being inspired essentially overrides the centuries-old, widely held notion that English translations such as the King James Bible are inerrant; yet, there remain King James inerrantists.

Regarding the canonical gospels, Dr. Erhman remarks: "We don't have the originals! We have only error-ridden copies..." Addressing the trend to assert the originals as inspired, in *Misquoting Jesus*, Ehrman further states:

> It is one thing to say that the originals were inspired, but the reality is that we don't have the originals—so saying they were inspired doesn't help me much, unless I can reconstruct the originals. Moreover, the vast majority of Christians for the entire history of the Church have not had access to the originals, making their inspiration a moot point.[1]

Ehrman also comments, "The mistake-ridden copies get copied; and the mistake-ridden copies of the copies get copied; and so on, down the line."[2]

Scribal Scalliwags

In discussing the evolution of New Testament texts, Ehrman relates an amusing anecdote concerning scribes who worked on the epistle to the Hebrews in the Codex

---

[1] Ehrman, *MJ*, 10.
[2] Ehrman, *MJ*, 59.

Vaticanus, one of the oldest complete biblical manuscripts in existence, dating to the fourth century. In response to a change made in the text of Hebrews by another scribe centuries earlier, a "medieval scribe" commented in the margin, "Fool and knave! Leave the old reading, don't change it!"[1] This episode illustrates how New Testament texts were copied, edited and interpolated by many people, some of whom unquestionably made *errors*—an important point, in consideration of the fact that some believers have also asserted that even certain copies are "inerrant," such as the very flawed Textus Receptus upon which the King James Bible was founded in large part. As we have seen, the Catholic Encyclopedia accepts some verses as inspired that were evidently written not by the evangelist Mark but by an unknown scribe.

These scribes were frequently not particularly well educated and often consisted of members of the "common people." Their inclusion into the equation allows for us to concur with another of Ehrman's statements regarding the Bible being a "human book."[2] Adding to this sentiment is the sixth principle for "understanding apparent discrepancies in the Bible," as laid out by Christian apologist Josh McDowell in *The New Evidence that Demands a Verdict*. Says McDowell, "The Bible is a human book with human characteristics."[3] As such, we simply must inquire as to the Bible's sloppy history, with a number of those entrusted with its care clearly describable as "bumbling." Indeed, as we have seen abundantly, the enterprise in general has been extremely disorganized, to say the least.

The fact that scriptures had been tampered with at some point is alluded to at the end of the Bible itself, in the warning at Revelation 22:18-19:

> "I warn every one who hears the words of the prophecy of this book: if any one adds to them, God will add to him the plagues described in this book, and if any one takes away from the words of the book of this prophecy, God will take away his share in the

---

[1] Ehrman, *MJ*, 56.
[2] Ehrman, *MJ*, 12.
[3] McDowell, 47.

tree of life and in the holy city, which are described in this book."

The sloppiness of the scribes and the mess they had made of the texts were remarked upon also by early Church father and apologist Origen (3rd cent.), in his *Commentary on Matthew* (15.14):

> It is an obvious fact today that there is much diversity among the manuscripts, due either to the carelessness of the scribes, or to the perverse audacity of some people in correcting the text, or again to the fact that there are those who add or delete as they please, setting themselves up as correctors.[1]

In fact, the earlier periods were the most error-ridden, as conservative Protestant Tenney comments: "The major divergences in the readings of the New Testament text date from the period before Constantine, and may reflect the stress and confusion prevailing in the Christian world."[2] Hence, uniformity in the New Testament—and indeed in the Christian doctrine as a whole—was not achieved but for the passage of much time, along with bitter and bloody battling between sects and denominations over a period of centuries.

New Testament scholarship has thus shown that the ancient texts used in the translation of the Bible vary greatly, and it has further sought to disentangle the original texts, or autographs, from the many thousands of alterations made by subsequent scribes. In other words, we do not possess the original gospels, and it is an indisputable fact that even the most ancient copies of the New Testament have been worked over repeatedly by a number of individuals and do not agree with each other in many places, making the task of determining what was in the originals extremely difficult, if not impossible. The importance of this fact needs to be emphasized, as no book in the New Testament has been untouched by numerous human hands, including those texts used by the translators of the editions still believed today to be 'inerrant" and "infallibly inspired."

---

[1] Hamblin and Peterson
[2] Tenney, 415.

Error-Filled Copies

The truth is that in many cases we are simply not dealing with the original words intended by the authors of the canonical gospels, which is to say that frequently we do not really know what they meant to convey. In such an atmosphere, it is logical to ask whether or not the Bible as we have it could possibly be considered the "inerrant word of God." One response to this dilemma asserts that not only were the evangelists under the guidance of the Holy Spirit but so too were the copyists who made all these alterations. This solution creates a new problem in that it suggests the Holy Spirit made so many errors to begin with that the texts required numerous corrections by the subsequent copyists. Indeed, if the original gospels were actually recording factual events and sayings exactly as they had occurred, a testimony created not only via eyewitnesses but also with the added assurance of being guided by God himself as the Holy Spirit, why would these texts *ever* need to be changed?

Moreover, numerous New Testament scholars have been aware of these many thousands of "variant readings," and some have blatantly called them "errors." In other words, within the higher ranks of New Testament scholarship, it is acknowledged that many of the scribes and copyists made *errors*, and this fact has in large part been a motivating factor behind the clamor to return to the original texts, devoid of these clearly *erroneous* revisions. Consider, for example, the words of the pious Christian scholar Fenton John Anthony Hort (1828-1892), who, Dr. Ehrman states, was "arguably the most brilliant mind to apply himself" to the task of discerning the originals of the New Testament texts under all of the subsequent changes. Hort described his task as "nothing more than the detection and rejection of error."[1] Hort further called "vile" the Greek New Testament edition deemed the Textus Receptus, again upon which the King James Version was based in large part. In such an environment of acknowledging error and striving to get back to the elusive "pristine" originals, it would appear unscientific and intellectually dishonest to assert that the Bible as we have it is "inerrant," regardless of the edition.

---

[1] Erhman, "Text and Tradition."

Perfect Harmony?

Even if we could get back to the originals, we would find it tricky to reconstruct the details of Christ's life and teachings. Indeed, the many difficulties and differences *between* the canonical gospels *themselves alone* highlight the reason why there has existed such an enormous amount of New Testament scholarship, and why a complex process of harmonization has been developed to deal with the numerous discrepancies in the gospel accounts of Christ's life. Some examples of harmonization have already been given, but the process is ongoing, as the divergences are profound and seemingly unsolvable in certain cases. As another example of working with the principles of harmonization to overcome these discrepancies, one explanation for the differences in chronology between the gospels is that Matthew, for example, organized his material according to subject or theme, rather than chronologically, combining "facts and precepts of a like nature."

While the thematic approach to gospel chronology is satisfying enough regarding some of the problems, still others are not so easily solved, such as the raising of Jairus's daughter. It is evident from this narrative that neither Matthew nor Luke was arranging the event thematically; yet, they depict it as having occurred at different times. Both of them cannot be correct, unless the daughter was raised twice, a scenario that some literalists have proposed. Many people, however, will not find that answer to be satisfactory, and the only logical conclusion is that one or the other of the texts is incorrect.

Concerning some of the most blatant discrepancies and the attempts at their harmonization, evangelical writers Botti, Dixon and Steinman remark:

> ...well-meaning Christians posit absurd theories to explain gospel phenomena that conflict with their view that the gospels are chronologically arranged. As a result, Jesus is claimed to have raised Jairus' daughter twice from the dead, was twice crowned with thorns, was denied by Peter six or more times, and so on.

Thus, within Christian apologetics we will encounter "absurd theories," a fact we must keep in mind on our quest to determine who Jesus was.

In another example of an attempt at harmonization, it is asserted that the sermon on the *mount* (Mt 5-7) and the sermon on the *plain* (Lk 6) are "probably different discourses."

Moreover, in the exorcism of the demoniac, Matthew, Mark and Luke refer to the country of the "Gerasenes," "Gadarenes" and "Gergesenes," depending on which manuscript and translation are relied upon. In this regard, the KJV of Matthew 8:28 calls the people "Gergesenes," while the RSV uses much earlier Greek texts that label them "Gadarenes." Apologists claim that these names refer to the inhabitants of two different cities in that country.

One more difficulty arises when Jesus is anointed with oil by a woman in the house of someone named Simon. Matthew, Mark and John place the anointment at the end of their gospels, in Bethany, while Luke places it early in his gospel as having occurred in Galilee. The solution has been to suggest that Jesus was anointed twice in two different houses owned by two people named Simon.

Regarding the messy ordering of the temple-cleansing and fig tree-cursing pericopes found in Matthew and Mark, Tom Dixon comments, "It is not hard to imagine that Matthew would want to simplify the complexity of Mark's account by grouping the cursing and discovery of the fig tree in one pericope." That reasoning may suffice to explain the fig-tree pericope ordering, but what about the rest of the chronology? Does Jesus spend the night in Bethany *before* or *after* he cleanses the temple? The solution to this problem is *both*: Jesus spends the night in Bethany both before and after he cleanses the temple.

In analyzing attempts at harmonizing the widely diverging gospels, apologists Botti, et al., further state:

> The Evangelical believer needs to approach the synoptic gospels with the clear understanding that each author has intentionally omitted certain things that the other authors did not, and that each author intentionally re-arranged certain passages for didactic purposes. As many scholars have recognized, when

we approach the gospels with this understanding, many of the apparent chronological problems evaporate.

Yet what is most important is that believers in inerrancy train their eye to discern when an author is clearly making a claim to chronology and when he is not. It is not enough to wave off every issue of apparent chronological contradiction with a simple appeal to topical rearrangement, as many Evangelical scholars seem to do. We need to have sharper answers.

Sharper answers are needed indeed, as the biblical difficulties are such that massive volumes of apologetics have been published over many centuries in order to address them all—yet, many quandaries remain, as can be inferred from the call by modern apologists Botti, et al., for "sharper answers."

Eyewitness Accounts or Compilations?

The statement that the evangelists "intentionally re-arranged certain passages" reiterates the fact that they were working with source texts or with each other's gospels, as previously noted. This observation that the evangelists were using other texts, certain of them shared, and did not just record from scratch what they themselves had witnessed, is widely known among Christian scholars, both Catholic and Protestant. Many of the rank-and-file believers, however, are unaware that *the gospels in numerous places represent a reworking of preceding texts*.

As they have been taught, many Christians believe that the gospels constitute translations of originals straight from the pens of eyewitnesses faithfully and infallibly recording what each had seen of the Lord's advent. Even from a conservative perspective this perception is erroneous, obviously, since Luke was never claimed to have been an eyewitness to any of the events in the gospel; nor is Mark a direct disciple or known witness to the Lord. In fact, the opening statement by the author of the Gospel of Luke indicates that he possessed a number of the *many* narratives in existence by his time, which would be the only way he could strive to improve upon their accuracy. Hence, his gospel was based on these texts, not on his own memories or even those of anyone close to him. This development provokes the question as to why the Holy Spirit needed these other, previous texts to record the gospel story. Wouldn't the Holy Spirit, who is God/Jesus, already know the story in perfect detail, such that he could supernaturally convey it to the evangelists pristinely and without error?

Furthermore, many of the variant readings within the gospels and in the different ancient manuscripts of each gospel appear in the quotations of Christ's *sayings*. If these gospels truly constitute the inerrant records of direct eyewitnesses infallibly recording the events in Jesus's life, why do Jesus's *sayings* vary from one source to the next? Should not the precise words of the Lord himself be quoted *verbatim*? Why does the Lord's Prayer, for example, differ between gospels and from one manuscript to another? Wouldn't it make sense for the Lord, as the Holy Spirit, to refresh his disciples' memories as to his exact words? If these are the precious words from the Almighty God, how could they be changed? And why? Did God make *mistakes* in his original statements that needed correcting? What would be the point of having the Holy Spirit infallibly guiding the all-important endeavor of recording the Lord's life, if his speeches were not to be recorded verbatim? In other words, *what is the purpose of the Holy Spirit if not to correct the errors?* And if these scriptures are not verbatim records, how can they be called "inerrant?"

In any event, the methodology of harmonization has been in the works for so many centuries and by so many individuals that there is practically no objection that it does not cover. Much clever thought and many machinations have been accorded to the discipline of harmonization, and euphemistic terms have been used to describe the chronological discrepancies, for example, calling them "dislocations" rather than errors. Over the centuries, millions of words have been written and numerous courses on apologetics designed specifically to overcome objections. Regardless of these proposed solutions, the question is begged as to why God would write an "infallible" and "inerrant" Word which is so full of problems and difficulties that it has required many centuries to iron them all out—a task that remains incomplete to a significant degree. It seems logical and rational to ask again, could it not be that the fallible human beings who wrote, edited and translated the gospels simply made mistakes? Naturally, this position casts doubt on the concept of biblical inerrancy, but in our quest for honesty and truthfulness—the hallmarks of religiousness—can we really afford to ignore this logic?

The Gospel Dates

"It's important to acknowledge that strictly speaking, the gospels are anonymous."

Dr. Craig L. Blomberg, *The Case for Christ* (26)

Because of the lack of original texts, it has been very difficult to date the canonical gospels as to when they were written or even when they first emerge in the historical record, as these two dates may differ. The gospels have been dated variously from shortly after the crucifixion, traditionally placed around 30 AD/CE, to as late as a century and a half afterwards.[1] The currently accepted dates are as follows, from the earliest by conservative, believing scholars to the latest by liberal and sometimes secular scholars:

Matthew: 37 to 100 AD/CE
Mark: 40 to 73 AD/CE
Luke: 50 to 100 AD/CE
John: 65 to 100 AD/CE

Many reasons have been given for these dates, from one end of the spectrum to the other, the earliest dates being based on the events recounted in the gospels themselves. The later dates are based also on this timeframe, but the difference is that they account for the mention of the destruction of the Jerusalem temple, which occurred in 70 AD/CE. According to this scholarship, the gospels must have been written after the devastation because they refer to it. However, conservative believers maintain the early dates and assert that the destruction of the temple and Judea mentioned in the gospels constitutes "prophecy," demonstrating Jesus's divine powers. The substantiation for this early, first-century range of dates, both conservative and liberal, is internal *only*, as there is *no* external evidence, whether historical or archaeological, for the existence of *any* gospels

---

[1] See "The 'Historical' Jesus?" chapter in my book *Suns of God* for more discussion of the scholarship over the centuries regarding the dating and order of the canonical gospels.

at that time. Nevertheless, fundamentalist Christian apologists such as Norman Geisler make misleading assertions such as that "many of the original manuscripts date from within twenty to thirty years of the events in Jesus' life, that is, from contemporaries and eyewitnesses."[1] Scrutinizing the evidence forensically, however, it is impossible honestly to make such a conclusion.

Moreover, even the latest of the accepted gospel dates are not based on evidence from the historical, literary or archaeological record, and over the centuries a more "radical" school of thought has placed the creation or emergence of the canonical gospels as we have them at a much later date, more towards the *end of the second century*.

Anonymous and Pseudonymous Authors

Based on the dating difficulties and other problems, many scholars and researchers over the centuries have become convinced that the gospels were not written by the people to whom they are ascribed. As can be concluded from the remarks of fundamentalist Christian and biblical scholar Dr. Craig L. Blomberg, the gospels are in fact *anonymous*.[2] Indeed, the belief in the authorship of the gospels by Matthew, Mark, Luke and John is a matter of *faith*, as such an opinion is not merited in light of detailed textual and historical analysis. In reality, it was a fairly common practice in ancient times to attribute falsely to one person a book or letter written by another or others, and this *pseudepigraphical* attribution of authorship was especially rampant with religious texts, occurring with several Old Testament figures and early Church fathers, for example, as well as with known forgeries in the name of characters from the New Testament such as the Gospel of Peter, et al.

In actuality, there were gospels composed in the name of *every* apostle, including Thomas, Bartholomew and Phillip, but these texts are considered "spurious" and unauthorized. Although it would be logical for all those directly involved with Jesus to have recorded their own memoirs, is it not odd

---

[1] Geisler, *CA*, 327.
[2] Strobel, 26.

that there are so many *bogus* manuscripts? What does it all mean? If Peter didn't write the Gospel of Peter, then who did? And why? Is not the practice of pseudepigraphy—the false attribution of a work by one author to another—an admission that *there were many people within Christianity engaging in forgery*? If these apostles themselves had gospels forged in their names, how can we be certain that Matthew, Mark, Luke and John did not likewise have gospels falsified in *their* names? And even if they did not, but so much of these texts has been changed, how do we know what really happened or even *if* anything did occur?

According to Whom?

What we *do* know for a fact—admitted even by the *Catholic Encyclopedia*—is that the titles attached to the gospels, "The Gospel According to Matthew," etc., are not original to the texts but were added later. Indeed, the term "according to" in the original Greek—*kata*—could be interpreted to suggest that the texts were understood to be relating a *tradition of* these individuals, rather than having been *written by* them. In reality, *none* of the evangelists identifies himself as a character in the gospel story. As one glaring example of this detachment, it is claimed that Matthew was recording events he himself had witnessed, but the gospel attributed to him begins before he had been called by Jesus and speaks of Matthew in the third person. If Matthew wrote his gospel, why does he describe his meeting with Jesus in this manner: "As Jesus passed on from there, he saw a man called Matthew sitting at the tax office?" (Mt 9:9) Why does the gospel writer speak of himself in the third person and never even state that he was there or that he had witnessed anything? A similar sentiment may be expressed regarding the author of the gospel of John: If the author is really John, and John is the disciple "whom Jesus loved," why would he write about himself in the third person, as at John 20:2? Regarding John, in *The Pre-Nicene New Testament*, biblical scholar Dr. Robert Price concludes, "As for the vexing question of gospel authorship, we may immediately dismiss the claim that it was one of the twelve disciples of Jesus."[1]

---

[1] Price, 667

This subject of attribution is extremely important, because, as Tenney asserts, "if it could be shown that any of the books of the New Testament was falsely attributed to the person whose name it bears, its place in the canon would be endangered."[1]

"Back in the Day..."

Furthermore, there are places in the New Testament that imply the books were written long after the purported events, such as when the text reads, "In the days of John the Baptist," which indicates that the writer is set far ahead in time and is looking back. As another example, regarding Jesus's body being stolen, Matthew's gospel claims that "this story has been spread among the Jews to this day." The phrase "to this day" indicates that the writer is talking about a significant length of time, not shortly after the resurrection as some have attempted to place the composition and emergence of this gospel. In fact, we do not have any mention in the historical record of the story of Christ's body being stolen having been spread among the Jews until the *second* century. It is possible that this particular verse was not added until that time, which means that it is not original to the gospel and that Matthew certainly is not its author. Also, Luke's gospel discusses an apparent myriad of preceding gospels written "by those who from the beginning were eyewitnesses..." The phrase "from the beginning" likewise implies a passage of time, as does the fact that there were "many" who preceded Luke in writing gospels.

The Lukan Prologue

For a closer look at the pertinent Lukan verses regarding the possible dates of the canonical gospels, I provide here my own translation of Luke 1:1-4 from Stephens's Greek "Textus Receptus," used also by the translators of the King James Bible. In making this *very literal* translation of the Textus Receptus, I also consulted over 20 English editions, as well as the Latin Vulgate:

> Seeing that many had put their hand to set in order (*anatassomai*) a narrative (*diegesis*) about those things

---

[1] Tenney, 402.

fulfilled (*plerophoreo*) among us, as they delivered them to us—they (*hoi*) who from the beginning (*arche*) became eyewitnesses and servants/preachers of the Word—it seemed to me also, having closely traced (*parakoloutheo*) from the beginning (*anothen*) all of the things exactly (*akribos*) in order (*kathexes*), to write to you, most excellent Theophilus....

The term *plerophoreo*, as referring to "those things," i.e., the events of Jesus's advent, comes from the root *pleroo*, which means "to carry into effect, bring to realisation, realise," as in bringing to pass *prophecies*. Hence, Luke is evidently supposing that the events of the narrative constitute the fulfillment of messianic prophecies. It seems, then, that the narrative has been *derived* in order to "fulfill" this all-important occurrence of the messiah's advent, so highly and passionately anticipated. In other words, the Old Testament "prophecies" have been used as a *blueprint* to compose the gospel tale.

In a display of how translators can muddle original meaning, some translations render the term *hoi*—"they"—as referring to the preceding "us," implying that Luke himself was among those who "from the beginning became eyewitnesses and ministers." In fact the masculine plural article *hoi* is in the nominative and must refer to the "they" who delivered "those things," meaning Luke was *not* among the eyewitnesses and ministers from the beginning. The translation of *hoi* that makes Luke appear to be among the eyewitnesses is not only erroneous but also illogical: Why would "they" deliver to "us" the narrative, if "we" ourselves were eyewitnesses? Going against this erroneous tendency, the Darby, HNIV and AMP editions do indeed associate the article *hoi* with "they" rather than "us."

Although it also means "from above," many if not most translations in English of the term *anothen* render it as "from the first," "from the very first" "from the beginning," "some time past" or "from the origin," etc. The point here is that Luke—set apart in time from the events—is researching the story clear back to its beginning, not that Luke was there, following the story from its beginning, as it was happening.

As can be seen, Luke's gospel itself indicates a passage of time, during which *many* people had attempted to write the narrative of the purported eyewitnesses "from the beginning," again signifying significant time had elapsed.

Irenaeus, "Father of the Catholic Canon."

In addition to the issues already discussed in support of the later dates is the important fact that *the four canonical gospels were not mentioned or named as such by anyone until the time of Church father Irenaeus*, Bishop of Lyons (c. 120/140-c. 200/203 AD/CE). In *Against All Heresies* (III, 11.8), written around 180 AD/CE, Irenaeus is the first to name the canonical gospels and give reasons for their inclusion and number in the New Testament:

> It is not possible that the Gospels can be either more or fewer in number than they are. For, since there are four zones of the world in which we live, and four principal winds, while the Church is scattered throughout all the world, and the "pillar and ground" of the Church is the Gospel and the spirit of life; it is fitting that she should have four pillars, breathing out immortality on every side, and vivifying men afresh. From which fact, it is evident that the Word, the Artificer of all, He that sits upon the cherubim, and contains all things, He who was manifested to men, has given us the Gospel under four aspects, but bound together by one Spirit.

These remarks by Irenaeus represent the first mention of all four canonical gospels together. In fact, *prior to the end of the second century, there is no clear evidence of the existence of the canonical gospels as we have them.*

Church Father and Bishop Papias

Christian apologetics for the early gospel dates rely on the slimmest of evidence, including a very late third-hand testimony of a late second-hand testimony that "Mark" had written a narrative, supposedly based on the experiences of Peter as related by the apostle himself. In the fourth century, Church historian Eusebius quoted early Church father and bishop Papias of Hierapolis (c. 70?-c. 155? AD/CE) as referring to the "presbyter John" and stating:

This, too, the presbyter used to say. "Mark, who had been Peter's interpreter, wrote down carefully, but not in order, all that he remembered of the Lord's sayings and doings. *For he had not heard the Lord or been one of His followers*, but later, as I said, one of Peter's. Peter used to adapt his teachings to the occasion, without making a systematic arrangement of the Lord's sayings, so that Mark was quite justified in writing down some things just as he remembered them. For he had one purpose only—to leave out nothing that he had heard, and to make no misstatement about it.[1]

Regarding the bishop of Hierapolis, the Catholic Encyclopedia says, "Of Papias's life nothing is known."[2] In other words, we do not even know who this person is whom Eusebius is allegedly quoting regarding these purported earlier texts. According to Eusebius—in disagreement with Irenaeus, who suggested Papias *had* known the apostle John—Papias had no direct acquaintance with *any* of the apostles:

...Papias himself in the preface to his work makes it clear that he was never a hearer or eyewitness of the holy apostles, and tells us that he learnt the essentials of the faith from their former pupils.[3]

The assumption that the "presbyter John" with whom Papias apparently had a relationship was the same as the apostle John is evidently incorrect. Papias himself remarked that he received his knowledge second-hand, even about the apostle John, when he stated:

And whenever anyone came who had been a follower of the presbyters, I inquired into the words of the presbyters, what Andrew or Peter had said, or Philip or Thomas or James or John or Matthew, or any other disciple of the Lord, were still saying.[4]

---

[1] Eusebius (III, 39), 103-104. (Emph. added.)
[2] *CE*, "St. Papias."
[3] Eusebius (III, 39:2), 101-102.
[4] Eusebius (III, 39), 103.

These comments indicate that the bishop was not in direct communication with *any* of the immediate apostles or disciples of the Lord. Indeed, Papias is merely passing along what he had heard from the disciples' "former pupils." What exactly is meant by "*former* pupils?" Such a statement implies that these individuals were either no longer followers or were deceased. If these individuals Papias is relying on were not even Christ's followers at that time, why should we trust their statements? Many of Papias's remarks, according to Eusebius, involved miracles, such as the raising of the dead, which stretch the credulity. Are we supposed merely to take Papias's word on what else he was told by these "former followers?" Moreover, even Eusebius does not think highly of Papias, remarking, "For he seems to have been a man of very small intelligence, to judge from his books."[1]

Regarding Papias's purported discussion of an original "Gospel of Matthew," a collection of Jesus's sayings in "Hebrew" or, rather, *Aramaic*, Tenney comments:

> The testimony of Papias has been frequently rejected, since no trace of an Aramaic original has survived and the language of the Gospel bears no marks of being a Greek translation.[2]

Nevertheless, Papias's remarks about a book of *sayings* in Aramaic by Matthew may well refer to a text extant in his time, which may have been used by the evangelists.

Indeed, in some early Christian texts there appear *sayings* that seem to correspond to some found in the gospels, but these isolated *logia* could easily be from earlier source texts utilized by the evangelists as well. In "The Use of the Logia of Matthew in the Gospel of Mark," Charles A. Briggs remarks:

> The Logia of the apostle Matthew, written in the Hebrew language, according to the testimony of Papias, in the citation of Eusebius, was one of the most important sources of the Gospels. Certainly a considerable portion of the Sayings of Jesus given in the Gospels of Matthew and Luke came from this

---

[1] Eusebius (III, 39), 103.
[2] Tenney, 150.

source. It is still in dispute, however, whether the Logia of Matthew was used by the Gospels of Mark and John.[1]

Modern scholars have struck upon a sayings gospel called "Q" for the German term *Quelle*, meaning "source." In *New Testament Documents*, Christian scholar F.F. Bruce logically posits that Q is in fact based on the Matthaean logia, or sayings found in the Aramaic Gospel of Matthew. Again, it would be reasonable to suggest that such a text or texts had been used by both the evangelists and early Christian writers; thus, the existence of sayings in early Christian texts that parallel those found in the canonical gospels does *not* prove the existence of the latter at the time the former were composed.

Despite all these factors, Papias is one of the only pieces of evidence Christian apologetics offers as to the dating of the gospels—yet, his testimony concerning these writings of Mark and Matthew is not only second-hand but also too late to possess any value as concerns the earliest of the gospels dates. Moreover, Papias only speaks about a *narrative* by Mark, which by no means conclusively refers to the canonical Mark as we have it. Nor, as we have seen, is the Aramaic gospel of Matthew the same as the canonical Matthew. Furthermore, from Papias's comments we can adduce that Mark was never a disciple who had ever heard or followed Christ, as has been erroneously asserted by a number of apologists claiming that Mark may have been one of the 70 or 72 disciples mentioned in the gospel of Luke (10:1).

In addition, from Eusebius it appears that Papias— rumored to have some relationship with the apostle John— does not mention any gospel of John! From this fact and other reasons, it can be safely stated that the gospel of John did not exist at that time, i.e., the first quarter of the second century. Nor does Papias mention Luke or give any indication of a narrative gospel of Matthew.

Justin Martyr

As proof of the existence of the gospels prior to the end of the second century, it is claimed that Church father Justin

---

[1] Briggs, "TULM."

Martyr (c. 110-c. 165 AD/CE) included *268* "quotations of the New Testament" in his writings, an extraordinary figure from a chart in Josh McDowell's book *New Evidence that Demands a Verdict*.[1] However, the various assertions regarding "quotes" from biblical texts in early Christian writings rank as highly misleading. In the first place, there appears nothing prior to Justin Martyr (c. 150 AD/CE) that we can point to as real evidence of the existence of the canonical gospels, which is why Justin Martyr heads the chart in McDowell's book. In fact, virtually all of the numerous quotes purportedly from the New Testament listed in the Catholic Encyclopedia,[2] for example, as found in earlier Christian writings constitute *sayings* that may have been transmitted orally or in other source texts such as the Aramaic Gospel of Matthew or Q. Next, upon close inspection, the material from Justin Martyr—such as the "Memoirs of the Apostles"—does *not* correspond well enough to that found in the canonical gospels and is likely from another common source text or texts. Indeed, renowned biblical scholar Tischendorf only managed to find *two* pertinent quotations in Justin Martyr's works that could possibly come from the gospel of Matthew, for example.[3] Again, these miniscule passages could very well come from a shared source text.

The Rylands Papyrus

Aside from various sayings within the writings of the Church fathers that resemble those found in the gospels but may well come from common source texts, the *only* widely accepted evidence that places the emergence of *any* of the canonical gospels before the end of the *second* century is a small scrap of papyrus called the "Rylands fragment" or P52, which contains several dozen letters scattered across four verses of John's gospel (18:31-33). The dates for this tiny fragment—the provenance of which is unknown and the authenticity of which has been disputed—are by no means set in stone and have been posited from the "wishful

---

[1] McDowell, 43.
[2] *CE*, "Gospel of St. Matthew."
[3] See also *Suns of God* for a thorough discussion about the value of Justin Martyr as well as other Christian and non-Christian evidences.

thinking" of 90 AD/CE all the way to the end of the second century. The presumed dating of P52 to the first half of the second century has been called "sensational" and seems untenable. One significant argument against the early dating of P52 is that the fragment was part of a codex, or book, rather than a scroll, and there are few examples of such books in existence at such an early date. Moreover, in a fairly recent paleographical study published in the *Archiv für Papyrusforschung* 35 (1989), German scholar Andreas Schmidt suggested a date for P52 of 170 AD/CE +/- 25 years. The fact is that paleography is a difficult and imprecise science, especially for as tiny a fragment as P52, which means that caution is warranted in making definitive declarations, particularly in regard to the earlier dates. As New Testament professor and Christian manuscript expert Dr. Larry Hurtado states:

> ...because paleographical dating can rarely be more precise than +/- 25 to 50 years, the proposed dating of many manuscripts will lie across two centuries (e.g., second/third century CE).[1]

Combined with these factors, since the gospel of John does not appear in the literary record until the end of the second century, logic would suggest the later dating of P52 to be more accurate. The debate continues, but the value of P52 in providing evidence of a *first* century date for John's gospel seems to be nil.

The same may be said of the other early papyri fragments, P90 (Jn 18:36-40; 19:1-7), P98 (Rev 1:13-20) and P104 (Mt 21:34-37; 43, 45?), speculatively dated to the middle of the second century +/- 50 years. These fragments—two of which, P90 and P104, are from the massive collection found at Oxyrhynchus in Egypt—may well be from the *end* of the second century at the earliest, particularly since they are evidently in the uncial style of Greek writing, which apparently began to emerge at the end of the second century or into the third century. Early to mid-second century dates for other papyri such as P1, P66 or P77 are not accepted by mainstream scholarship and likely

---

[1] Hurtado, 45.

constitute wishful thinking that assumes the gospel history, rather than seeking a scientific assessment.

Late Dating of the Gospels?

It is not within the scope of this present work to examine thoroughly the alternative argument for a late dating of the gospels. This important scholarship is based principally on a close examination of the most ancient Christian texts,[1] as well as archaeological evidence—or lack thereof—and various anachronisms. The result is that there is good reason to include these late dates in our investigation, and doing so may yield some surprising results concerning the authorship of the gospels.

Engaging for a moment in "outrageous speculation" to demonstrate how alternative dating of at least one of the gospels may provide solutions to outstanding problems, we will take as an example the gospel of Luke, particularly since it is asserted that "the key to dating the Gospels is the Book of Luke."[2]

In dating Luke's gospel, which is addressed to "most excellent Theophilus," it should first be noted that nowhere does the author identify himself as the Luke who was a companion of Paul, mentioned in three Pauline epistles. In fact, other than the title "the Gospel according to Luke"— which is admitted by all authorities to be an addition and not original to the text—Luke's name does not show up in *any* gospel. Despite outward appearances, it is by no means certain that the author of Luke, who was neither an apostle nor a known disciple, was anywhere near in time to the events he is recording. When we factor in the Acts of the Apostles, which is widely regarded as having been written by the same person as the gospel of Luke and which likewise addresses "Theophilus," a whole new can of worms is opened, as there is also no record of *that* book having been written or existing before the *end of the second century.* Furthermore, other than the Jewish high priest Theophilus

---

[1] The minutiae of this subject can be studied in Walter Richard Cassels's exhaustive analysis *Supernatural Religion*, an comprehensive survey of all of the early Christian writings in the original Greek and Latin, with English translations and commentary.
[2] Geisler, *CA*, 312.

(37-41 AD/CE) briefly mentioned in Josephus (*Ant.*, XVIII, 5, 3)—a highly unlikely candidate for Luke's pen-pal, particularly since Josephus certainly says nothing about what would constitute a stunning conversion to Christianity—*there is no appearance in the historical record of any other "Theophilus" earlier than the bishop of Antioch* (fl. c. 168-c. 181/188 AD/CE). Thus, the identity of Luke's Theophilus has never been explained adequately in terms of the purported era of Christ's advent.

Some scholars and apologists have sought to explain this name "Theophilus" as more of an epithet, meaning "Lover of God"; hence, it has been suggested that Luke was addressing his text to "God-lovers" in general. Among other reasons, the fact that Acts also begins with a greeting to this "Theophilus" makes it more likely that it is a name of an individual, not simply a title. In the original Greek, Luke calls Theophilus "*kratistos*," a term used biblically with the following meaning, per Strong's Biblical Concordance (G2903):

1) mightiest, strongest, noblest, most illustrious, best, most excellent
   a) used in addressing men of prominent rank or office

In discussing the word "Theophilus," Strong's asserts that it is a *single individual* to whom Luke is addressing his gospel and Acts. In addition, someone with the title *kratistos* is likely not to be an obscure, lower-class individual but, rather, a person of rank.

Theophilus, Bishop of Antioch

Concerning Theophilus, Christian biblical commentator David Brown (1871) remarks, "It is likely 'Theophilus' was chief magistrate of some city in Greece or Asia Minor." Could not this "chief magistrate" be a *bishop*, and this "city in Asia Minor" be *Antioch*? Especially since it was asserted by ancient authorities that Luke himself was from Antioch? And that the Christians were first so-called at Antioch? It is possible that Luke's Theophilus is indeed the bishop of Antioch, who was a "Pagan"[1] convert to Christianity, fitting

---

[1] The word "pagan" meaning "peasant" in Latin was used as a pejorative term to make non-Christians seem backward and foolish.

in with Luke's assertions concerning Theophilus's instruction in Christian doctrine. In fact, Bishop Theophilus (c. 115-c. 181/188 AD/CE) was one of the early Christian apologists, composing an apology called *Ad Autolychum* (c. 176), in which the author describes himself as a convert from "heathenism."[1] It is singularly noticeable that, despite his sincerity as a Christian convert, in this work Theophilus does not discuss *any* of the synoptic gospels, a fact which tends to validate the notion that the gospels were not in circulation at that point and that Luke may have been composing his gospel specifically to encourage the bishop in his apologetics.

In book II, chapter XXII of *Ad Autolychum*, Theophilus does bring up a "spirit-bearing" man named John, giving some language that appears to be from the first chapter of the Gospel of John. However, we cannot be certain that this brief mention is not a later interpolation by a Christian scribe, and, even if we accept that this passage genuinely came from Theophilus's hand, he does not state that John was an apostle or immediate disciple of Christ's. Moreover, in his apology Theophilus specifically says that he was converted to Christianity through reading the *Jewish* scriptures. If the gospels had been known at that time, why would Theophilus need to rely on the Jewish scriptures for his conversion from Paganism? In discussing his own conversion, would a proselyte to Christianity refer only to the "sacred scriptures of the holy prophets," as Theophilus does in chapter 14 of his apology? Could it be that these canonical gospels—the most valuable tool for proselytizing—were not yet in existence by that time?

In any event, with this reference in his apology and a purported text of commentaries on the gospels, *Bishop Theophilus becomes the first Church father clearly to discuss the canonical gospels*! Indeed, in the "Introductory Note" to one authoritative translation of *Ad Autolychum*, Rev. Marcus Dods remarks of Theophilus:

> *He was one of the earliest commentators upon the Gospels, **if not the first**; and he seems to have been*

---

[1] *CE*, "Theophilus."

the earliest Christian historian of the Church of the Old Testament.[1]

In this astounding admission, Rev. Dods is referring to one of Theophilus's lost works, apparently his commentary on the Gnostic-Christian "heretic" Marcion (fl. c. 155-166 AD/CE), the originator of the New Testament. Dods also names Theophilus the "founder of the science of Biblical Chronology among Christians." Why, then, is this important Christian authority rarely discussed? Is it because, perhaps, Theophilus represents a "smoking gun" when it comes to unraveling the era of the canonical gospels' composition? Moreover, Dods further acclaims Theophilus's ability in his apology to describe "the Antioch of the early Christians," which is fitting for the bishop of the place where Christ's followers were first called Christians. In fact, it may be surprising for many to discover that it was in the *Syrian* city of Antioch, rather than anywhere in Judea, that Christ's followers were first named "Christians." Does that fact make any sense, if Christ had a large following originating in Judea beginning decades earlier? Why would they not have been named *there*? Why Syria? It is evident Antioch played a significant role in the development of Christianity that is not widely addressed.

Who are the "Many?"

The fact that Luke is superseding "many" narratives also fits in with the idea that his gospel was composed at the end of the second century, as there *were many* gospels by that time.[2] Trying to fit Luke into the middle or end of the first century, however, is an endeavor rife with problems, including that there certainly were not "many" gospels in circulation or even in existence by that time. This suggestion also presents us with some clarity on the tradition beginning in the late second century that Luke's gospel supposedly had

---

[1] Dods, "Introductory Note to Theophilus of Antioch."

[2] Waite notes that the German critic Schleiermacher determined Luke's gospel to have been compiled from 33 different manuscripts, and he shows the very divisions upon which these are delineated (Waite, 379-380). According to Waite's survey of Church fathers and other Christian authorities, "It is the universal conclusion, that the author of Luke does not here refer to any of the canonical gospels." (385)

been corrupted by Marcion during the middle of the second century. In reality, it seems the author of Luke may have based his gospel on Marcion's "Gospel of the Lord," rather than vice versa. Furthermore, in determining which texts Luke may be referring to, a number of Church fathers, including Origen, Epiphanius and Jerome, as well as other Christian authorities such as the Venerable Bede (8th cent.), evidently named books from authors of the *second century* such as the Gospels of the Egyptians and the Twelve Apostles, as well as the writings of the Gnostic-Christian heretic Cerinthus.[1]

In Origen's *Homily on Luke 1.1*, the original Latin edition reads:

> Ecclesia quator habet evangelia, haeresis plurima, e quibus quoddam scribitur secundum Aegyptios, aliud iuxta duodecim apostolos. ausus fuit et Basilides scribere evangelium et suo illud nomine titulare.

This passage is translated as:

> The church has four gospels, heresy many, from among which a certain one is written according to the Egyptians, another according to the twelve apostles. Even Basilides dared to write a gospel and to entitle it by his own name.[2]

The Greek edition of this quote does not contain the word "twelve" in numbering the apostles. In his *Homily on Luke 1.1*, Origen argues that none of these "many" could be the canonical gospels because the authors of these preceding efforts were "trying" to write the gospel, whereas "Matthew, Mark, John, and Luke did not 'try' to write..."[3] Instead, in consideration of the fact that Origen is addressing his Homily specifically to Luke 1:1, in which the evangelist discusses the "many," it would appear that the Church father is counting among these "many" the *haeresis plurima*—or, "heresy many"—such as the Gospel of the Egyptians and the Gospel of the Twelve Apostles. Origen's aside about the Gospel of Basilides cannot be deemed for certain to mean that Luke

---

[1] Waite, 385-6.
[2] Smith, "The Jewish-Christian gospels."
[3] Lienhard.

used the Gnostic-Christian "heretic's" work as well. The best evidence indicates a middle to late second-century date for the existence of these texts, with the earliest dates (c. 100-150 AD/CE) based on the *a priori* presumption that the received gospel and church history are factual.

In reality, the earliest mentions of the Gospel of the Egyptians appear to be in the writings of Church fathers at the end of the second century to the fourth century, such as Clement Alexandrinus, Origen, Hippolytus and Epiphanius. But, even the earliest of the dates for this gospel and that of the Twelve Apostles would place the composition of Luke at the end of the first century at the very earliest. Moreover, Basilides supposedly thrived during Hadrian's reign, which ended in 138 AD/CE. Any work of Basilides would date to no earlier than the first quarter of the second century.

Another Church father who mentions various writers in his discussion of Luke's "many" is Epiphanius of Salamis (c. 310-403 AD/CE), who in his *Panarion* names "Cerinthus, Merinthus and others" in response to Luke 1:1 (in the original Greek):

Επειδηπερ πολλοι επεχειρησαν ινα τινας μεν επιχειρη τας δειξη Φημι δε τους περι Κηρινθον, και Μηρινθον, και τους αλλους.[1]

Waite translates this passage thus:

"Forasmuch as many have taken in hand," by which he would intimate that there have been many undertakers of the like work. Among them, I suppose, were Cerinthus, Merinthus, and others.[2]

The dating of the Gnostic-Christian heretic Cerinthus to the beginning of the second century is likewise based on the circular reasoning which presupposes that the gospel and church history are true, particularly upon the claims by Irenaeus and Jerome that John's gospel was written against Cerinthus. If John was composed by the end of the first century, it is reasoned, then Cerinthus must have existed at that time as well. In any event, Cerinthus cannot be dated to any earlier than 100 AD/CE, and some have placed him in the

---

[1] Epiphanius, *Heresy* II, VII.
[2] Waite, 386.

middle of the second century,[1] although he may have flourished prior to around 120. Hence, if Luke based his gospel on Cerinthus's writings, the emergence of Luke again needs to be pushed into the second century.

Following Epiphanius, in the "Preface" to his *Commentary on Matthew*, St. Jerome (c. 340-2 to 420) made some extremely interesting statements in the same vein:

> The evangelist Luke declares that there were many who wrote gospels, when he says, "forasmuch as many, etc...", which being published by various authors, gave rise to several heresies. They were such as that according to the Egyptians, and Thomas, and Matthias, and Bartholomew, that of the Twelve Apostles, and Basilides, and Apelles, and others which it would be tedious to enumerate.[2]

Theron's translation of these surprising remarks occurs as follows:

> Luke, the Evangelist, also testifies that there have been many who wrote Gospels, saying: "For many, indeed..." and up to the present time they are declaring with perseverance the records which have been published by diverse authors as the beginning of diverse heresies: as, for instance, "those" [Gospels] according to the Egyptians and [according to] Thomas and Matthias and Bartholomew, and also [that] of the twelve Apostles and of both Basilides and Apelles and of the rest, which to enumerate is too long...[3]

---

[1] Waite, 400.

[2] Waite, 385. The Latin original for this quote of Jerome's is: "Plures fuisse qui euangelia scripserunt, et Lucas euangelista testatur dicens Quoniam quidem multi conati sunt ordinare narrationem rerum, quae in nobis completae sunt, sicut tradiderunt nobis qui ab initio ipsi underunt sermonem et ministrauerunt ei, et perseurantia usque ad praesens tempus monumenta declarant, quae a diuersis auctoribus edita, diuersarum haeresium fuere principia, ut est illud iuxta Aegyptios et Thomamet Matthiamet Barthlomeum duodecin quoque apostolurm et Basilids atque Apellis ac reliquorum, quos enumerare longissimum est, cum hoc tantum in praesnetiarum necesse sit dicere, extitisse quosdam, qui sine spiritu et gratia dei conati sun magis ordinare narrationem, quam historiae texere ueritatem." (Theron, 50.)

[3] Theron, 51.

From these translations of the original Latin, it appears that Jerome is stating that the texts of the "many" to whom Luke refers include the gospels of the Egyptians and the Twelve Apostles, as well as those of Thomas, Matthias, Bartholomew, Basilides and Appelles. With this evident validation, Jerome dropped a bombshell which might have shaken the foundations of the Church but which has apparently been ignored, with translations omitting this part of the saint's Preface, and the original Latin of which possibly difficult to track down outside of a major university. Whether or not Luke used these particular texts is immaterial, as what is important is that, in referring to these writers at all, Luke must have composed his gospel *after* these heretical books already existed. Like those of the Egyptians and Twelve Apostles, none of the gospels of Thomas, Matthias and Bartholomew can be placed earlier than the second century, although there are "wishful-thinking" first-century arguments for Thomas, evidently the earliest of the three.

This interpretation of Jerome's remarks regarding the gospels of Basilides and Apelles as two of the persons to whom Luke refers was evidently upheld by the respected theologian Venerable Bede in his *In Lucae Evangelium Expositio* (734 AD/CE).[1] Slightly later than Basilides, the Gnostic-Christian "heretic" Apelles thrived in the middle of the second century and was said to be a disciple of Marcion who redacted the latter's Gospel of the Lord.[2] Thus, if Luke's gospel postdated their texts, his own could date to no earlier than the second quarter to the middle of the second century. Moreover, the association of Apelles with Luke adds to the argument that Luke based his gospel largely on Marcion's Gospel, and not vice versa.

Luke's Use of Josephus?

Another longstanding argument for a later date for Luke's gospel is that the evangelist used the works of Jewish historian Josephus to pad out his history. Although Christian apologetics argues for the opposite influence, when the most scientific criteria are applied to the investigation, Josephus comes up first, with Luke following. These arguments are

---

[1] Waite, 386. See Giles, *The Complete Works of the Venerable Bede*, vol. X, p. 273.
[2] Schneemelcher, 400.

lengthy but include Luke's inclusion of the following episodes found in Josephus:

- The census under Quirinius/Cyrenius
- The three Jewish rebel leaders
- The death of Herod Agrippa
- Various aspects of Felix's life
- The tetrarch Lysanias
- The "parable of the hated king"
- The famine during the reign of Claudius
- Pilate's aggressions[1]

If we factor into this discussion the work released in 1995 by Dr. G.J. Goldberg, based on a search of the massive *Thesaurus Linguae Graecae* database concerning the TF and Luke's "Emmaus" passage (24:19-21, 25-27), we are left with the distinct impression that Josephus and Luke are inextricably linked. Indeed, the TF/Emmaus comparison, done using a database of all extant Greek and Latin texts up to the year 600 AD/CE, strongly indicates that one borrowed from the other or both used a common source text. In consideration of the facts outlined here regarding the gospel dates, however, it becomes reasonable to state that Luke used Josephus, and not the other way around. Or, at least, Josephus's use of a common source or sources occurred decades before Luke's use of the same texts. Considering that the Luke/Josephus connection goes beyond just a couple of similarities, and that Josephus clearly did not have before him Luke's gospel, it would be further reasonable to suggest that it was Josephus's work used by the author of Luke, rather than a common source text, unless that too was based on Josephus, which makes the point rather moot. All in all, the scientific, "forensic" evidence points to Luke using Josephus.

In this scenario of Luke using Josephus, the earliest time for the composition of Luke's gospel would be the last decade of the first century. However, as we have seen, there is reason to suspect that it was composed much later, nevertheless using possibly the best known history of that era, the works of Josephus.

---

[1] Carrier, "Luke and Josephus."

There are thus several good and valid reasons to suspect that, despite current beliefs regarding its date, the gospel of Luke as we have it represents a late second-century creation.

John's Gospel

As noted, despite familiarity with John, Papias does not identify any *gospel* of John. Nor, in reality, is there any clear evidence that Justin Martyr knew about the Johannine writings. Again, the first notice of John's gospel emerges around the time of Bishop Theophilus, who, while he does name a "John" as the author of verses seemingly from the first chapter of the gospel of John, does not identify the author as a direct apostle or disciple of Christ.

Other mentions of John's gospel occur around the same time by Clement Alexandrinus (d. c. 215), as well as commentary by Tatian (fl. 160-185), and then a grandiose and strident apology by Irenaeus, from whose pen it has been suspected the gospel originally emanated, as a defense against the "heretical" but powerful Gnostic sect of Docetism. In fact, the evidence points to the existence of Docetism, *which denied Christ had come in the flesh, prior* to the emergence of the Catholic Church, which did not formally come into being until this very period, under the impetus of Irenaeus. The argument for this assertion that Irenaeus himself authored John includes the fact that the Church father was provoked passionately to defend the gospel, which he does with a fervor that often accompanies a "pet project." Even if John were composed by another's hand, this abundance of defense suggests that the gospel had not been in existence for a long time, as has been claimed, but had only recently emerged in the literary and historical record, leading to the gospel immediately being attacked and dismissed.

In his defense, Irenaeus claims that John was written against the heretic Cerinthus, who was spreading the error of "gnosis," but it seems as if John was also written in order to combat the "heresy" of Christ not coming in the flesh, which was called "Docetism." In fact, Irenaeus fairly foams at the mouth when going after these heretics who did not confess Christ had come in the flesh. In other words, Jesus's very incarnation was at stake, and Irenaeus's goal was to wipe out two Gnostic birds with one stone.

Gospel Anachronisms

In addition to these profound reasons for a later dating of the canonical gospels as we have them, some of the variant readings and assorted other anachronisms within the gospels tend to confirm these late dates in terms of words used, writing style, and politics of the day as well. As examples of terms anachronistically used that indicate a late dating for at least parts of the gospels, a number of word usages supposedly articulated by Jesus were not "in vogue" until after the destruction of the Jewish temple in 70 AD/CE. These terms used anachronistically in the gospels include: 1. "Gehenna" (Hell) as a place of punishment; 2. "synagogue" as concerns a place of prayer; 3. "sanhedrin" as referring to the Jewish court; and 4. "mammon" as meaning "money."[1] In the Sermon on the Mount in Matthew, Jesus is represented as assailing prayer in public, as in the synagogues, when in reality synagogues were never used as houses of prayer until after the temple was destroyed. Hence, this part of the Sermon could not have been written until after that time, which means either that the gospel itself dates to then, or the passage was a later interpolation and was certainly not spoken by Jesus. That the Sermon on the Mount represents a later patchwork is further evidenced by the fact that the Lord's Prayer, for example, appears nowhere in the rest of the early Christian writings, including the other canonical texts, as well as those of the Church fathers—an astounding omission in consideration of the fact that this prayer was supposedly ordained from on high by God/Jesus, during his advent. Indeed, it is possible to demonstrate that the Sermon as a whole was strung together using sayings from the Old Testament and the rabbinical tradition. As Jewish scholar Gerald Friedlander states in *The Jewish Sources of the Sermon on the Mount*, "Four-fifths of the Sermon on the Mount is exclusively Jewish."[2]

---

[1] Friedlander, xii, xviii, xxx-xxxi.
[2] Friedlander, 266.

Another noted Jewish scholar, Solomon Zeitlin, concurs with the assessment that the Sermon is an aggregation: "Many of the sayings were not uttered by Jesus, but are the product of the time of the compilations,"[1] after the destruction of the temple. After breaking down the Sermon into parts, and after showing Old Testament precedents for several of the Beatitudes, Friedlander remarks, "The Beatitudes have undoubtedly a lofty tone, but let us not forget that all that they teach can be found in Isaiah and the Psalms."[2] In another chapter entitled, "The Old Testament as the Source of the Lord's Prayer," Friedlander goes into further detail demonstrating the Hebrew scriptural basis for that part of the Sermon as well. Friedlander further comments, "Once again we can see how the Gospels have borrowed the entire framework of the Messianic conception from the Pharisaic Judaism, out of which Christianity grew."[3]

The end of the Lord's Prayer at Matthew 6:13, called the "Doxology," is also lacking in the earliest manuscripts, and appears to have been added from 1 Chronicles 29:11, as yet another piece of the patchwork of Old Testament scriptures that constitute the Sermon on the Mount. As Friedlander states, "Doxologies are by no means uncommon in Jewish literature."[4] Regarding the Lord's Prayer in general, Friedlander further remarks, "The Lord's Prayer is...lacking in originality. There is not a single idea or expression which cannot be found in pre-Christian literature of Israel."[5] Thus, in the Sermon on the Mount we possess further indication of the use of the Old Testament as a *blueprint* for the creation of the New Testament, constituting one of more germane "fingerprints of the Christ."

Another similar anachronism in the gospels appears in the description of the "disciples of the Pharisees," as at Mark 2:18 and Luke 5:33. Since the Pharisees were technically not "priests" *per se* but pious, unlearned laymen, it would be unusual for them to have "disciples" in the clerical sense.

---

[1] Friedlander, xv.
[2] Friedlander, 23.
[3] Friedlander, 153. (Emph. added.)
[4] Friedlander, 162.
[5] Friedlander, 163.

This phrase may not have come into use until after the destruction of the temple in 70 AD/CE, which would mean that the writers were distanced from the events by a considerable amount of time.[1]

The Canon: A Second-Century Composition

With such remarkable declarations of the Church fathers, et al., as well as other cogent arguments, we possess some salient evidence that the gospels of Luke and John represent late second-century works. In fact, *all* of the canonical gospels seem to emerge at the same time—first receiving their names and number by Irenaeus around 180 AD/CE, and possibly based on one or more of the same texts as Luke, especially an "Ur-Markus" that may have been related to Marcion's Gospel of the Lord. In addition to an "Ur-Markus" upon which the canonical gospels may have been based has also been posited an "Ur-Lukas," which may likewise have "Ur-Markus" at its basis.

The following may summarize the order of the gospels *as they appear in the historical and literary record*, beginning in the middle of the second century:

1. Ur-Markus (150)
2. Ur-Lukas (150+)
3. Luke (170)
4. Mark (175)
5. John (178)
6. Matthew (180)

To reiterate, these late dates represent the time when these specific texts undoubtedly emerge onto the scene.[2] If the canonical gospels *as we have them* existed anywhere previously, they were unknown, which makes it likely that they were not composed until that time or shortly before, based on earlier texts. Moreover, these dates correspond perfectly with Theophilus's bishopric of Antioch, which has been dated from about 168 to either 181 or 188 and during which the first definite indications of the canonical gospels begin to materialize. After this time, in fact, the floodgates open up, with Irenaeus's canon, followed by

---

[1] Meier, II, 112-113.
[2] See Waite for arguments supporting this dating and order.

gospel commentaries of all manner by Irenaeus, Tertullian (c. 160-?; fl. 197), Origen, Eusebius, Chrysostom, Jerome and Augustine, et al. At least three Church fathers, as we have seen, pointed to Gnostic heretics of the second century as some of the "many" in Luke's prologue, also verifying a late second-century date for the emergence of that gospel.

When one considers the amount of time, effort and resources put into New Testament studies and criticism over the centuries, it is understandable that the wagons would circle whenever someone comes along with suggestions seemingly out of the ordinary, such as asserting late dates for the canonical gospels. One must ask, however, if there is no clear scientific evidence for the existence of these gospels before that time, would it not be more honest to entertain at least the *possibility* of their having been composed at a later date? One reason why considering this possibility is so important is precisely because there *have* been so much time, effort and resources put into NT studies. Some of the hardest nuts to crack exist largely because of the early dates attached to these texts, without valid scientific evidence. Without proper dates for these gospels, we will have little luck in establishing who Jesus was.

Jesus Outside of the Bible

"Apart from the New Testament writings and later writings dependent on these, our sources of information about the life and teaching of Jesus are scanty and problematic."

F.F. Bruce, *New Testament History* (163)

"The only definite account of his life and teachings is contained in the four Gospels of the New Testament, *Matthew*, *Mark*, *Luke* and *John*. All other historical records of the time are silent about him. The brief mentions of Jesus in the writings of Josephus, Tacitus and Suetonius have been generally regarded as not genuine and as Christian interpolations; in Jewish writings there is no report about Jesus that has historical value. Some scholars have even gone so far as to hold that the entire Jesus story is a myth..."

The Universal Jewish Encyclopedia (v. 6, 83)

The various problems with the numerous discrepancies and disputable dates of the canonical gospels suggest that these texts do not constitute entirely helpful or reliable biographies of Jesus Christ. It would thus be useful to turn our attention elsewhere for additional clues as to who Jesus was. However, when we go looking for material outside of the New Testament that might validate the events described there, we come up empty-handed, both textually and archaeologically. In other words, there is no *contemporaneous* evidence outside of the New Testament to attest to Christ's advent and ministry—or *even his existence*. This silence is singularly astounding, in consideration of the repeated assertions in the gospels that Christ was famed far and wide, drawing great crowds because of his miraculous healings, causing a fracas with the local and imperial authorities, and, upon his death, creating astonishing and awesome miracles and wonders the world had never seen before, including not only an earthquake and the darkening of the sun and moon, but also dead people rising from their graves and visiting people in town.[1] One would think that if all these things happened, someone somewhere would have written about them or otherwise recorded them for posterity. But, inspecting the literary, historical and archaeological record of the time produces *nothing*. The dearth of evidence is not for want of suitable reporters, as during the first century the following historians and writers depicted life in and around the Mediterranean, including in some of the very places that Jesus and his disciples purportedly moved about:

Aulus Perseus (60 AD)	Plutarch (c. 46-c. 119 AD)
Columella (1st cent. AD)	Pomponius Mela (40 AD)
Dio Chrysostom (c. 40-c. 112 AD)	Rufus Curtius (1st cent. AD)
Justus of Tiberius (c. 80 AD)	Quintilian (c. 35-c. 100 AD)
Livy (59 BC-17 AD)	Quintus Curtius (1st cent. AD)
Lucanus (fl. 63 AD)	Seneca (4 BC?-65 AD)
Lucius Florus (1st-2nd-cent. AD)	Silius Italicus (c. 25-101 AD)
Petronius (d. 66 AD)	Statius Caelicius (1st cent. AD)
Phaedrus (c. 15 BC-c. 50 AD)	Theon of Smyrna (c. 70-
Philo Judaeus (20 BC-50 AD)	c.135 AD)
Phlegon (1st cent. AD)	Valerius Flaccus (1st cent. AD)
Pliny the Elder (23?-69 AD)	Valerius Maximus (fl. c. 20 AD)

Oddly enough, not one of these writers recorded any of the amazing and earth-shaking events reported in the gospels, even though this period was one of the best documented in history and although some of these authors lived or traveled in the same small area in which the gospel story was set. Neither Jesus nor his disciples are mentioned by any of them—not a word about Christ, Christianity or Christians.

Concerning this peculiar deficiency of testimony, conservative Protestant writer Merrill Tenney remarks:

> One would naturally expect that the Lord Jesus Christ would be sufficiently important to receive ample notice in the literature of his time, and that extensive

---

[1] These "great crowds" and "multitudes," along with Jesus's fame, are repeatedly referred to in the gospels, including at the following: Mt 4:23-25, 5:1, 8:1, 8:18, 9:8, 9:31, 9:33, 9:36, 11:7, 12:15, 13:2, 14:1, 14:13, 14:22, 15:30, 19:2, 21:9, 26:55; Mk 1:28, 10:1; Lk 4:14, 4:37, 5:15, 14:25, etc.

biographical material would be available. He was observed by multitudes of people, and his own followers numbered into the hundreds (1 Cor. 15:6), whose witness was still living in the middle of the first century. As a matter of fact, the amount of information concerning him is comparatively meager. Aside from the four Gospels, and a few scattered allusions in the epistles, contemporary history is almost silent concerning him.[1]

Concurring with this assessment, Catholic University New Testament professor, ex-Catholic priest and monsignor Dr. John P. Meier, author of *A Marginal Jew*, states:

> ...there are very few sources for knowledge of the historical Jesus beyond the four canonical Gospels. Paul and Josephus offer little more than tidbits. Claims that later apocryphal Gospels and the Nag Hammadi material supply independent and reliable historical information about Jesus are largely fantasy. In the end, the historian is left with the difficult task of sifting through the Four Gospels for historical tradition.[2]

As we shall see, even the "tidbits" do not provide much sustenance.

Titus Flavius Josephus

To reiterate, there is in reality no acknowledgement of Christ's existence in *contemporary* history, which is in fact *entirely* silent concerning him. What we do find, however, are very short but much touted passages in the works of four writers of the *late first to early second century*, Josephus (37-c. 100 AD/CE), Tacitus (c. 107-116 AD/CE), Pliny (c. 111-113 AD/CE) and Suetonius (c. 110 AD/CE). As stated in the Universal Jewish Encyclopedia, the value and/or authenticity of these passages is disputed and questionable. For example, the passage in the works of Jewish historian Josephus called the "Testimonium Flavianum," which has been deemed by many the most valuable of this trifling

---

[1] Tenney, 203.
[2] Meier, II, 5.

collection of "proofs," has been assailed for centuries as a forgery in part or *in toto*, with a number of able critics putting forth an extensive case against its authenticity. Appearing in Josephus's *Antiquities of the Jews* (XVIII, III, 3), the Testimonium or "TF" goes as follows:

> Now, there was about this time, Jesus, a wise man, *if it be lawful to call him a man*, for he was a doer of wonderful works,—a teacher of such men as receive the truth with pleasure. He drew over to him both many of the Jews, and many of the Gentiles. *He was [the] Christ*; and when Pilate, at the suggestion of the principal men amongst us, had condemned him to the cross, those that loved him at the first did not forsake him, *for he appeared to them alive again the third day, as the divine prophets had foretold these and ten thousand other wonderful things concerning him*; and the tribe of Christians, so named from him, are not extinct at this day.[1]

Although at one point it was universally rejected by scholars as a forgery, in recent times there has been a clamor to establish the Josephus passage as genuine either wholly or partially, with Christian interpolations, as indicated by the italics. Reflecting the general impression of the earlier time regarding the TF, respected Jewish scholar Solomon Zeitlin remarked in 1969:

> Ever since Scalinger in the sixteenth century, the genuineness of the Christ passage in Josephus has been questioned. Friedlander, in following Niese, whom he regarded as the greatest authority on Josephus, considered this passage to be spurious. I fully share his opinion.[2]

Zeitlin continues by citing his published article, "The Christ Passage in Josephus," in which he sets out to prove that the TF was interpolated by Church historian Eusebius during the fourth century, when it first appears in the literary record.

---

[1] Whitson, 379. (Emph. added)
[2] Friedlander, xi.

Concerning the TF, Dr. Crossan comments, "It is either a total or partial interpolation by the Christian editors who preserved Josephus' works."[1] In evaluating this situation, it needs to be kept in mind that tampering and forgery were widespread in the ancient world, including in both non-Christian and Christian texts, as we have seen in the discussion regarding the massive amounts of variant readings in the copies of the New Testament, as well as the abundant creation of pseudepigraphical literature.

The arguments against the authenticity of the Testimonium Flavianum include that there is no mention of it before the time of Eusebius (c. 260-c. 339?). Indeed, no early Church father before then has taken the slightest notice of this very important testimony to the existence of the Lord and Savior, even though a number of them poured over the works of Josephus and other writers in order to find precisely such references to Christ, Christians or Christianity. Christian experts on Josephus such as Origen somehow missed this critical passage, the Church father even complaining that the Jewish historian did not consider Jesus to be the Christ.[2] Other arguments against the genuineness of the TF by a number of significant scholars, many of whom have been Christian, include, among several more: 1. It breaks the narrative preceding and succeeding it in an unnatural manner; 2. It is oddly brief in consideration of the numerous long passages Josephus writes regarding assorted other characters, such as some 20 *other* Jesuses; and, 3. The blatantly Christian language is likewise not natural to Josephus, a pious Jew. As another clue as to the possibly fraudulent nature of at least part of the TF, the Greek word *phylon*—"tribe"—in the TF constitutes a unique usage by Josephus, as he ordinarily utilizes it only to describe a nation, people or ethnicity, but never a religious group. Eusebius, however, does use the term *phylon* in this manner to describe Christians.

These contentions are hotly debated, of course, but even fervent Christian apologists such as Josh McDowell do not agitate for the TF's authenticity in toto, accepting instead the "partial interpolation theory," which asserts that the most

---

[1] Crossan, *THJ*, 373.
[2] Origen, *Contra Celsus*, I, 47.

Christian-sounding phrases were inserted into an existing passage genuine to Josephus.

One argument for the authenticity of the Testimonium as a whole contends that, since it is present in all existing copies of Josephus's *Antiquities*, it must have been in the original. This assertion sounds good, until it is realized that *there are no extant Greek copies of the Antiquities that predate the 9ᵗʰ to 11ᵗʰ century* (depending on the source), that all of these copies were made by Christians, and that all of them evidently were based on a single text. Regarding this argument that all copies of Josephus contain the TF, Meier cautions, "These facts must be balanced, however, by the sobering realization that we have only three Greek manuscripts of Book 18 of *The Antiquities*, the earliest which dates from the 11ᵗʰ century."[1] Moreover, the text of the TF differs significantly in an Arabic copy of the *Antiquities*, while an "old Russian" or Slavonic edition of the TF—which Meier calls a "clearly unauthentic text"[2]—appears not in the *Antiquities* but in Josephus's *Jewish War*. These facts tend to cast suspicion on the authenticity of the TF as a whole.

Another argument for the authenticity of the TF hinges on the fact that it represents a "neutral" or "ambiguous" depiction, which would explain why it was ignored by all the Church fathers prior to Eusebius.[3] In reality, the silence by the Church fathers regarding this passage, particularly if it was neutral or even negative, ranks as highly uncharacteristic. One would, in fact, expect a heated polemic, a critical analysis, an attempt at padding out the TF, or a long treatise called "Against Josephus" from the likes of Justin Martyr, Irenaeus, Origen and Tertullian, et al. Nevertheless, again, there remains nothing.

Our exploration of Luke's apparent usage of Josephus leads to another mystery regarding the TF: Relevant words from the TF—such as "Iesous," "man" and "deeds"—reveal a connection with *only* Luke and no other ancient text in the massive database searched by Dr. Goldberg, who discovered these correspondences between the original Greek of the TF and a scripture in Luke's "Emmaus passage" (Lk 24:19). The

---

[1] Meier, I, 62.
[2] Meier, I, 57.
[3] Meier, I, 68.

connection is so strong that one is almost certainly copied from the other. It would be mindboggling to think that Luke would copy his data about Jesus from Josephus, a notion that would, of course, suggest that the TF in part may be original to Josephus. However, a more scientifically satisfying suggestion posits that the forger of the pertinent part of the TF used Luke—and that Luke postdated the Jewish historian. Goldberg concludes that both the authors of Luke and the TF used a common Christian source-text, as possibly one of the "many" upon whose works the evangelist based his own material.

One argument against the TF being an interpolation contends that it closely mimics Josephus's style. However, again, the use of the term *phylon* is unprecedented in Josephus, as is the combination of the words "Iesous," "man" and "deeds," which appear to have come from Luke's gospel. Moreover, a skilled forger would be able to "digest" the style of his target (e.g., Josephus) in order to emulate him, and "regurgitate" using whatever source material he chose to best suit his purposes (Luke, *et al.*) In creating a passage out of whole cloth, there is no reason it could not be a piecemeal production from memory of a series of passages. The TF is short enough that such a solution does not seem implausible at all, even if there appears, as Goldberg suggests, no precise precedent in the long chronicle of Christian interpolations. The obscurity of the Emmaus passage only serves to make it more desirable to a forger, as such a fraud would be less likely detected. An accomplished counterfeiter knowing Josephus would surely attempt to emulate the style of not only the author but also the time. Arguing, as does Goldberg, that the TF more closely resembles an earlier phase in the Jewish-Christian depiction of the passion one presumes that the story truly happened as portrayed and during the era represented.

Regarding Josephus and the Testimonium, F.F. Bruce, one of the founders of the modern evangelical Christian movement, concludes:

> ...a paragraph about Jesus...was evidently modified
> and interpolated at an early stage in the course of

transmission to suit Christian tastes. *It cannot therefore be adduced with confidence as evidence...*[1]

The same determination of "modification" and "interpolation" has been made by those arguing against the authenticity of the phrase "brother of Jesus, who was called Christ" in the "James passage" in Josephus's *Antiquities* (XX, IX, 1)—at least as applies to the phrase "who was called Christ," which unnaturally breaks the text and seems to be an interpolation. The evidence against this latter phrase being genuine also includes that, again, Church father Origen—who studied Josephus's works and used them to refute critics such as Celsus—specifically complained that the Jewish historian did *not* consider Jesus to be the Christ. This phrase "who was called Christ" may have been copied from the gospel of Matthew (1:16), possibly long after Josephus's time. Furthermore, the James in this passage has not been concretely identified with the James in the gospel story, as Josephus's James died some seven years prior to the death of the New Testament's "James the Just."

Despite the conclusions reached by Bruce and many others that Josephus "cannot be adduced with confidence as evidence," Meier insists that this debate about Josephus becomes critical to proving that Christ even existed. Hence, Christ's very existence hangs on the slender thread of the TF. Since this debate about Josephus has gone on long enough and will seemingly never end, let us for a moment assume that the Testimonium Flavianum is genuine, in whole or in part. Even with such an assumption, the TF still does *not* constitute credible, scientific proof of the historicity of Jesus Christ, since it was not written by an eyewitness, nor is it based on any discernible documents of any authority. The TF reflects only a *tradition* or *rumor* of something that purportedly occurred 60 to 70 years earlier and made little to no impact upon anyone significant outside of immediate Christian circles.

Pliny the Younger

The writings of Roman authors Pliny, Suetonius and Tacitus held up as evidence of Christ's life are also very

---

[1] Bruce, *NTH*, 166. (Emph. added.)

questionable in their value, as they are either ambiguous as to who or what they are describing, or—in the case of Tacitus especially—may likewise be forgeries in part or in whole, as they have been considered to be at various points in the past.

In a letter to the Emperior Trajan (c. 100 AD/CE), Pliny, who was governor of Bithynia at the time, asks for assistance in dealing with "Christiani" brought before him in his court, complaining that these Christiani sing hymns or chant verses "in honor of Christ as if to a god." If Pliny's letter is genuine, it would serve only to demonstrate that there were people termed "Christians" who were singing hymns to a *god* with the *title* of "Christos" around the beginning of the second century. Neither Pliny's letter nor the response by Trajan mention anything about this god having a life on Earth; nor do they ever call him "Jesus." In reality, the epithet "Christos"—χριστος—is used *40 times* in the Septuagint version of the Old Testament, centuries before the Christian era, as applied to a variety of characters, including in several references to "the Lord's anointed."[1] Indeed, in 1 and 2 Samuel the first king of Israel, Saul, is repeatedly referred to as "Christos"—*Christ*—at least a couple of hundred years before Jesus was given the same title. By the end of 2 Samuel (23:1), it is David who is called "Christ." In 2 Chronicles 6:42, David's son Solomon becomes God's Christ, and at 2 Chronicles 22:7 it is Jehu who is the Lord's anointed. As can be seen, there have been *many* Christs—all leaving behind their own fingerprints.

From the foregoing facts, it can be asserted that Pliny provides no useful information either as to who Jesus was or even whether or not he existed. Like the missives of Pliny and Trajan, the letter or "rescript" of Emperor Hadrian to Minucius Fundanus, said by Eusebius to have been attached to Justin Martyr's *First Apology*, also cited as evidence of Christ's life, is doubtful as to both its genuineness and its usefulness. Even if it were authentic, the letter likewise is too late to serve as evidence of anything but the existence of Christians in the empire by Hadrian's time (117-138 AD/CE).

---

[1] 1 Sam 12:5, 16:6, 24:7, 24:11, 26:9, 26:11, 26:16; 2 Sam 1:14, 16; Lam 4:20, etc. These citations are from the Septuagint, which varies considerably in some places from the Hebrew or Masoretic Old Testament.

Gaius Suetonius Tranquillus

Other apologist "proofs" of the history of the gospel story occur in a couple of brief passages in the works of Roman historian and biographer Suetonius. In Suetonius's *Life of Claudius* (c. 113 AD/CE) appears the following passage:

> Iudaeos impulsore Chresto assidue tumultuantis Roma expulit.
>
> [Those] Jews impelled by Chrestos to assiduously cause tumult, [Claudius] expelled out of Rome.

The germane term here is "Chrestos," a widely used epithet meaning "good," "virtuous," "useful" or "easy," as at Matthew 11:30. Contrary to the claims of Christian apologists, however, *Chrestos* is *not* equivalent to, or interchangeable with, *Christos* or *Christ*, meaning "anointed," although Christian writers and scribes did confusedly utilize both epithets. Nevertheless, numerous individuals, including both gods and mortals, were called "Chrestos" or "Chrestus" during this era, so it is uncertain that this brief remark even concerns Jesus of Nazareth in the first place, especially since Jesus was never said to have been at Rome.

In his *Life of Nero* (c. 110 AD/CE), Suetonius also mentions "Christians" as involved in a "new and mischievous superstition" and being punished by Nero. It seems odd that a movement over 80 years old would be considered "new," particularly since both Peter and Paul were said to have proselytized at Rome. Indeed, the book of Acts claims Paul was such a known rabble-rouser that he was arrested and hauled before Roman authories, even appealing to Caesar himself! (Acts 26:32) Paul not only purportedly spent two years in prison in Rome, but it was there where he allegedly later experienced martyrdom in the arena "before a jeering crowd" during Nero's reign. Strangely, despite his noteworthy life Paul appears nowhere in the historical record. Moreover, this passage in Suetonius may have been another Christian interpolation, breaking the narrative in an unnatural manner. In any event, these brief mentions of "Chrestos" and "Christians" do not provide credible scientific evidence of the historicity of the gospel story; nor do they add anything to our quest to find out who Jesus was.

Publius/Gaius Cornelius Tacitus

Although dated by scholars to between 107 and 116 AD/CE, the vaunted passage in Roman senator and historian Tacitus's *Annals* (15:44) does not appear in the literary record until the 14th century, while the earliest extant manuscript possessing book 15 dates only to the 11th century. Hence, the authenticity and value of the Annals remain dubious. The pertinent passage in the Annals—considered by some apologists as the best evidence outside of the gospels for Christ's historicity—goes as follows:

> Therefore, in order to abolish that rumor, Nero falsely accused and executed with the most exquisite punishments those people called Christians, who were infamous for their abominations. The originator of the name, Christ, was executed as a criminal by the procurator Pontius Pilate during the reign of Tiberius; and though repressed, this destructive superstition erupted again, not only through Judea, which was the origin of this evil, but also through the city of Rome, to which all that is horrible and shameful floods together and is celebrated. Therefore, first those were seized who admitted their faith, and then, using the information they provided, a vast multitude were convicted, not so much for the crime of burning the city, but for hatred of the human race. And perishing they were additionally made into sports: they were killed by dogs by having the hides of beasts attached to them, or they were nailed to crosses or set aflame, and, when the daylight passed away, they were used as nighttime lamps. Nero gave his own gardens for this spectacle and performed a Circus game, in the habit of a charioteer mixing with the plebs or driving about the race-course. Even though they were clearly guilty and merited being made the most recent example of the consequences of crime, people began to pity these sufferers, because they were consumed not for the public good but on account of the fierceness of one man.[1]

---

[1] Hooker.

In the Latin manuscript that is the basis of this particular translation, Tacitus refers to a "Christus," with an "i," but he claims the "class hated for their abominations" were called "Chrestians," with an "e," meaning "the good" or "the useful," etc., rather than "followers of Christ." However, the manuscript tradition of the Annals also reveals that the word "Christus" has been interchanged with "Chrestus," presenting yet another difficulty in discerning an original, and reflecting that the text has been altered.[1]

Moreover, Tacitus's assertion that these Chrestians constituted a "vast multitude" at Rome by Nero's time (64 AD/CE) is incorrect, and, despite the repeated claim to the opposite, *there is no other evidence of a massive Neronian persecution of Christians for setting the fire at Rome*. Concerning this development, Drew University Professor of New Testament Darrell Doughty comments:

> ...it is highly remarkable that no other ancient source associates Christians with the burning of Rome until Sulpicius Serverus in the late fourth century... The dramatic and fantastic description of the tortures suffered by the scapegoats resembles the executions portrayed in later legendary Acts of Christian Martyrs.

Indeed, even though there is one mention in Tertullian of Nero being the first persecutor of Christians at Rome, his predecessor Irenaeus says nothing about it. Nor does Eusebius elaborate upon the Neronian persecution, neither associating it with the fire nor claiming that there were "vast multitudes" of Christians "thrown to the lions," so to speak. In addition, if there were a "vast multitude" of Christians in Rome by Nero's time, why would Suetonius write some 40 to 50 years later that Christianity was a "new" superstition? Particularly if these multitudes of Christians had notoriously been blamed for the fire and persecuted thereafter? How could Suetonius fail to discuss such a scenario in his *Life of Nero*, especially when the historian does record the fire but blames it on Nero himself, making no connection between the fire and the alleged punishment of Christians previously mentioned?

---

[1] Doughty.

Other arguments against the authenticity of this text include that it is written in different and rougher Latin than Tacitus's other, more well-known works. Furthermore, in all of Tacitus's other works, no mention is made of Christ, Christians or Christianity—how do we account for this fact, if there were already a "vast multitude" of Christians at Rome by the time of Nero, several decades earlier? And whom Nero supposedly had blamed for the infamous fire that almost destroyed Rome? And who were allegedly horribly persecuted—yet, not one other writer of the time or thereafter recorded these significant facts?

Also, this passage constitutes the *only* Pagan reference that specifically associates Pontius Pilate with Christ. In describing Pilate, Tacitus anachronistically uses the term "procurator," when it has been asserted that Pilate was a *prefect* and that there were no procurators until after his era.[1] Moreover, even though it was the passion and duty of Church historian Eusebius to compile all non-Christian references to Jesus in his work *History of the Church*, he failed to mention the Annals passage. All in all, the passage smacks of being a late Christian interpolation or at the least a redaction for the purpose of establishing not only the historicity of the gospel tale but also the early martyrdom of Christians, with the anti-Christian sentiment representing an attempt at "verisimilitude, reflecting what Christian apologists later attributed to pagans and what someone thought Tacitus also might have said."[2]

If, on the other hand, we are to accept this passage as genuine, the question needs to be asked why Tacitus—a Roman *senator*—himself would make such derogatory remarks about Rome, calling it the city "to which all that is horrible and shameful floods together and is celebrated?" Would a respected Roman senator and historian truly state that a multitude of people were hideously tortured and killed not for the crime of burning the city—for which they were

---

[1] The point seems to be moot as to whether or not Pilate was erroneously called "procurator" in the gospels, since in the Textus Receptus the Greek term is *hegemon* (Strong's G2232), which simply means "leader" and which is translated as either "procurator" or "prefect," among other designations, including the most common description of Pilate as "governor."
[2] Doughty.

"falsely accused and executed"—but in reality because they hated the human race? Why does Tacitus first say that the Christians were *falsely* accused and then conclude that they were "clearly guilty," yet they were not killed for the "public good" but because of the "fierceness of one man," i.e., Nero? Why is Tacitus so vicious towards the Christians, if they were not guilty of burning Rome? This passage is confused and hardly seems to reflect the thinking of "Rome's greatest historian," as Tacitus has been deemed.

These brief remarks represent all we find in Tacitus's writings concerning Christ or "Chrestians"; hence, there is no evidence whatsoever for the presumption by certain apologists that Tacitus utilized official Roman documents for his commentary. The biggest flaw in this argument would be the use of the epithet "Christ"—*and no other name*—in an imperial document, as no Roman record would refer to an executed criminal as "the anointed" or "the messiah." Nor would someone interested in historical accuracy—particularly "Rome's greatest historian" Tacitus—refer to Pilate as a "procurator," especially if he had Roman records in front of him.

Nevertheless, Meier considers the Tacitus passage to be "obviously genuine" and attempts to show it as a Christian interpolation to be "feeble."[1] Yet, he also admits that Tacitus is of little value as an independent source and additionally remarks that "Josephus is our only independent non-Christian source of information about the historical Jesus in the first century."[2] Nor does Meier consider Pliny and Suetonius of any value as independent witnesses, as "they are simply reporting something about what early Christians say or do..."[3]

References in the works of other non-Christian sources such as Lucian of Samosata (2nd cent.)—who doesn't even mention Jesus Christ by name—are far too late to serve as evidence of anything other than a *tradition* established by that time. Much too late also is the testimony of the Pagan critic Celsus, who, instead of serving as "evidence" of any historical Jesus, essentially focuses on shredding to pieces

---

[1] Meier, I, 90.
[2] Meier, I, 92.
[3] Meier, I, 91.

any rationality or logic claimed of Christianity. His purported testimony to the life of Christ constitutes an attack rather than a validation.

Even if we were to accept these writings in the works of Jewish and Roman authors as genuine and relevant, they represent *traditions* and emerge too late to serve as eyewitness accounts demonstrating that any of the gospel events happened at any time in history. Indeed, these resources do not provide us with any biographical material useful in our quest to find out who Jesus was, an assessment also averred by Bruce and Meier, to name a few Christian scholars.[1]

Thallus, Phlegon and Mara Bar-Serapion, et al.

A close study of the purported evidence outside of the New Testament discloses a disturbing trend on the part of Christian apologists: The efforts to demonstrate *any* kind of pertinent, non-Christian testimony for the historicity of the gospel story display a seemingly desperate situation in which apologists glom onto suspect "references" and "artifacts" that, upon scrutiny, reveal little more than the practice within apologetics of misinterpreting and misrepresenting data.

For example, within mainstream apologetics we find a much-ballyhooed passage in the works of Christian monk George Syncellus (9th cent.) relating that in the writings of an early Church father named Julius Africanus (c. 160-c. 240) appears a brief mention of a Roman writer named Thallus or Thallos, who purportedly reported on an eclipse sometime during the first century, which is *interpreted* to be the darkness that allegedly accompanied Christ's death. Hence, playing the children's game "Telephone," we possess a testimony several times removed from what Thallus actually wrote. Firstly, we know practically nothing about this Thallus—a common name of the time—and cannot determine with certainty whether or not he was discussing an eclipse that occurred during the first century AD/CE. We do not even know when Thallus lived, as it could have been

---

[1] For a more thorough discussion of the supposed testimony of Josephus, Pliny, Suetonius and Tacitus, see *The Christ Conspiracy* and *Suns of God*.

anytime well into the second century; nor do we even know for certain if he was a Samaritan, as has been asserted previously. The contention by apologists that Thallus wrote around 52 AD/CE appears to be mere wishful thinking, based not on any concrete evidence but only on the assumption that he penned his work shortly after the end of the 207th Olympiad or Olympic games. Since we possess only a rumor that Thallus wrote about an Olympiad, we can only guess which one, with three candidates for determining the *terminus a quo* for the composition of his "Histories": the Olympiads of 109 BCE, 52 AD/CE or 92 CE.[1]

According to Syncellus's account, after referring to the darkness that allegedly fell and the earthquake that purportedly struck upon Christ's death, what Africanus literally said was:

τουτο το σκοτος εκλειψιν του ηλιου Θαλλος αποκαλει εν τριτη των ιστοριων, ως εμοι δοκει, αλογως.

This darkness—"an eclipse of the sun," Thallos calls [it] in the third of the histories, which to me seems unreasonable.[2]

The phrase "this darkness" refers to the subject of the discussion preceding this sentence, which is not necessarily a reflection of what Thallus himself was discussing. As this report stands, considering that Africanus apparently never made any comment whatsoever that Thallus had actually mentioned either Christ or his crucifixion, the most logical conclusion regarding this remark is that Thallus was merely reporting on a solar eclipse that later Christians themselves associated with the crucifixion of Christ. Since, according to our knowledge of his work, Thallus *only* mentions a solar eclipse and nothing more, unless Christ is the *sun* Thallus's writing is useless in demonstrating anything about Jesus.

In addition, nowhere else does anyone claim that Thallus himself associated this eclipse with the darkness upon Jesus's demise. All of these details and interpretations are by Julius Africanus or Syncellus, writing decades to centuries afterwards. These facts of the absolute uselessness of

---

[1] Carrier, "Thallus."

[2] This very literal translation is mine, from the original Greek found at Smith's "Thallus on the passion phenomena," a misleading title.

Thallus in the quest for a historical Jesus are entirely ignored by apologists, who even go to the misleading lengths of such sophistry as: "One of the first secular writers who mentions Christ is Thallus!"[1] This statement is utterly erroneous, but it has been repeated numerous times within the apologist community. As another example of an inaccurate conclusion, in *The Historical Jesus* Christian apologist and evangelical scholar Dr. Gary Habermas also remarks of Thallus: "At least the death of Jesus was mentioned in an ancient history..."[2] Yet again, it is dishonestly and inaccurately claimed that Thallus serves as one of the "ancient secular sources [who] mention various aspects of Jesus' life."[3] Even noted Christian scholar and evangelist F.F. Bruce bizarrely falls into this trap, erroneously claiming, "Thallus did not doubt that Jesus had been crucified..."[4] In making such a misstatement, Bruce gives the impression that Thallus did in fact mention Jesus, when, in reality, there is no evidence at all of such a remark. Apologists will also make the contention that Thallus "did not deny the existence of Jesus," when, again, in reality there is no evidence that Thallus—whoever he was and whenever he lived—had ever even heard of Jesus Christ!

Regarding Thallus, Bruce concludes:

> But the writings of Thallus have disappeared; we know them only in fragments cited by later writers. Apart from him, no certain reference is made to Christianity in any extant non-Christian Gentile writing of the first century.[5]

To reiterate, the evidence demonstrates that even *not apart from Thallus* we *possess no certain references to Christ, Christians or Christianity in non-Christian works of the first century*.

In the same passage by Syncellus appears a passing remark regarding a Roman writer named "Phlegon," who apparently lived during the second century. This Phlegon evidently reported on an eclipse and earthquake, which is

---

[1] McDowell, 122.
[2] Habermas, *THJ*, ch. 9.
[3] Harbermas, "WIBTNT."
[4] McDowell, 122.
[5] Bruce, *NTD*, ch. X.

associated by a couple of early Church fathers with Christ's death. Indeed, Origen mentions Phlegon in his *Contra Celsus* (II, 14):

> Now Phlegon, in the thirteenth or fourteenth book, *I think*, of his Chronicles, not only ascribed to Jesus a knowledge of future events (although falling into confusion about some things which refer to Peter, as if they referred to Jesus), but also testified that the result corresponded to His predictions. (Emph. added)

Later in the same discourse (II, 33), Origen remarks:

> And with regard to the eclipse in the time of Tiberius Cæsar, in whose reign Jesus appears to have been crucified, and the great earthquakes which then took place, Phlegon too, *I think*, has written in the thirteenth or fourteenth book of his Chronicles. (Emph. added)

And again, Origen brings up Phlegon (II, 59):

> He imagines also that both the earthquake and the darkness were an invention; but regarding these, we have in the preceding pages, made our defence, according to our ability, adducing the testimony of Phlegon, who relates that these events took place at the time when our Saviour suffered.

Whether or not the passage concerning Phlegon in Syncellus/Africanus is an interpolation or error is immaterial. Nor does the oblique testimony in Origen provide evidence of who Jesus was, as it is too late, and we cannot be certain, *I think*, what Phlegon actually said about Christ, or even if he did say anything about him at all. It is very odd that, if this testimony is original to Origen and not an interpolation, no other Christian writer who discusses Phlegon, including Eusebius (*Chronicle*, II) and Michael the Syrian (12th cent.), claims that he said anything whatsoever about Christ. Nor does Eusebius mention Phlegon at all in his *History*—if Phlegon had truly written so much about Jesus as Origen suggests, Eusebius surely would have cited him as one of his proofs, especially since the Church historian does discuss the purported evidences in Josephus and Pliny. Oddly enough, Eusebius also does not mention Suetonius or Tacitus as providing testimony to Christ. It is possible that Eusebius ignored Suetonius because he discussed "Chrestos," not "Christos," and Tacitus because the passage in *The Annals* was unknown at the time and may well be a forgery. In any event, it appears that, if this material were known to Eusebius, he did not find it helpful in his passionate defense of the faith.

Another source cited by apologists is a passage in the writing of a Syrian author named Mara Bar-Serapion—who wrote anywhere from sometime after 73 AD/CE all the way up to the 3rd century. Thus, several decades to a couple of *centuries* after the alleged advent of Christ, Bar-Serapion purportedly made a passing reference to a "wise king" of the Jews, after whose "execution" the Jewish "kingdom was abolished." Bar-Serapion, in fact, does not identify this "wise king" as Jesus but could be referring to a number of individuals in Jewish history. Upon scrutiny, this source does not provide valid, scientific evidence for the existence of Christ or the historicity of the gospel accounts.

For those who are sincere about discovering information regarding who Jesus was, it is disturbing that we must rely on such sketchy and basically useless sources. It is especially peculiar that under scientific scrutiny there is no evidence to back the contentions in the gospels regarding the astounding supernatural events that purportedly occurred upon Jesus's death—in reality, not a word of these incredible occurrences was recorded by anyone anywhere obvious.

The Talmud

Despite claims to the contrary, the Jewish composition the Talmud rates as worthless in establishing the existence of Christ and the historicity of the gospel tale. The supposed references in the Talmud—largely consisting of unflattering commentary about Jesus—are all too late to demonstrate anything more than *traditions* passed along decades to centuries later. Furthermore, some of the passages cited do not seem to refer to the gospel Jesus at all. Moreover, the earliest stratum of the Talmud, the Mishna, is virtually silent on the subject of Jesus, while it is only the later commentary on the Mishna called the Gemara (4th-5th cents.) that

contains any solid reference to "Jesus of Nazareth."[1] As the
Catholic priest Meier says:

> ...scholars of rabbinic tradition do not agree among
> themselves on whether even a single text from the
> Mishna, Tosefta, or Talmud really refers to Jesus of
> Nazareth. For instance, a radical position is represented
> by Johann Maier, who maintains that not only the
> Mishna but also both Talmuds lack any authentic,
> direct mention of Jesus of Nazareth.... His conclusion
> is that even the original text of the two Talmuds
> never mentioned Jesus of Nazareth; all such references
> to Jesus are later interpolations inserted in the Middle
> Ages.[2]

While Meier is wary of Maier's overall thesis, he too
concludes, "Jesus of Nazareth is simply absent from the
Mishna and other early rabbinic traditions." Meier further
states that "apart from Josephus, Jewish literature of the
early Christian period offers no independent sources for
inquiry into the historical Jesus."[3]

Concerning the dates of the Talmud, Meier also remarks
that the "earliest collection of rabbinic material," the Mishna,
emerges at the end of the second to beginning of the third

---

[1] The phrase "Jesus of Nazareth" appears in quotations because in the
"original" Greek of the Bible (Textus Receptus) the term often translated as
"of Nazareth" in actuality reflects three different Greek words. Although the
phrase "Jesus of Nazareth" appears 29 times in the King James Bible, the
original Greek phrase is "Jesus the *Nazarene*" the majority of the time. In
fact, the Greek word for "Nazareth" (Strong's G3478) appears 11 times total
in the gospels: three times in Matthew, once in Mark, five times in Luke and
twice in John. The word for "Nazarene, Nazarite" or "Nazarite"—*Nazaraios*
(G3480)—appears in the Greek 15 times, but it is only translated as such
twice, the remaining 13 rendered as "of Nazareth." Another version of
"Nazarene, Nazarite"—*Nazarenos* (G3479)—appears four times but is
always translated as "of Nazareth." This fact is significant in that it seems
the term "Nazareth"—*which was not much of a place for people to inhabit, if
it even existed at the time*—was used, as stated at Matthew 2:23, to make
Jesus a "Nazarene." Rather than being inhabitants of a particular town, the
Nazarenes or Nazarites were members of a certain sect, to which the Old
Testament hero Samson likewise belonged. It is possible that the
mistranslations occur in order to cloak the fact of this pre-Christian sect that
contributed much to Christianity. (See *The Christ Conspiracy* and *Suns of
God* for more information on the Nazarenes.)
[2] Meier, I, 95.
[3] Meier, I, 98.

century, while "all other collections are later still."[1] Hence, it could be stated that the earlier dates given by apologists for Talmudic references to Jesus are simply erroneous and represent not science but wishful thinking. Meier further admonishes against placing too much value on these Talmudic accounts, such as claiming they represent "independent traditions," and reminds of the words of Jewish scholar Joseph Klausner "who wrote...that the very few references to Jesus in the Talmud are of little historical value..."[2] As we have seen, the Universal Jewish Encyclopedia concurs with this assessment.

Obviously, the Talmud is not an "eyewitness" account of the events of the Christian tale. In fact, whatever statements appear in the Talmud occur in response to later Christian legends already in existence and do not serve as a record of actual events. Therefore, the Talmud is worthless as a non-Christian source demonstrating the historicity of the gospel tale and does not add much acceptable material to our quest to find out Jesus was.

Gnostic Sources

There have existed many texts classified under the genre of "Gnosticism," which is asserted to be a Christian heresy that rose to prominence in the second century and for a couple of centuries afterwards. While these texts provide interesting insights into the myriad Gnostic-Christian sects, they are not seriously considered by most scholars to provide any useful data concerning the "historical" Jesus. In the first place, the Gnostic texts are generally composed in a highly fanciful manner that does not come across as being either historical or biographical. Secondly, these texts are all too late to provide any evidence as to the historicity of Jesus Christ, although if we accept that there was such a person, it appears permissible at least to consider the fanciful tales and peculiar sayings found within these texts in our attempts to pad out a biography for Christ. Nevertheless, fundamentalist and evangelical Christians do not allow anything about Jesus found within Gnosticism that is not already present within

---

[1] Meier, I, 91.
[2] Meier, I, 95.

traditional Christianity as based on the New Testament. In reality, these texts could be used to cast doubt upon the historicity of the gospel tale, as they contain much material that is both mythical and contrary to that found within the canon.

Extrabiblical Christian Sources

Concerning the issue of extrabiblical *Christian* testimony for Christ, F.F. Bruce concludes:

> Of independent Christian information about Jesus, beyond what the New Testament writers supply, there is nothing apart from a number of sayings attributed to him. The best-known collection of these [sayings] belongs to the second century, and is extant in a fourth-century Coptic translation from the Greek, the *Gospel of Thomas*...[1]

Of course, there were several Church fathers of the second century who wrote about Jesus the Christ, including Ignatius, Barnabas, Justin Martyr, Theophilus, Irenaeus and Clement of Alexandria, while Clement of Rome may have written during the last decade of the first century. A survey of the writings of these Church fathers would require another volume. However, as Bruce asserts, these commentaries provide us with only a slight amount more than what is found in the New Testament—such as Irenaeus's claim that Christ was "more than fifty" when he died, nevertheless based on the gospel of John (8:57)[2]—and they do not serve as valid scientific, eyewitness evidence of the historicity of the gospel tale.

The Stones are Silent

Contrary to the claims of Christian apologists, there is no valid credible and scientific archaeological evidence for the historicity of Jesus Christ or the gospel story. In the first place, archaeological artifacts thus far known such as those from the Christian catacombs at Rome or papyri fragments from Egypt are useless in our quest, dating too late to serve

---

[1] Bruce, *NTH*, 167.
[2] Irenaeus, *AH*, II, 22.

as evidence of the gospel tale. Indeed, other than some possibly earlier papyri fragments there are no solid Christian artifacts earlier than the third century. This fact begs the question as to why, if there were a multitude of Christians at Rome a century and a half earlier for instance, there are no certain artifacts of their existence.

The James Ossuary

Also marring the field of Christian archaeology are such artifacts as the notorious James ossuary and the Jesus tomb found at Talpiot in Jerusalem, as well as the fake relics and artifacts peddled throughout Christendom over the centuries. In the first place, the inscription "brother of Jesus" on the ossuary or bone box was determined by several scholars within a number of disciplines to have been a forgery.[1] Even if it were not, it would not establish anything more than that there was a James who had a brother named Jesus—two *very* common names in the ancient Jewish world. This fact did not prevent Christian advocates from jumping on the bandwagon and making such statements as those by Dr. Crossan:

> If the inscription is authentic, then the ossuary not only once housed the bones of James the brother of Jesus and leader of the early Church, it also provides to date the earliest tangible evidence of Jesus.[2]

In this commentary, Crossan is presuming that any bone box from the general era with the inscription of "James, brother of Jesus" would in fact be that of the famous apostle, which is in reality not an automatic assumption, in consideration of the commonality of both these names. Moreover, the assertion—made many times in the press— that the ossuary would in reality represent the "earliest tangible evidence of Jesus" is striking, in that it reveals *there currently exists no "tangible evidence of Jesus" from the era of his alleged advent.*

---

[1] See my article "Bone Box No Proof of Jesus."
[2] Crossan, *EJ*, 2

The Many Jesus Tombs and Bone Boxes

The infamous "Jesus Family Tomb" at Talpiot in Jerusalem thus reflects little more than the common usage of the names found therein. Since the modern archaeological era, there have been *several* tombs not only with the name of Jesus in them but also with the phrase "son of Joseph." There was, in effect, nothing sensational about this decades-old discovery. Regarding the Jesus tomb, Dr. Habermas remarks:

> The Names "Joseph" and "Jesus" were very popular in the 1st century. "Jesus" appears in at least 99 tombs and on 22 ossuaries. "Joseph" appears on 45 ossuaries.... "Mary" is the most common female name in the ancient Jewish world.[1]

Illustrating how widespread was the name "Jesus," in 1945 at another Talpiot site Professor E.L. Sukenik found two ossuaries with name "Jesus" inscribed on them and crosses carved into them. Sukenik subsequently pronounced these discoveries the "earliest Christian evidence." Despite Sukenik's enthusiasm, these ossuaries have now been excluded as evidence, as discussed by Bruce in *New Testament Documents*:

> ...it now seems fairly certain that the inscriptions have nothing to do with Christianity, but refer to two separate first century individuals named Jesus, neither of them being Jesus of Nazareth.[2]

In fact, the inscription on the ossuary first unveiled by Sukenik was "Jesus, Son of Joseph," which stunned his audience until he informed them that the two names were very common during the first century. Moreover, in 1873 French archaeologist Charles Clermont-Ganneau had discovered some 30 ossuaries near Jerusalem, some of which contained the names Jesus, Judah and Salome on them. As these artifacts were inscribed with crosses, Ganneau made the case that they were Christian.[3] The fact remains, however, that these artifacts too have since been

---

[1] Habermas, "LTJ."
[2] Bruce, *NTD*, ch. VIII.
[3] Taylor, 5.

determined to be Jewish, not Christian. Signs of the cross, in fact, do not necessarily represent a Christian symbol, and artifacts possessing them cannot automatically be deemed Christian. Pre-Christian Jews and Pagans also used the symbol of the cross, particularly within the context of religion. This fact of the pre-Christian cross may explain why in the gospels Christ is depicted as telling his followers to "take up" their "crosses." (Mk 8:34)

Over 50 years prior to the discovery of the notorious "Jesus Family Tomb" at Talpiot there occurred other finds of similar significance at the Dominus Flevit site in Jerusalem, with some 40 ossuaries, upon certain of which appeared the names Jairus, Jesus, Joseph, Mary, Martha, Matthew, Lazarus, Salome and Zechariah—all appellations appearing in the New Testament. These discoveries have all been ruled out as evidence of the historical Jesus and the gospel tale. Another tomb at the same site, which was excavated by the Italian archaeologist P. Bagatti, yielded a bone box or ossuary with the name of "Shimon bar Yonah," which was deemed in 1962 to be that of the apostle Peter. The brouhaha about that discovery petered out quickly, especially since tradition depicts the apostle dying at *Rome*, not Jerusalem, and being buried under St. Peter's Basilica in the Vatican. In fact, the discovery of the purported tomb of Peter at Rome was announced by the Pope in 1950, making it obvious why this later find at Jerusalem escaped notice. Peter's relics themselves were purportedly found in 1968 in the same Roman tomb. Few people outside of Catholicism have taken these claims seriously, and the skepticism regarding all such discoveries is well placed, in consideration of the vast bogus relic and artifact industry that has been in play for millennia.

Indeed, one fact which needs to be kept in mind whenever we hear about archaeological discoveries that may be pertinent to biblical lore: The forgery and fraud within this field have been *rampant* over the past centuries, beginning in earnest with the Christian convictions of Emperor Constantine's mother, Helena. Those individuals who stood to benefit financially from Helena's religious fervor were only too happy to provide her with whatever "artifacts" she desired—and the result has been the highly profitable and widespread counterfeit relic and artifact industry. Included among these countless bogus artifacts and sites are the "one True Cross," the Holy Sepulcher at Jerusalem, and, apparently, the supposed house of St. Peter at Capernaum. Of course, Christianity has not been alone in this practice of fabricating relics and artifacts; in reality, it has built upon and perfected a longtime habit of the priesthood in general around the world.

The Pilate Inscription and Caiaphas Tomb

One archaeological find that is widely hyped as providing "evidence" of the gospel story is a Latin inscription on a stone that purportedly mentions Pilate. The pertinent part of this inscription is peculiar in that it has been cramped in below a neatly laid-out phrase referring to a previously unknown term "Tiberium," possibly a temple of Tiberias. Indeed, it seems as if the "I" and "T" in the word "PILATUS" have been sloppily inserted into another word. Be that as it may, the existence of Pontius Pilate is not in question here, as we already know much about him from Josephus and Philo. Even if this inscription is original, it proves little more than that the gospel story was placed in a particular historical setting using a number of historical characters. Another of these figures would be the high priest Caiaphas, whose family tomb was apparently found in 1990. Again, the discovery of this artifact serves only to validate that the gospel story was given a historical setting; it does not verify the events of the tale or the historicity of its other main characters. Nor do either of these finds add anything to our knowledge of who Jesus was.

The Crucified John

Apologists also hold up the bones of a crucified victim from the first century named Yehochanan as evidence of the grotesque practice of crucifixion. It is odd that there are no other such discoveries, in consideration of the impression given by Christian history that this practice was significantly widespread in Judea. In any event, such finds, along with those of coins, boats, diaper pins and assorted other artifacts and relics simply establish a historical or quasi-historical milieu into which the gospel story was placed, rather than providing evidence that the tale is true.

The other archaeological discoveries listed by apologists such as F.F. Bruce to demonstrate the purported historical reliability of the New Testament consists almost exclusively of the same type of circumstantial evidence, such as an inscription defining a "wall of partition" in the Jewish temple, the "Pool of Bethesda" at Jerusalem, or inscriptions found at Corinth in Greece naming an "Erastus" and apparently concerning a "synagogue of the Hebrews."

Furthermore, there are countless temples, precincts, statues, inscriptions, pottery and other artifacts of the Greek gods all over Greece and elsewhere—many in the exact places where ancient authorities such as Herodotus and Pausanias recorded they would be. Does that fact mean the stories of the Greek myths are true? Was Zeus Pateras—*God the Father*—a real being who impregnated the virgin Danae by way of a golden shower? Was their offspring, the virgin-born Son of God, Perseus, a real person who walked the earth? The swampy site of the water-monster the Hydra has been found in Lerna, Greece—does this discovery mean that its killer, the hero and demigod Hercules, also born of a mortal woman and God the Father, really existed and performed the miraculous deeds he was supposed to have accomplished? And so on, through many *thousands* of such archaeological sites and finds around the world that relate to gods and goddesses of antiquity. Indeed, the archaeological finds that *prove* the historical setting and background of many myths, Greek, Roman and otherwise, are extremely abundant—*much* more so than those corresponding to Christianity. If we were to apply the "argument of abundance" used in the discussion of the New Testament texts to the archaeological finds of ancient Greece, we would need to admit that the Greek gods were "authentic!"

Again, upon close inspection, it is clear that *all* of the archaeological finds held up as proofs of early Christianity constitute *circumstantial evidence*. After all these centuries, there has emerged, in fact, not one solid scrap of evidence of Christ's advent or even the existence of his immediate followers. It seems amazing that so many people for so long have been fervently and diligently seeking evidence to prove or at least flesh out the gospel story—yet, they have invariably come up empty-handed!

Despite the lack of hard, scientific evidence, and after making erroneous claims as to the discredited textual "evidence" regarding the existence of Jesus Christ and the historicity of the gospel tale, Christian apologists nevertheless set forth declarations such as the following from Dr. Geisler:

> The primary sources of the life of Christ are the four Gospels. However there are considerable reports from non-Christian sources that supplement and confirm the Gospel accounts. These come largely from Greek, Roman, Jewish, and Samaritan sources of the first century.[1]

Here Geisler is evidently referring to Suetonius, Pliny, Tacitus, Josephus and Thallus; however, as has been demonstrated, the value of these "considerable reports" is dubious to non-existent. Moreover, the assertion that all these "sources" come from the "first century" is extremely misleading.[2] In this same apologetic vein, Habermas also concludes that "ancient extra biblical sources do present a surprisingly large amount of detail concerning both the life of Jesus and the nature of early Christianity."[3] Christian scholar Dr. Ben Witherington likewise puts forth the same sort of conclusion: "It is simply not true...that we have had no hard evidence for Jesus' existence before now except in the Bible. That ignores mentions in ancient Roman and Jewish historians such Tacitus, Suetonius and Josephus."[4] As we have seen, this assessment cannot be reasonably and scientifically upheld.

Ignoring all these facts, and using a logical fallacy of appealing to authority and not on the basis of any valid

---

[1] McDowell, 60.

[2] In discussing the "Christian era," it should be noted that such a period differed widely in diverse places. For example, while the Christian era in Rome began in earnest during the fourth century, with the endorsement of Constantine, the country of Lithuania remained *pre-Christian* until the 14th-15th centuries. Moreover, the dating of the "Christian era" did not exist until the 6th century, when Christian monk Dionysius attempted to discern the year of Christ's birth. Hence, the idea of the "Christian era" and "pre-Christian" times depends on the location in question, and using phrases like "during the first century" is misleading in that no such division existed at the time.

[3] Habermas, *THJ*, ch. IX.

[4] Witherington, "Tomb of the (Still) Unknown Ancients."

credible and scientific evidence, Christian scholars and apologists also make statements such as those of F.F. Bruce:

> Some writers may toy with the fancy of a "Christ-myth," but they do not do so on the ground of historical evidence. The historicity of Christ is as axiomatic for an unbiased historian as the historicity of Julius Caesar. It is not historians who propagate the "Christ-myth" theories.[1]

After investigating these purported evidences from Josephus, Suetonius, Pliny and Tacitus, however, Bruce further acknowledges, "We are thus thrown back on the New Testament writings as our primary documents,"[2] evincing that the New Testament itself constitutes "well-tested... source-material." Yet, in a footnote to these remarks, Bruce further comments:

> *The NT writings were not, of course, designed as historians' source-material*, and apart from Luke-Acts are not written in historiographical style... (Emph. added)

Hence, while admitting that there is no historical evidence for the life of Christ, and noting that the gospels themselves were *not* "designed as historians' source-materials," Bruce nevertheless dismisses the rational deduction that Christ himself may not be historical, going so far as to imply that anyone who comes to such a conclusion cannot be considered a historian—despite the fact that there is essentially no history to go on! To put it another way, after discovering that there is basically no historical evidence for Jesus, with not even the gospels serving as "historian's source-material," it is asserted that no "unbiased historian" can reach the conclusion that Christ may be non-historical. In dealing with the investigation of a "historical" Jesus, then, we are faced with a hopeless and absurd Catch-22.

In reality, the puzzling and embarrassing deficiency of historical and archaeological evidence for the greatest man who ever lived and who was famed far and wide has made many people wonder about the story itself, causing them to

---

[1] Bruce, *NTD*, ch. X.
[2] Bruce, *NTH*, 167.

doubt the most fantastic elements, including the bulk of Christ's signs of divinity. In order to add to our picture of who Jesus was, we will therefore need to inquire elsewhere, in light of this paucity of data, keeping in mind that, again, we cannot afford to avoid disquieting conclusions in our quest for truth.

Who are Elijah and Elisha?

Now it happened that as he was praying alone the disciples were with him; and he asked them, "Who do the people say that I am?" And they answered, "John the Baptist; but others say, Eli'jah; and others, that one of the old prophets has risen."

Luke 9:18-19

We cannot look to contemporary extrabiblical evidence to determine who Jesus really was. We may, however, follow certain internal clues that might give us some ideas. For example, at Luke 9, when discussing who people say he is, Jesus's disciples respond that some believe him to be "Elijah." In Matthew (11:14), Jesus identifies John the Baptist as Elijah instead. Who was Elijah? Why does he appear with Moses next to Jesus during one of Christ's most miraculous events, the Transfiguration?

In the Old Testament (2 Kings 2:11), the esteemed Jewish prophet Elijah ended his earthly career by being taken up into heaven alive, such that "the Jews expected he would return just before the advent of the Messiah, whom he would prepare the minds of the Israelites to receive."[1] In the last book before the New Testament, the prophet Malachi ("My messenger") says:

"Remember the law of my servant Moses, the statutes and ordinances that I commanded him at Horeb for all Israel.

"Behold, I will send you Elijah the prophet before the great and terrible day of the Lord comes. And he will turn the hearts of fathers to their children and the hearts of children to their fathers, lest I come and smite the land with a curse." (Mal 4:4-5)

Thus, in the biblical book, chapter and verses directly preceding the gospel of Matthew it is said that Elijah would appear "before the great and terrible day of the Lord," an

---

[1] *Blue Letter Bible*, "Elijah."

interpreted reference to the coming of Jesus Christ. Therefore, Elijah is the messiah's forerunner, the same as John the Baptist.

Concerning the transfiguration scene in the gospels, which places both Elijah and Moses on either side of Jesus, Christian commentator Matthew Henry (1706-1714) states:

> These two were Moses and Elias [Elijah], men very eminent in their day. They had both fasted forty days and forty nights, as Christ did, and wrought other miracles, and were both remarkable at their going out of the world as well as in their living in the world. Elias was carried to heaven in a fiery chariot, and died not. The body of Moses was never found, possibly it was preserved from corruption, and reserved for this appearance. The Jews had great respect for the memory of Moses and Elias, and therefore they came to witness of him, they came to carry tidings concerning him to the upper world. In them the law and the prophets honoured Christ, and bore testimony to him. Moses and Elias appeared to the disciples; they saw them, and heard them talk, and, either by their discourse or by information from Christ, they knew them to be Moses and Elias; glorified saints shall know one another in heaven. They talked with Christ. Note, Christ has communion with the blessed, and will be no stranger to any of the members of that glorified corporation. Christ was now to be sealed in his prophetic office, and therefore these two great prophets were fittest to attend him, as transferring all their honour and interest to him; for in these last days God speaks to us by his Son, Heb. 1:1.[1]

Hence, Moses and Elijah materialize next to Jesus in order to confer their authority on him, and, therefore, as the voice of God commands at Matthew 17:5, we should "listen to him." Regarding these events, David Brown remarks:

> Moses represented "the law," Elijah "the prophets," and both together the whole testimony of the Old

---

[1] *BLB*, "Commentary on Matthew 17."

Testament Scriptures, and the Old Testament saints, to Christ; now not borne in a book, but by living men, not to a coming, but a come Messiah, visibly, for they "appeared," and audibly, for they "spake."[1]

Jesus is made to appear talking with Moses in order to show that he is the fulfillment of Mosaic law, while Elijah is there in order to demonstrate that Jesus is his heir, i.e., the messiah, as well as the fulfillment of the prophets. As Jesus says at Matthew 5:17, "Think not that I have come to abolish the law and the prophets; I have come not to abolish them but to fulfil them." Furthermore, by God's voice booming from the heavens, Jesus's place as His Son is exalted higher than the law and the prophets. The scene also serves to illustrate that Jesus could not *be* Elijah, as was suggested by some in the gospel story, because Elijah is there with him.

Moreover, if, as Jesus says, John the Baptist is Elijah, then logically Jesus would be equivalent to Elijah's Old Testament successor, Elisha. Indeed, as "Elisha" means "God is salvation," so too does "Jesus." Who is Elisha? Why would he be comparable to Jesus himself? Let us look at the events in the life of Elisha in comparison to that of Jesus. Elisha's life, it should be noted, is portrayed in the Old Testament in greater detail than that of Elijah, which indicates that he possesses some importance.

Elisha and Jesus Comparison

Elisha	Jesus
Anointed or *christed* by his forerunner, Elijah. (1 Kings 19:16)	Baptized or "cleansed" by his forerunner, John. (Mt 3:13)
Associated specifically with the number 12. (1 Kings 19:19)	Has a circle of 12 disciples. (Mt 10:2)
Immediately leaves his mother and father to follow Elijah. (1 Kings 19:20)	Directs disciples to immediately leave their parents in order to follow him. (Mt 4:22)
Goes to Gilgal ("a wheel,	Goes to Galilee (Heb:

---

[1] *BLB*, "Commentary on Matthew 17."

rolling"). (2 Kings 2:1)	"Galiyl": "circuit") and Golgotha (Heb: "galal": "to roll").
Appears in Bethel ("house of God"). (2 Kings 2:2)	Appears in Bethlehem ("house of bread").
Goes to Jericho. (2 Kings 2:4)	Goes to Jericho. (Mk 10:46)
Takes on the mantle of Elijah (John). (2 Kings 2:13)	Takes on the mantle of John (Elijah).
Crosses the Jordan river by miraculously parting the waters. (2 Kings 2:14)	Crosses the sea of Galilee by miraculously walking on the water. (Mt 14:24)
Curses some boys, destroying them. (2 Kings 2:24)	Curses a fig tree, destroying it. (Mt 21:9)
Replenishes the land with water. (2 Kings 3:20)	Gives the woman at the well the "living water." (Jn 4:10-11) Replenishes the "heart" with "living water." (Jn 7:38)
Miraculously increases oil to fill empty jars. (2 Kings 4:1-6)	Miraculously turns water in jars into wine. (Jn 2:7-9)
Causes an old woman to conceive miraculously. (2 Kings 4:14)	Is the product of a miraculous conception.
Called the "man of God." (2 Kings 4:16)	Called the "son of God."
Prays to the Lord in a room with the door shut. (2 Kings 4:33)	Specifically instructs on prayer to the Lord in a room with the door shut. (Mt 6:6)
Raises a child from the dead. (2 Kings 4:34)	Raises a child from the dead. (Mt 9:25)
Miraculously feeds the multitudes, starting with small amounts of food and ending up with leftovers. (2 Kings 42-44)	Miraculously feeds the multitudes, starting with small amounts of food and ending up with leftovers. (Mt 15:34-37)
Heals a leper. (2 Kings 5:12-14)	Heals lepers.
Restores sight to the blind.	Restores sight to the blind.

(2 Kings 6:20)	
Saves Israel from foreign invasions and influences; is Israel's savior. (2 Kings 6:8-23; 9:1-3)	Saves the lost sheep of Israel from foreign influences; is Israel's savior.
Is threatened with death by Israel's king. (2 Kings 6:31)	Is threatened with death by Israel's king. (Mt 2:13)
Delivers Israel in a day of "good news." (Gk: "evangelias") (2 Kings 7:9)	Delivers Israel with his "good news." (Eng: "gospel"; Gk: "evangelion")
Predicts famine in Israel. (2 Kings 8:1)	Predicts famines and other disasters. (Mt 24:7)
The man of god wept. (2 Kings 8:11)	The son of God wept. (Jn 11:35)
Elisha's "servant" becomes king of Syria, "betrays" Israel. (2 Kings 8:13)	Jesus's disciple betrays him, the Lord of Israel.

As can be seen, the lives of these two figures, Elisha, the Old Testament man of God named "God saves," and Jesus, the New Testament son of God named "God saves," run very closely in several salient instances. At first glance, there also seem to be some serious differences between Elisha and the later Jesus, such as Elisha's display of wrath when he destroys boys and causes blindness and leprosy. Even here, however, Elisha and Jesus are alike, as in the non-canonical early Christian text depicting Christ's childhood, *The Infancy Gospel of Thomas* (c. 185 AD/CE?), a "lost book of the Bible," Jesus is portrayed as an angry boy who kills and maims people. In one episode (3:1-3), a furious five-year-old Jesus calls the young son of Annas the scribe a "godless, brainless moron" and vows to make him "wither away," instantly killing him. In the next chapter, Jesus kills a boy who bumps into him. When the parents of the murdered child complain, Jesus causes them to go blind. (5:2) Jesus next sasses his stepfather, Joseph, when the latter goes to punish him for these deeds. When a teacher tells Joseph that he should commit Jesus to his care, the young savior laughs and remarks:

> "Really, teacher, what my father has said to you is true. I am the Lord of this people and am here in

your presence and have been born among you and am with you. I know where you are from and how many years there will be in your lives. I am telling you the truth, teacher, when you were born, I existed. And if you want to be a perfect teacher, listen to me and I will teach you wisdom which nobody knows except me and the one who sent me to you. For you are my disciple and I know you, how old you are and how old you will live to be. And when you see the cross my father has described, you will believe that everything I have said to you is true."[1]

Throughout the Infancy Gospel, Jesus is portrayed as a belligerent and arrogant little boy, as well as a violent killer who soon makes everyone afraid of him. He is also depicted as the lord and savior who raises up a playmate who had fallen off a roof and died. (9:5) The boy Jesus further saves a man who had chopped off his own foot with an axe, and he creates clay birds that he miraculously animates, among other miracles. Even without using this non-canonical Christian text, Jesus's fiery personality can be seen in the gospel accounts, as at Mark 1:43, when Jesus "sternly charges" and sends away a leper who was pestering him. At Mark 3:5, Jesus becomes peeved with the Jewish authorities: "And he looked around at them in anger..." In the well-known pericope of the moneychangers, Jesus takes a whip and violently and angrily overturns their tables. Mark 10:14 also depicts Christ as "indignant" at not being allowed to touch the children brought to him for healing, rebuking his disciples for preventing the exchange. While such an emotion might seem understandable, Matthew (Mt 19:14) and Luke (Lk 18:16) both omit it, possibly for purposes of public relations.

Joseph, A Type of Jesus

Another prominent Old Testament figure who shares some interesting parallels with Jesus is Joseph, son of Jacob/Israel, famed for his "coat of many colors." The correspondences between Joseph and Jesus include the following:

---

[1] Bernhard, 6:4-7.

- Jesus, also a "son of Jacob/Israel" (Mt 1:2) is born of a miraculous birth, as is Joseph, whose mother, Rachel, was previously barren but miraculously conceives. (Gen 30:22-24)
- Jesus has 12 disciples; Joseph is one of 12 brothers. (Gen 35:22)
- Joseph is a shepherd (Gen 37:2); Jesus is the "Good Shepherd."
- Joseph was rejected by his family, as was Jesus.
- Jesus is betrayed for silver pieces by Judas, while Joseph is sold for silver pieces by Judah, et al. (Gen 37:26-28)[1]
- Both Joseph and Jesus go into Egypt as youngsters to avoid danger. (Gen 37:28)
- Joseph and Jesus both are imprisoned.
- Joseph is confined with two other prisoners (Gen 40:2-3); Jesus is condemned between two criminals.
- Both Joseph and Jesus attain notoriety for feeding bread to hungry people.
- The age of 30 is noteworthy in the lives of both Joseph (Gen 41:46) and Jesus (Lk 3:23).
- Joseph and Jesus alike possess divine powers to predict the future. (Gen 44:15)
- Joseph's father "prays" him to "forgive" his brothers' "transgression" and "sin." (Gen 50:17) Jesus is prayed to for forgiveness of transgressions and sins.
- Joseph is the "deliverer of his family." Jesus is the deliverer of the family of mankind.
- Jesus is the "savior of the world," while at Genesis 41:45, Pharaoh calls Joseph the "savior of the world."[2]

---

[1] In fact, the word for "Judah" or "Juda" in the Greek Old Testament, the Septuagint, is exactly the same as the word for "Judas" in the New Testament: "Ιουδας."

[2] This definition of the name Pharaoh gave Joseph comes from the Catholic Bible, the Douay-Rheims, based on Jerome's Latin Vulgate, which translates the original Egyptian name as "Salvatorem mundi," or "savior of the world." Other versions do not translate this name, commonly transliterated from the Egyptian as "Zaph'enath-pane'ah," glossing over the meaning ascribed by Jerome and, where defined, giving the name a different meaning. The Hebrew is "Tsophnath Pa'neach," while the Septuagint gives the name as "Tsonthomphanеех." Strong's defines the Hebrew/Egyptian as "treasury of the glorious rest," while the Genesius Lexicon avers that the Septuagint

Regarding the correlations between Joseph and Jesus, the Catholic Encyclopedia remarks:

> A character so beautiful made Joseph a most worthy type of Christ, the model of all perfection, and it is comparatively easy to point out some of the traits of resemblance between Jacob's beloved son and the dearly beloved Son of God. Like Jesus, Joseph was hated and cast out by his brethren, and yet wrought out their salvation through the sufferings they had brought upon him. Like Jesus, Joseph obtained his exaltation only after passing through the deepest and most undeserved humiliations; and, in the kingdom over which he ruled, he invited his brethren to join those whom heretofore they had looked upon as strangers, in order that they also might enjoy the blessings which he had stored up for them. Like the Saviour of the world, Joseph had but words of forgiveness and blessing for all who, recognizing their misery, had recourse to his supreme power. It was to Joseph of old, as to Jesus, that all had to appeal for relief, offer homages of the deepest respect, and yield ready obedience in all things. Finally, to the Patriarch Joseph, as to Jesus, it was given to inaugurate a new order of things for the greater power and glory of the monarch to whom he owed his exaltation.[1]

Hence, the CE acknowledges that Joseph is a "type of Christ," which is to say a "prefiguring," precursor or foreshadowing of Jesus. As discussed by early Church fathers such as Justin Martyr and Tertullian, there were several "types of Christ" in the Old Testament, including Isaac, Jonah, Ezekiel, Saul, David, Solomon, Jeremiah, Moses and Moses's successor Joshua, likewise named "*Jesus*" in the Septuagint, two to three centuries prior to the Christian era.[2]

---

contains a "more accurate" Egyptian form that means "saviour of the age," the latter term being *aion* in Greek. In turn, the Greek word *aion* means both "world" and "age." Hence, the translation of this Egyptian name for Joseph may be accurately stated as "savior of the world."

[1] *CE*, "Joseph."

[2] An extensive discussion of the Joshua-Jesus connection may be found in my book *Suns of God*.

In consideration of the numerous, detailed and remarkable correspondences between Elisha ("God saves") and Jesus ("God saves"), and between Joseph and Jesus, as well as many other "types of Christ" in Jewish and Pagan literature, as remarked upon even by the early Church fathers, it is fair to ask whether or not the gospel writers had in mind closely reproducing in Jesus these other esteemed figures. Such a suggestion, of course, would imply that the gospels are not necessarily biographies of actual occurrences in the life of an historical figure but could represent a fictionalized compilation of characters.

Jesus as Fulfillment of Prophecy

"But all this has taken place, that the scriptures of the prophets might be fulfilled." Then all the disciples forsook him and fled.

Matthew 26:56

"Hide the prophecy, tell the narrative, and invent the history."

Dr. John D. Crossan, The Historical Jesus (372)

In addition to various Old Testament characters serving to "prefigure" the person of Jesus Christ are the numerous Old Testament scriptures held up as "prophecies" of the messiah fulfilled in Christ. Over the centuries, in fact, since the story of Jesus began to be circulated, believers have appealed to these scriptures to demonstrate that Jesus was indeed the messiah. These prophetic scriptures number in the hundreds, depending on the apologetic text consulted, with upwards of 1,000 in some circles, the book of Psalms alone possessing almost 100 by some counts—all these have been cited as "fulfillment of prophecy" in the purported advent of Jesus Christ.

When these scriptures deemed prophetic of the coming messiah are placed side by side with the characteristics and sayings of Jesus, as well as the events of his life, a startling and convincing comparison is apparent. Many of these comparisons or "prophecies," however, are highly tenuous and in reality have little if anything to do with the coming messiah; nor are they truly "prophecies." Indeed, it is not just the Christian apologists but the gospel writers themselves, and perhaps interpolating later scribes, who have glommed onto OT scriptures that are *not* "prophecies," trying to make them appear to be predicting Jesus's advent. When the list is critically pared down, many fewer scriptures are possibly applicable.

It is important to note also that Jesus himself is reported to say that he did not come to "abolish the law or the prophets" but to fulfill them. (Mt 5:17) In Luke (24:25-27) the resurrected Jesus scolds the dimwitted disciples who are "slow of heart to believe all that the prophets have spoken!" He then reminds them that "the Christ" needs to endure "these things" in order to "enter into his glory," and he proceeds to expound upon "Moses and all the prophets," interpreting the characteristics found in these scriptures as applicable to himself. At Luke 24:44, Jesus states that "everything written about me in the law of Moses and the prophets and the psalms must be fulfilled." At John 5:39, Christ mentions the scriptures about eternal life that "bear witness" to him, and at 5:46 he states that Moses wrote about him. Other books in the New Testament, such as Acts and certain of the epistles likewise testify to Christ's fulfillment of prophecy.

The following chart highlights some of the better-known and more obvious scriptures illustrating the Old Testament "messianic prophecies" and their relationship to the New Testament gospel of Jesus. Many of these purportedly prophetic fulfillments are included because of the specific mention in the New Testament of "prophets," "prophecy" or otherwise identified by such phrases as "in fulfillment of scripture" or "it is written." Also included here are other verses utilized in the creation of the gospels, such as those appearing in the Sermon on the Mount, previously discussed as having been strung together from Old Testament scriptures.

Old Testament	New Testament
Jewish tradition based on scriptural interpretation held that there would be a messiah from the house of David, descended from Abraham. (Gen 12:3, 18:18; Is 9:7) The messiah would also be a "star out of Jacob" (Num 24:17) and a "branch of Jesse." (Is 11:1)	In the genealogies of Matthew and Luke—which are not the same—Jesus is said to have descended from Abraham and David. (Mt 1:1; Lk 1:32-33; 3:34) The genealogies also list Jacob and Jesse as Jesus's ancestors. (Mt 1:2, 1:6; Lk 3:34, 3:32)
"Behold, a young woman shall conceive and bear a son, and shall call his name Immanuel." (Is 7:14; RSV)	"Now the birth of Jesus Christ took place in this way…. All this took place to fulfil what the Lord had

"Therefore the Lord himself shall give you a sign; Behold, a virgin shall conceive, and bear a son, and shall call his name Immanuel." (Is 7:14; KJV)	spoken by the prophet: 'Behold, a virgin shall conceive and bear a son, and his name shall be called Emmanuel.'" (Mt 1:18-23; Lk 1:27-31)
"The scepter shall not depart from Judah, nor the ruler's staff from between his feet, until he comes to whom it belongs; and to him shall be the obedience of the peoples." (Gen 49:10) "But you, O Bethlehem, Ephrathah, who are little to be among the clans of Judah, from you shall come forth for me one who is to be ruler in Israel, whose origin is from old, from ancient days." (Micah 5:2)	Jesus is a descendant of Judah. (Mt 2:6; Lk 3:33) After Jesus is born in Bethlehem, Herod asks the wise men where he is. They answer that he is in Bethlehem, "so it is written by the prophet: 'And you, O Bethlehem, in the land of Judah, are by no means least among the rulers of Judah; for from you shall come a ruler who will govern my people Israel.'" (Mt 2:1-6)
"May the kings of Tarshish and of the isles render him tribute, may the kings of Sheba and Seba bring gifts!" (Ps 72:10) "...all those from Sheba shall come. They shall bring gold and frankincense..." (Is 60:6)	"...behold, wise men from the East came to Jerusalem... (Mt 2:1) "...they offered him gifts, gold and frankincense and myrrh." (Mt 2:11)
"When Israel was a child, I loved him, and out of Egypt I called my son." (Hosea 11:1)	"And he rose and took the child and his mother by night, and departed to Egypt, and remained there until the death of Herod. This was to fulfil what the Lord had spoken by the prophet, "Out of Egypt have I called my son." (Mt 2:14-15)
"Thus says the Lord: 'A voice is heard in Ramah, lamentation and bitter	"Then was fulfilled what was spoken by the prophet Jeremiah: 'A voice was heard

weeping. Rachel is weeping for her children; she refuses to be comforted for her children, because they are not.'" (Jer 31:15)	in Ramah, wailing and loud lamentation, Rachel weeping for her children; she refused to be consoled, because they were no more.'" (Mt 2:17-18)
"'Therefore beware, and drink no wine or strong drink, and eat nothing unclean, for lo, you shall conceive and bear a son. No razor shall come upon his head, for the boy shall be a Nazirite to God from birth; and he shall begin to deliver Israel from the hand of the Philistines.'" (Judg 13:4-5)	"And he went and dwelt in a city called Nazareth, that what was spoken by the prophets might be fulfilled, 'He shall be called a Nazarene.'" (Mt 2:23)
"A voice cries: 'In the wilderness prepare the way of the Lord, make straight in the desert a highway for God.'" (Is 40:3)	"For this is he who was spoken of by the prophet Isaiah when he said, 'The voice of one crying in the wilderness: Prepare the way of the Lord, make his paths straight.'" (Mt 3:3) "He said, "I am the voice of one crying in the wilderness, 'Make straight the way of the Lord,' as the prophet Isaiah said." (Jn 1:23) "As it is written in the book of the words of Isaiah the prophet, 'The voice of one crying in the wilderness: Prepare the way of the lord, make his paths straight.'" (Lk 3:3-6)
"I will tell of the decree of the Lord: He said to me, 'You are	"...and lo, a voice from heaven, saying, 'This is my

my son, today I have begotten you.'" (Ps 2:7)	beloved Son, with whom I am well pleased.'"[1] (Mt 3:17)
"The Spirit of the Lord God is upon me, because the Lord has anointed me to bring good tidings to all the afflicted; he has sent me to bind up the brokenhearted, to proclaim liberty to the captives, and the opening of the prison to those who are bound; to proclaim the year of the Lord's favor... (Is 61:1-2)	"And [Jesus] stood up to read; and there was given to him the book of the prophet Isaiah. He opened the book and found the place where it was written, 'The Spirit of the Lord is upon me, because he has anointed me to preach good news to the poor. He has sent me to proclaim release to the captives and recovering of sight to the blind, to set at liberty those who are oppressed, to proclaim the acceptable year of the Lord.'" (Lk 4:16-19)
"... In the former time he brought into contempt the land of Zebulun and the land of Naphtali, but in the latter time he will make glorious the way of the sea, the land beyond the Jordan, Galilee of the nations." (Is 9:1-2)	"...and leaving Nazareth he went and dwelt in Capernaum by the sea, in the territory of Zebulun and Naphtali, that what was spoken by the prophet Isaiah might be fulfilled: 'The land of Zebulun and the land of Naphtali, toward the sea, across the Jordan, Galilee of the Gentiles...'" (Mt 4:13-15)
"And I will sanctify my great name..." (Ezek 36:23) (KJV)	"...Hallowed be thy name." (Mt 6:9)[2]

---

[1] Per Ehrman, some copies of Matthew repeat the pertinent psalm verbatim: "This is my beloved Son, whom I have begotten." The scribes doing so apparently felt perfectly comfortable adjusting the Lord's alleged words to suit themselves and to fit better with scripture. (See below for further discussion.)

[2] The term for "hallowed" in the Greek is the same in the Septuagint, or Greek Old Testament, as that which is translated as "sanctified": *hagiazo* or *hagiaso*.

"Then the LORD said to Moses, 'Behold, I will rain bread from heaven for you; and the people shall go out and gather a day's portion every day....'" (Ex 16:4)	"Give us this day our daily bread." (Mt 6:11) "Give us day by day our daily bread." (Lk 11:3)
"Thine, O LORD, [is] the greatness, and the power, and the glory... thine [is] the kingdom, O LORD, and thou art exalted as head above all." (1 Chron 29:11) (KJV)	"For thine is the kingdom, and the power, and the glory, for ever. Amen." (Mt 6:13) (KJV)
"Ask of me, and I will make the nations your heritage, and the ends of the earth your possession." (Ps 2:8) "You will seek me and find me..." (Jer 29:13) "...[it is] the voice of my beloved that knocketh, [saying], Open to me..." (Sgs 5:2) (KJV)	"Ask, and it will be given you; seek, and you will find; knock, and it will be opened to you..." (Mt 7:7)
"...you shall love your neighbor as yourself..." (Lev 19:18)	"So whatever you wish that men would do to you, do so to them; for this is the law and the prophets." (Mt 7:12)
"He was despised and rejected by men; a man of sorrows, and acquainted with grief... "Surely he has borne our griefs and carried our sorrows; yet we esteemed him stricken, smitten by God, and afflicted. But he was wounded for our transgressions, he was bruised for our iniquities; upon him was the chastisement that made us whole, and with his stripes	"That evening they brought to him many who were possessed with demons; and he cast out the spirits with a word, and healed all who were sick. This was to fulfil what was spoken by the prophet Isaiah, 'He took our infirmities and bore our diseases.'" (Mt 8:16-17)

we are healed.... "...yet he bore the sin of many, and made intercession for the transgressors." (Is 53:4-32)	
"For I will pour water on the thirsty land, and streams on the dry ground..." (Is 44:3) "Ho, every one who thirsts, come to the waters..." (Is 55:1)	"He who believes in me, as the scriptures has said, 'Out of his heart shall flow rivers of living water.'" (Jn 7:38)
"Then the eyes of the blind shall be opened, and the ears of the deaf unstopped; then shall the lame man leap like a hart, and the tongue of the dumb sing for joy..." (Is 35:5-6)	"...the blind receive their sight and the lame walk, lepers are cleansed and the deaf hear..." (Mt 11:5; Mk 7:35-37) "And when the demon had been cast out, the dumb man spoke..." (Mt 9:33)
"Behold, I send my messenger to prepare the way before me..." (Mal 3:1)	"This is he of whom it is written, 'Behold, I send my messenger before thy face, who shall prepare thy way before thee.'" (Mt 11:10; Lk 7:27)
"Behold, I will send you Elijah the prophet before the great and terrible day of the Lord comes." (Mal 4:5)	"For all the prophets and the law prophesied until John; and if you were willing to accept it, he is Elijah, who is to come." (Mt 11:13-14)
"Behold my servant, whom I uphold, my chosen, in whom my soul delights; I have put my Spirit upon him, he will bring forth justice to the nations. He will not cry or lift up his voice, or make it heard in the street; a bruised reed he will not break, and a dimly burning wick he will not quench; he will faithfully	"...he healed them all, and ordered them not to make him known. This was to fulfil what was spoken by the prophet Isaiah: 'Behold, my servant whom I have chosen, my beloved with whom my soul is well pleased. I will put my Spirit upon him, and he shall proclaim justice to the

bring forth justice. He will not fail or be discouraged till he has established justice in the earth; and the coastlands wait for his law." (Is 42:1-4)	Gentiles. He will not wrangle or cry aloud, nor will any one hear his voice in the streets; he will not break a bruised reed or quench a smoldering wick, till he brings justice to victory; and in his names will the Gentiles hope'." (Mt 12:15-21)
"I will open my mouth in a parable; I will utter dark sayings from of old, things that we have heard and known, that our fathers have told us. We will not hide them from their children, but tell to the coming generation..." (Ps 78:2-4)	"All this Jesus said to the crowds in parables; indeed he said nothing to them without a parable. This was to fulfil what was spoken by the prophet: 'I will open my mouth in parables, I will utter what has been hidden since the foundation of the world.'" (Mt 13:34-35)
"The Lord your God will raise up for you a prophet like me from among you, from your brethren--him you shall heed..." (Deut 18:15)	"When the people saw the sign which he had done, they said, 'This is indeed the prophet who is to come into the world!'" (Jn 6:14) "Moses said, 'The Lord God will raise up for you a prophet from your brethren as he raised me up. You shall listen to him in whatever you he tells you." (Acts 3:22)
"Binding his foal to the vine and his ass's colt to the choice vine..." (Gen 49:11) "Lo, your king comes to you; triumphant and victorious is he, humble and riding on an ass, on a colt the foal of an ass." (Zech 9:9)	"So they took branches of palm trees and went out to meet him, crying, 'Hosanna! Blessed is he who comes in the name of the Lord, even the King of Israel!' And Jesus found a young ass and sat upon it; as it is written, 'Fear not, daughter of Zion; behold, your king is coming,

	sitting on an ass's colt!'" (Jn 12:13-14) "Tell the daughter of Zion, Behold, your king is coming to you, humble, and mounted on an ass, and on a colt, the foal of an ass." (Mt 21:2-5)
"And there shall no longer be a trader in the house of the Lord of hosts on that day." (Zech 14:21) "Has this house, which is called by my name, become a den of robbers in your eyes? (Jer 7:11)	"And Jesus entered the temple of God and drove out all who sold and bought in the temple, and he overturned the tables of the money-changers and the seats of those who sold pigeons. He said to them, 'It is written, "My house shall be called a house of prayer"; but you make it a den of robbers.'" (Mt 21:12-13)
"I thank thee that thou hast answered me and hast become my salvation [Yeshuwah]. The stone which the builders rejected has become the head of the corner." (Ps 118:21-22)	"Jesus [Yeshua] said to them, 'Have you never read in the scriptures: "The very stone which the builders rejected has become the head of the corner..."'" (Mt 21:42)
"...and upon the wing of abominations shall come one who makes desolate, until the decreed end is poured out on the desolator." (Dan 9:27) "Forces from him shall appear and profane the temple and fortress, and shall take away the continual burnt offering. And they shall set up the abomination that makes desolate." (Dan 11:31)	"So when you seed the desolating sacrilege spoken of by the prophet Daniel, standing in the holy place (let the reader understand), then let those who are in Judea flee to the mountains..." (Mt 24:15-16)

"And from the time that the continual burnt offering is taken away, and the abomination that makes desolate is set up..." (Dan 12:11)	
"Then I said to them, 'If it seems right to you, give me my wages; but if not, keep them.' And they weighed out as my wages thirty shekels of silver." (Zech 11:12)	"and [Judas] said, 'What will you give me if I deliver him to you?' And they paid him thirty pieces of silver." (Mt. 26:15)
"Strike the shepherd, that the sheep may be scattered..." (Zech 13:7)	"Then Jesus said to them, 'You will all fall away because of me this night; for it is written, "I will strike the shepherd, and the sheep of the flock will be scattered."'" (Mt 26:31; Mk 14:27)
"...let not those wink the eye who hate me without cause." (Ps 35:19) "More in number than the hairs of my head are those who hate me without cause..." (Ps 69:4)	"It is to fulfil the word that is written in their law, 'They hated me without a cause.'" (Jn 15:25)
"Even my bosom friend in whom I trusted, who ate of my bread, has lifted his heel against me." (Ps 41:9)	"...Jesus took bread, and blessed, and broke it, and gave it to the disciples..." (Mt 26:26) "Jesus said to him, 'Friend, why are you here?' Then they came up and laid hands on Jesus and seized him." (Mt 26:50; Jn 13:21)
"I gave my back to the smiters, and my cheeks to those who pulled out the beard; I hid not my face from shame and spitting." (Is 50:6)	"Then they spat in his face, and struck him; and some slapped him..." (Mt 26:67)

"...So I took the thirty shekels of silver and cast them into the treasury in the house of the LORD." (Zech 11:13) "And the LORD said unto me, Cast it unto the potter: a goodly price that I was prised at of them. And I took the thirty [pieces] of silver, and cast them to the potter in the house of the LORD." (Zech 11:13) (KJV)	"And throwing down the pieces of silver in the temple, he departed..." (Mt 27:5) "So they took counsel, and bought with them the potter's field, to bury strangers in." (Mt 27:7)
"Arise, and go down to the potter's house, and there I will let you hear my words." (Jer 18:2) "And I bought the field at An'athoth from Han'amel my cousin, and weighed out the money to him, seventeen shekels of silver." (Jer 32:9)	"Then was fulfilled what had been spoken by the prophet Jeremiah, saying, "And they took the thirty pieces of silver, the price of him on whom a price had been set by some of the sons of Israel, and they gave them for the potter's field, as the Lord directed me." (Mt 27:9-10)
"He was oppressed, and he was afflicted, yet he opened not his mouth..." (Zech 53:7)	"But when he was accused by the chief priests and elders, he made no answer." (Mt 27:12)
"And all the elders of that city nearest to the slain man shall wash their hands over the heifer whose neck was broken in the valley; and they shall testify, 'Our hands did not shed this blood, neither did our eyes see it shed. Forgive, O LORD, thy people Israel, whom thou hast redeemed, and set not the guilt of innocent blood in the midst of thy people Israel; but let the guilt of	"So when Pilate saw that he was gaining nothing, but rather that a riot was beginning, he took water and washed his hands before the crowd, saying, 'I am innocent of this man's blood; see to it yourselves.' And all the people answered, 'His blood be on us and on our children!'" (Mt 27:24-25)

blood be forgiven them.' So you shall purge the guilt of innocent blood from your midst, when you do what is right in the sight of the LORD." (Deut 21:6-9) "I wash my hands in innocence..." (Ps 26:6) "If any one goes out of the doors of your house into the street, his blood shall be upon his head, and we shall be guiltless; but if a hand is laid upon any one who is with you in the house, his blood shall be on our head." (Josh 2:19)	
"They gave me poison for food, and for my thirst they gave me vinegar to drink." (Ps 69:21)	"...they offered him wine to drink, mingled with gall..." (Mt 27:34) "After this Jesus, knowing that all was now finished, said (to fulfil the scripture), "I thirst." A bowl full of vinegar stood there; so they put a sponge full of vinegar on hyssop and held it to his mouth." (Jn 19:28-29)
"...they divide my garments among them, and for my raiment they cast lots." (Ps 22:18)	"And when they had crucified him, they divided his garments among them by casting lots..." (Mt 27:35) "When the soldiers had crucified Jesus they took his garments and made four parts.... So they said to one another, 'Let us not tear it, but cast lots for it to see whose it shall be.' This was to fulfil the scripture, 'They parted my garments among

	them, and for my clothing they cast lots.'" (Jn 19:23-24)
"...because he poured out his soul to death, and was numbered with the transgressors; yet he bore the sin of many, and made intercession for the transgressors." (Is 53:12)	"Then two robbers were crucified with him, one on the right and one on the left." (Mt 27:38) "The next day he saw Jesus coming toward him, and said, "Behold, the Lamb of God, who takes away the sin of the world!" (Jn 1:29)
"So Moses returned to the LORD and said, 'Alas, this people have sinned a great sin... But now, if thou wilt forgive their sin..." (Ex 32:31-32)	"And Jesus said, 'Father, forgive them; for they know not what they do.'..." (Lk 23:34)
"All who see me mock at me, they make mouths at me, they wag their heads;" (Ps 22:7) "I am an object of scorn to my accusers; when they see me, they wag their heads." (Ps 109:25)	"And those who passed by derided him, wagging their heads." (Mt 27:39)
"'And on that day,'" says the Lord GOD, "I will make the sun go down at noon, and darken the earth in broad daylight." (Amos 8:9)	"Now from the sixth hour there was darkness over all the land until the ninth hour." (Mt 27:45)
"My God, my God, why hast thou forsaken me?" (Ps 22:1)	"...My God, my God, why hast thou forsaken me?" (Mt 27:46)
"Into thy hand I commit my spirit; thou hast redeemed me, O LORD, faithful God." (Ps 31:5)	Then Jesus, crying with a loud voice, said, "Father, into thy hands I commit my spirit!"... (Lk 23:46)
"Thy dead men shall live, together with my dead body shall they arise. Awake and	"...the tombs also were opened, and many bodies of the saints who had fallen

sing, ye that dwell in dust: for thy dew is as the dew of herbs, and the earth shall cast out the dead." (Is 26:19) (KJV)	asleep were raised, and coming out of the tombs after his resurrection they went into the holy city and appeared to many." (Mt 27:52-53)
"'And I will pour out on the house of David and the inhabitants of Jerusalem a spirit of compassion and supplication, so that when they look on him whom they have pierced, they shall mourn for him...The land shall mourn...'" (Zech 12:10) "Yea, dogs are round about me; a company of evildoers encircle me; they have pierced my hands and feet..." (Ps 22:16) "He keeps all his bones; not one of them is broken." (Ps 34:20)	"...when they came to Jesus and saw that he was already dead, they did not break his legs. But one of the soldiers pierced his side with a spear... For these things took place that the scripture might be fulfilled, 'Not a bone of him shall be broken.' And again another scripture says, 'They shall look on him whom they have pierced.'" (Jn 19:33-37)
"My friends and companions stand aloof from my plague, and my kinsmen stand afar off." (Ps 38:11)	"And all his acquaintances and the women who had followed him from Galilee stood at a distance and saw these things." (Lk 23:49)
"And he made his grave with the wicked, and with the rich in his death..." (Is 53:9)	"When it was evening, there came a rich man from Arimathe'a, named Joseph, who also was a disciple of Jesus.... And Joseph took the body, and wrapped it in a clean linen shroud, And laid it in his own new tomb..." (Mt 27:57, 59-60)
"After two days he will revive us; on the third day he will raise us up, that we may live before him." (Hos 6:2)	"...the Son of man must be delivered into the hands of sinful men, and be crucified, and on the third day rise."

	(Lk 24:7)
"Thou didst ascend the high mount..." (Ps 68:18) "You have ascended on high..." (Ps 68:18) (NKJV)	"So then after the Lord had spoken unto them, he was received up into heaven, and sat on the right hand of God." (Mk 16:19) (KJV) "...he was parted from them, and carried up into heaven." (Lk 24:51) (KJV)
"Your divine throne endures for ever and ever. Your royal scepter is a scepter of equity; you love righteousness and hate wickedness. Therefore God, your God, has anointed you with the oil of gladness above your fellows..." (Ps 45:6-7)	"But the Son he says, 'Thy throne, O God, is for ever and ever, the righteous scepter is the scepter of thy kingdom. Thou has loved righteousness and hated lawlessness; therefore God, thy God, has anointed thee with the oil of gladness beyond thy comrades.'" (Heb 1:8-9)
"The Lord has sworn and will not change his mind, 'You are a priest for ever after the order of Melchizedek.'" (Ps 110:4)	"So also Christ did not exalt himself to be made a high priest, but was appointed by him who said to him, 'Thou are my Son, today I have begotten thee'; as he says also in another place, 'Thou are a priest for ever, after the order of Melchizedek.'" (Heb 5:5-6)

These numerous correlations and many others between the Old and New Testaments may be found in the footnotes of the RSV and other versions, and need not be reproduced in full here. Suffice it to say that the writers of the New Testament were very familiar with the Old Testament—the only "scriptures" of the time to which they could possibly refer—and that many of these scriptures were adapted from the Greek OT or Septuagint. In fact, almost *all* the Old Testament scriptures common to Matthew, Mark and Luke come from the Septuagint, rather than the Hebrew OT. As today, pious Jews at the time when the gospel story supposedly occurred studied the scriptures intensely and knew them very well—including and *especially* those interpreted to apply to the coming messiah, for whom they were desperately waiting.

On the surface of it, if taken literally the New Testament seems to record the advent of the messiah, as prophesied in the Old Testament. However, there may be a different reason for this appearance. In scrutinizing all of the Old Testament "prophecies" that purportedly relate to the coming messiah, it is evident that the gospels were deliberately designed to show that these scriptures had been fulfilled in Jesus Christ. When these and other OT scriptures are studied and seriously considered, therefore, it is logical to ask if they constitute "prophecies" and "prefiguring" of the advent of a historical Jesus Christ—or if they were used as a *blueprint* in the *creation* of a *fictional* messiah.

The suggestion that the gospel story constitutes a patchwork of Old Testament scriptures used as a framework throws light upon some of the more illogical parts of the tale, such as at Matthew 27:12, when Jesus is being accused by the chief priests and elders yet says nothing. If we consider that this passage was written in order to "fulfill prophecy" at Zechariah 53:7, the pericope takes on greater sense.

The deliberate historicizing of "prophecies" by ancient writers is well known among biblical scholars, as reflected in the discussion by Dr. Crossan of a reconstructed text called the "Cross Gospel," the author of which, Crossan states, "attempts to write, from prophetic allusions, a first 'historical narrative' about the passion of Jesus." Concerning the Old Testament scriptures purportedly prophesying Christ's passion, Crossan remarks that "historicized narratives were created out of those prophetic complexes, stories so good that their prophetic origins were almost totally obliterated."[1] Hence, over the centuries stories have been created using "prophecies"; based on the evidence presented above, it is not unreasonable to aver that the gospel tale is one of them, with its prophetic origins obscured.

---

[1] Crossan, *THJ*, 382.

Questions about the Gospel Story

"The Bible is a human book with human characteristics."

Josh McDowell, *The New Evidence that Demands a Verdict*

If you have been told repeatedly by authorities, usually since you were very young, that the gospel story is true in every fact and detail, and that the Bible is the inerrant Word of God, you may very well believe it. After all, aren't the people in authority there for a reason, and don't they always tell the truth? Nevertheless, over the centuries many people have not been convinced that the miracles recounted in the gospels really happened, believing instead that Jesus's zealous followers added these stories to his biography in order to convince others that he was divine. These people who are skeptical cite other tales and myths that contain similar miracles and magic tricks to show that the gospel story is not unique.

In addition, many people have problems accepting all the obvious contradictions in the Bible as a whole but also in the gospel story, as well as apparent mistakes, failed prophecies and repugnant doctrines. The objections raised by Bible critics include questions and concerns about the following:

- Miracles and impossibilities
- Failed prophecies
- Contradictions and inconsistencies
- Errors in time and place
- Chronological discrepancies
- Erroneous translations and interpretations
- Illogic and Irrationality
- Lack of character
- Repulsive deeds, sayings and doctrines

Although comprehensive in some aspects, the scope of this present work is not to list and address all of the problems with the gospel texts but to provide an appropriate sampling instead. It probably need not be stated that these are quandaries the average priest or pastor does not generally discuss with the congregation.

Miracles, Impossibilities and Implausibilities

In the New Testament, there are so many miracles, including feeding the multitudes and walking on water, it would require too much space to elucidate upon all of them, so we will examine only some of the most spectacular and unbelievable.

From the very beginning we find implausible fables that cast doubt upon the gospel story's historicity. Not only are we faced with the incredible story of Mary's impregnation by the Holy Spirit, but at Luke 1:41-44 John the Baptist is depicted as "leaping" in his mother's womb at the sound of Mary's voice, because she is carrying "the Lord." Hence, John miraculously recognizes Jesus before either is born. As an adult, upon first sight John pronounces Jesus "the Lamb of God who takes away the sin of the world" (Jn 1:29), and he is a witness to the heavens opening up, "Spirit of God descending like a dove" upon Christ, and God's voice establishing Jesus as his Son. At this development, John the Baptist asserts, "I have seen and have borne witness that this is the Son of God" (Jn 1:33-34). Yet, after all the signs and wonders, why does the Baptist later send word from prison, asking Christ if he is the messiah? (Lk 7:18-23) Does this scenario truly seem realistic?

Also, if John's mother, Elizabeth, and Jesus's mother, Mary, are cousins, meaning John and Jesus are also cousins, how is it that John did not grow up around Jesus, such that the two meet as complete strangers as adults? The area being discussed is only 90 miles in length—is it logical that these two families would never have met again, particularly since John's mother, Elizabeth, whose husband was a *priest* in the Temple, was aware that Mary's baby, Jesus, was *her Lord*? Would the pious Elizabeth—like so many other Jews of her time, possibly desperately awaiting the messiah—truly spend the next decades at such a distance as not to know Christ at all? Moreover, many women who have given birth in proximity of one another become very friendly and dependent on each other, *especially if they are relatives*—

could Elizabeth and Mary really have visited with each other only prior to Mary giving birth?

Regarding this pericope, biblical scholar Meier casts doubt as to the inerrancy of Luke's gospel by arguing that the evangelist's assertion that Jesus was conceived six months after John (Lk 1:26-28), and is therefore a "younger relative" than John, finds no support anywhere else in the New Testament and is "of doubtful historicity."[1] The whole pericope has an air of cartoonish artifice about it, and logic and honesty dictate that we ask whether or not it is fiction.

The Events of the Baptism

The descent of the Holy Spirit as a dove represents a highly implausible part of the tale, as does the booming voice of God. Rather than being a fact, the dove motif may have come from the prevalence of doves in pre-Christian religion around the same basic area, or from a combination of Isaiah 11:2 and Isaiah 42:1, regarding the "Spirit of the LORD" resting upon God's "Servant."[2] Concerning the dove motif, Meier notes:

> The debate over the precise meaning of the dove as the symbol of the spirit continues unresolved: allusion to the spirit of God over the waters in Gen. 1:2... [or] the dove as a symbol of a goddess in the ancient Near East or as a messenger of the gods... For supposed mythological parallels, see Bultmann, *Geschichte*, 264-69.[3]

In *Paganism of the Roman Empire*, scholar Ramsay MacMullen, PhD—deemed by the American Historical Association "the greatest historian of the Roman Empire alive today"—discusses the sacred doves in the holy city of Hierapolis, described by Jewish historian Philo (1st cent AD/CE) as possessing an "enormous population of doves."[4] Indeed, dove worship was associated with several pre-Christian cults, including those found in Samaria/Palestine and elsewhere:

---

[1] Meier, II, 208.
[2] In *New Testament History* (168), F.F. Bruce points out the possible correlation of the dove motif to the passages in Isaiah.
[3] Meier, II, 188.
[4] Ramsay, 35.

"Evidence for domestication extends back to 4500 BC in ancient Iraq, and the bird was sacred to the early Middle Eastern cultures, being associated with Astarte, the goddess of love and fertility; later, in ancient Greece, it was sacred to Aphrodite and in Roman times to Venus."[1] In any event, rather than implausibly representing history, couldn't it be that the dove motif was "borrowed" from the OT, Pagan religion or both?

Jesus's Temptation

Another implausibility occurs in the story of Jesus's temptation by the devil. In the first place, we are asked to believe that a cosmic and very powerful creature called "the devil" can appear as a human being and was needed as such in the gospel story in order to "tempt" Jesus, who himself is in reality God and who, therefore, created the devil in the first place! The Greek word for "temptation," *peirasmos*, is also translated as "rebellion against God." Hence, the all-powerful God causes and/or allows his own creation to rebel against him for dramatic and seemingly nonsensical purposes. It would appear to be a strange and one-sided battle, the outcome of which one would hope would have been obvious; for, if Satan had won, Satan would be God! Perhaps, it is argued, Jesus did not know himself fully as God, which seems bizarre if God is all powerful and omniscient—why separate himself out as Jesus, to forget who he is and then tempt himself? Yet, if God the Father is somewhere "out there" directing the show, would he then not be in two places at once? If not, where *is* God physically in relation to Jesus? This tale is extremely illogical and irrational.

Turning Water into Wine

Still one more miracle that is difficult to believe and that makes little sense even if it *could* happen occurs when Christ turns water into wine at the wedding feast of Cana—a pericope found *only* in John. The immense amount of wine created by Jesus equaled about 100 to 160 *gallons*! (Jn 2:6) The guests had apparently already drunk quite a bit of wine

---

[1] *Encyclopedia Britannica*, "Sacred Doves."

at the time when Jesus conjured up this mind-boggling amount. If this story is true, we must ask whether or not it is a righteous and moral act to supply so much alcohol to people who've already been drinking—what would be the point of creating such an excessive amount of wine?

Moreover, providing tangible physical and archaeological evidence of a "Christian" motif in pre-Christian times, within the sanctuary of the Greek temple of Apollo at Corinth (c. 540 BCE)—where Paul preached to the Corinthians—exists to this day *a stone sluice used by the Corinthian Pagan priesthood to turn water into wine.* At one end of this sluice water was poured in, while a priest in a hidden compartment diverted the water and poured wine out the other end. This water-to-wine contraption was created at least two centuries before the Christian era. Could it be that, rather than a "true story," the water-to-wine motif in John's gospel was based in part on this previously known "miracle," which was part of the priestly repertoire?

The Resurrection of Dead People

The resurrection of dead people is a theme found within the Old Testament, in the story of Elijah raising the widow's son at 1 Kings 17:22, and in that of Elisha with a comparable resurrection miracle of his own at 2 Kings 4:34. In the New Testament, Christ's own resurrection is preceded by that of Jairus's daughter. In addition to these implausible tales appears that of Jesus raising a man named "Lazarus" from the dead. Not only is it difficult to believe the Lazarus-resurrection pericope in itself, but also the fact that it appears *only* in the gospel of John—by most accounts the latest of the gospels—makes one wonder why the first three evangelists would overlook such a momentous event! The logical suggestion may be that the raising of Lazarus did not really happen but was an afterthought by either the writer of John or a later scribe. Since the idea of the resurrection of the dead is so important to Christian doctrine, it is crucial to investigate this oversight by the synoptists more fully and not simply wave it away. Could it be that Christ's implausible resurrection was not "historical" at all but, like the water-to-wine miracle, based on a motif found in other religions within the Roman Empire?

The Raising of the Saints

In addition to the improbable Lazarus resurrection, it also seems inconceivable that if, upon Jesus' death, the saints rose up out of their graves and went into Jerusalem, appearing to many people, the Jewish scribes—who are everywhere present in the gospel story—would not have chronicled such a supernatural phenomenon somewhere in their books. Jewish scribes were known to record practically everything significant that affected them, especially purported supernatural events. They often wrote long screeds against individuals, however minor, who may have irritated them. **Surely, if Jesus had caused such a ruckus throughout their country, overturning tables in their sacrosanct temple, threatening to throw the temple itself to the ground, and then having their dead rise and walk through their holy city, the Jewish scribes would have recorded Christ somewhere!** But *they did not*, as if Jesus never existed, and they had never heard of the story.

This bizarre and grotesque episode remains more logically explained not as a real, historical event that was somehow overlooked by everyone of the day, but as a reworking of Old Testament "messianic" scriptures:

> Thy dead shall live, their bodies shall rise. O dwellers in the dust, awake and sing for joy!... (Is 26:19)

> And many of those who sleep in the dust of the earth shall awake, some to everlasting life... (Dan 12:2)

Indeed, it is evident that the gospel writers were once more using OT scriptures as a *blueprint* in their creation.

The Ascension into Heaven

Another detail that makes the gospel story difficult to swallow is that the ascension—one of the most miraculous events to happen to Jesus—is not even mentioned by Matthew or John. It is stunning to consider that only the *non-eyewitnesses* Mark and Luke report the ascension—and, as noted earlier, both of those brief passages are widely considered later interpolations by unknown scribes! How could Christ's faithful *apostles* possibly fail to relate such a momentous occurrence, if it really happened? It is clear that

Matthew is very concerned about recording the major, miraculous events of Christ's life, some of which he allegedly witnessed, and that John is quite obviously interested in showing everything that could possibly be considered an indication of Christ's divinity—and the ascension is surely one of the biggest qualifications—yet, no word of it? People today become all excited and agog by alleged images of Jesus Christ in stains on a sidewalk, but Christ's ascension—the floating up into the air and disappearance of a man—somehow failed to make enough of an impression on Matthew and John for them to write about it in their gospels! This glaring omission seems very odd to the logical mind, to say the least.

To reiterate, even the accounts of the ascension in Mark and Luke are doubtful and are missing in some early manuscripts, causing these verses to be omitted in some translations. We have seen that the pertinent verses in Mark (16:9-20) are not included in the earliest manuscripts. In addition, Christ's ascension is absent in the RSV translation of Luke 24:51, which notes that "[o]ther ancient authorities add *and was carried up into heaven*." Which version is correct, and what is the original? It is sensible and honest to ask, did the ascension really happen, or was it an afterthought? Could it not be that the ascension was added later in order to explain what happened to Jesus after he was resurrected, since he was obviously not still on Earth, walking around in a state of immortality? It is not only possible but probable that any hearer of the story, being convinced of it, would excitedly want to meet the living Christ—maybe the scribes who later interpolated the ascension were basing it on traditions created by Christian preachers in response to requests to meet the Lord, in essence giving an excuse for why they could not produce him? Or perhaps there was another political reason for its inclusion?

Assuming we accept that miracles can and do happen, we must nevertheless ask ourselves why the miracles of Jesus are more significant and truthful than those of other individuals throughout history. As Dr. Meier remarks:

> In the ancient Mediterranean world, most people readily granted the possibility and reality of miracles. But precisely because of this, sociology and anthropology

raise a question many believers may find uncomfortable: is there any justification for seeing a significant distinction between the miracles attributed to Jesus in the Gospels and the magical practices widely reflected in Greco-Roman writings, including magical papyri and popular novels? Are these magical practices anything more than the "bad" miracles of pagans, while the Gospel miracles are simply the "good" magical practices of Jesus? In other words, is there any real difference between magic and miracle? Or is the only difference in the eye of the beholder who happens to be a Christian apologist?[1]

In further discussing the miracles of Jesus as reflections of the "literary forms, themes, and motifs found in the Pagan and Jewish miracles stories circulating in the Mediterranean world around the turn of the era," Meier states that there is a "great deal of truth to this claim," although he follows this remark with a caution that "distinctions are in order" and "respect for the differences" must be kept in mind.[2] Yet, Meier also comments that "the miracle stories of the Gospels do in fact parallel *literary forms* found in pagan and Jewish miracle stories."[3]

In reality, if all these miracles were true, and Jesus displayed numerous such wonders and signs of divinity, as well as fulfilling so many characteristics and prophecies of the messiah in the Jewish scriptures, *it is impossible to fathom how Christ could possibly be rejected by the Jews in the end*. Rather than serving as an exhibition of Jewish folly in rejecting Christ, the lack of notice by the "chosen people" and the many difficulties surrounding the gospel story must make one wonder—based on honesty and logic—whether or not the story is fiction, explaining precisely why the Jews did not believe it: They could not, obviously, if it didn't happen! In fact, the Jews of "this generation," i.e., the time of Jesus's purported advent, would not have been aware of the existence of the story even as *fiction*, since, in such a scenario, the tale would not have been composed yet. In all

---

[1] Meier, II, 511.
[2] Meier, II, 536.
[3] Meier, II, 536.

fairness to the Jewish culture, and with an eye to the honesty and integrity claimed to be hallmarks of religion, *we must inspect these beliefs scientifically and not take them simply on faith*.

When scrutinized scientifically, the entire gospel story demonstrates a profoundly artificial feel about it, including the fact that the whole tale could be compressed into a timeframe of a week or two, coming across more as a *play* than a factual biography or history. Even removing the natural-law-bending miracles, the tale reads not as if it were "history" or "biography" but as if it were *fiction*. Instead of engaging in illogical machinations involving supernatural events that go against the laws of physics, it is reasonable to ask whether or not the evangelists and later scribes were writing *fictional*, and not historical, accounts.

Failed Prophecies

Continuing with the miraculous events, when the material is analyzed, it becomes difficult to claim that *any* of the purported "prophecies" in the gospels have been fulfilled, including the destruction of the temple, which is accepted by numerous mainstream scholars as having occurred *before* it was discussed in the New Testament. As one more glaring example of failed prophecy, many people point to Christ's assertions that he would be coming back "soon" and that certain other incredible events would take place, before "this generation" would pass away. Jesus said that there were some present who "will not have gone through all the towns of Israel, before the Son of man comes." (Mt 10:23) He also stated that they would not "taste death before they see the Son of man coming in his kingdom." (Mt 16:28) So far, there has been no "Second Coming," if ever there was a first. Indeed, *none* of these things have happened yet, and these people are all long dead. Certainly, one could argue that, per Christ's "predictions" at Matthew 24:7, etc., nation *has* risen up against nation and kingdom against kingdom, and there *have* been famines and earthquakes, as well as wars, "rumors of wars" and the rest supposedly prophesied in the New Testament. Such vague predictions about the already obvious nature of this world and of mankind would be about as earth-shattering as "prophesying" that tomorrow someone's car will break down somewhere.

Contradictions and Inconsistencies

Like the miracles and failed prophecies, there are enough contradictions and inconsistencies in the gospels to warrant questioning their historical value. Yet, in the frantic effort to maintain the tale as credible and inerrant history, we are asked to subscribe to some irrational and illogical gyrations in order to harmonize or reconcile these many problems. For example, the names in the genealogies differ between gospels: In his genealogy, Matthew lists 28 generations from King David to Jesus Christ, while in Luke (3:23-38) the number is 43 generations. Also, if Jesus is not related to Joseph, who is not his real father, he cannot be considered a genetic "son of David," one of the main qualifications for messiahship. Apologists attempt to reconcile these difficulties by tracing Jesus through *Mary* to King David, although the genealogy lists in Matthew and Luke clearly trace Christ to David through *Joseph*—in fact, in Matthew (1:7) Joseph descends from David's son Solomon, while in Luke (3:31) Joseph is descended from David's son Nathan! In addition to this contradiction of the evangelists' claims, there is no precedent in the Bible for a *female* genealogy. In this manner, a significant amount of ink has been spilled in order to reconcile these lists, but a simpler and more logical solution would be to ask, perhaps somebody made mistakes? Or, maybe these lists are not historical in the first place but contrived to show that Jesus fulfilled prophecy?

Appearing later in his gospel than in Matthew's, Luke's genealogy, in fact, plainly breaks the narrative and was interpolated into the text in the midst of the pericope about Jesus at the Jordan. Oddly enough, Luke's mundane genealogical digression directly follows the astounding events of the baptism by John, during which the Holy Spirit descends on Christ, the heavens open up, and the voice of God pronounces Jesus his own Son. The insertion at this point of Jesus's earthly pedigree appears to have been done to abrogate God's genealogy, instead demonstrating that Christ nevertheless possesses the divine right to rule by being a descendant of King David. This situation is unrealistic, evidently reflecting not actual "history" but political propaganda and a deliberate attempt at depicting Christ as having "fulfilled prophecy."

Another apparent contradiction warranting commentary emerges at John 1:18, where it is said, "No one has ever seen God"; yet, in the same chapter (Jn 1:32) John the Baptist is depicted as *seeing* "the Spirit" as a dove descending upon Jesus. The original Greek word for "Spirit" is πνευμα—*pneuma*—for which Strong's gives the first definition as:

> 1) the third person of the triune God, the Holy Spirit, coequal, coeternal with the Father and the Son

Hence, despite earlier declaring that no one has ever seen God, the evangelist then claims that John the Baptist *has* seen God. It has been proposed that this pericope serves to impress that *only* John had seen God, by emphasizing that, previously, no one else had ever seen God. John also portrays Jesus as saying that, because he and the Father are one, by knowing Christ his disciples to "have *seen*" the Father. Even so, one would think that such a mind-boggling bending of biblical doctrine and natural law would merit more than one brief mention, if it really happened!

In the temptation accounts, Matthew depicts the temptation as occurring at the end of the 40-day fast, while Luke portrays the devil as tempting Jesus throughout the period. Oddly enough, Mark doesn't portray Jesus as fasting at all during the 40 days when he is in the desert, and John does not even report on this all-important event in Christ's life! Bizarrely, the battle between Jesus and the devil is composed of quotes from the Old Testament, specifically Deuteronomy and Psalms 91.[1] If this strange and incredible occurrence really happened, why would the characters involved be recorded as quoting little else but the Old Testament? Is this story realistic? Regarding this peculiar pericope, Dr. Meier remarks, "Granted the paucity of sources and their conflicting presentations of the temptation of Jesus, any judgment about a historical event is extremely

---

[1] Meier, II, 271.

difficult."[1] Rather than serving as a "historical event," is it not more plausible that this episode represents a fictional account cobbled together from scriptures and mythical motifs?[2]

At John 3:13, Christ says, "No man has ascended into heaven..." This assertion appears to contradict the claim in the Old Testament that Elijah had ascended into heaven (2 Kings 2:11). The apology for this apparent contradiction speculates that Jesus is saying that he is the only one who has ever *come back* from heaven to speak of it from "firsthand knowledge."[3]

The calling by Jesus of his disciples is also portrayed in various manners in the different gospels. The variances are such that it is impossible to insist that all of the evangelists recorded the scene correctly, if they are indeed depicting an historical event. Therefore, one or more of the accounts must be incorrect.

Moreover, in Matthew 5 and 6, Christ first advises his followers to "let their light shine before men"—i.e., in public—so that others can see their "good works." Later, Jesus admonishes that we should pray and give alms in secret. Which are we to do? Why do we pray aloud in church, when Christ makes much ado about praying in secret in a room with the door shut?

At one point (Mt 5:22), Jesus admonishes us not be angry with our brother, but he also says that our foes will be those of our own household, including our brothers. Christ later states that we should confront our brother for sinning against us. Can we do both of these things? Is it rational and compassionate to force us to forgive our brother, no matter what he has done? This verse provides yet another illustration of how biblical texts have been changed, as some

---

[1] Meier, II, 271.

[2] The tale of Christ's temptation becomes doubly peculiar when it is understood that, in a famous *myth*, Lord Buddha too was subjected to, and overcame, the temptation by the evil being Mara. This tradition dates to at least the 2nd century AD/CE, as evidenced by Indian sculptures depicting the scene, and as found in the Padhana Sutta, parts of which may date to the time of Ashoka (3rd cent. BCE). According to this scripture, Buddha is tempted nearby the "river Nerañjara," which bears a resemblance to the "River Jordan." (Ireland)

[3] Geisler, *WCA*, 407.

manuscripts of the New Testament insert "without cause" or "without a cause" into the admonition that we should not be angry with our brother, making this scripture more sensible.

At Matthew 5:34, Christ admonishes his followers not to swear oaths, but he himself repeatedly states, "Amen, I say to you," which constitutes an utterance of an oath.[1] In fact, the word "amen," usually translated as "verily," appears over 100 times in the gospels alone, while the oath "verily I say unto you" occurs almost 70 times in quotes by Jesus! Isn't that quite a bit of oath-swearing by Jesus?

Jesus also tells us at Matthew 5:44 to "love our enemies," which sounds utopian but impossible, and which also contradicts Christ's own sentiments when he angrily excoriates the cities of Chorazin, Bethsaida and Capernaum (Mt 11:21, 23). As an illustration of the difficulty in following this command, are Christians supposed to love those who are not Christian and who therefore deny Christ? Should we love Satan as well, since he is our biggest enemy?

In the Sermon on the Mount, Christ first tells us not to judge anyone, but then advises us to determine who are "dogs" and "swine," so we don't give them what is holy and throw our "pearls" before them. (Mt 7:6) How are we to decide who or what are swine, if we can't judge anyone? Isn't pronouncing people "dogs" and "swine" *judgmental*?

In the pericope of the mission of the 12, in Matthew (10:10) and Luke (9:3) Jesus is quoted as telling his disciples *not* to take a staff with them, but Mark (6:8) relates Jesus as charging them *to* take a staff. Obviously, one of these accounts is wrong, unless Jesus changed his mind from one second to the next.

Yet another contradiction and implausibility occurs when Christ is pressed by the Pharisees and scribes for a "sign" that he is the messiah, in Matthew (12:38-39; 16:1-4) and Luke (11:28). Jesus replies none will be given but the "sign of Jonah"—that is, being dead and resurrected in three days.[2] Providing a contradiction, Mark reports Jesus as *denying* the Jewish authorities and others *any* sign: "...no sign shall be given to this generation." (Mk 18:12) In any

---

[1] Cf. Zeitlin in Friedlander, xxvii.
[2] The name "Jonah" means "dove," which suggests that the "sign of Jonah" may also be the descent of the dove upon Jesus.

event, at this point in the story Jesus had already displayed constant miracles, wonders and signs that should have sufficed to convince even the most skeptical, if it all really happened. Like many others, this pericope seems contrived and artificial.

Christ first tells his followers to *hate* their mother and father but later exhorts them to *honor* their mother and father (Mt 15:4). How can we do both?

Another contradiction appears at Mark 10:35, where it is not their mother, as in Matthew (20:20), but James and John, the sons of Zebedee, *themselves* who ask to sit at Jesus's right hand. Which is it?

When at Mark 12:32 Jesus is depicted as saying that no one knows when the Second Coming will be, not even himself, but only the Father, Christ appears to be saying that he himself is not the omniscient Lord. Geisler's apology for this evident contradiction is that there were times when Jesus was God and times when he was not: "We must distinguish between what Jesus knew *as God* (everything) and what He knew *as man*. As God, Jesus was omniscient (all-knowing), but as man He was limited in His knowledge."[1] These remarks seem to be stating that Jesus turns off his omniscience at various times. If Christ is omnipotent, however, he can turn his omniscience back on whenever he wants, so it must be a question of him *desiring* not to be all knowing. Why would God play such a strange game with himself and with us? When do we know if Christ is speaking from his limited human knowledge and when he is speaking as God? If he doesn't know the time of his own coming, because he is a man, what else did he not know during his advent on Earth? Couldn't Jesus have made mistakes because of his limited knowledge?

Regarding the scriptures at Genesis 49:11 and Zechariah 9:9 about the "ass and colt" that were supposedly fulfilled in Jesus's triumphal entry into Jerusalem, Mark (11:1-7), Luke (19:29-35) and John (12:12-16) sensibly omit one of the animals, since Christ could hardly have ridden *two* asses. Matthew (21:1-7), on the other hand, depicts Jesus as riding on *two* asses, leaving one to wonder where was the Holy

---

[1] Geisler, *WCA*, 374.

Spirit to guide the evangelists, and why, if they were recording eyewitness accounts, rather than relying on a purported "prophecy," would they not know whether or not Jesus took and rode one or two asses? It would be honest and logical to ask whether or not the evangelists made an error, thus demonstrating that the Bible is not "inerrant." What this problem also strongly suggests is that, rather than depicting an actual event that he had witnessed, Matthew— who is nevertheless *claimed* to have been an *eyewitness*— simply cut and paste scriptures supposedly having to do with the coming messiah.

One more inconsistency occurs in the commonly held idea that Jesus was a "political rebel" fighting against the vested interests of both Judea and Rome. Despite this "freedom fighter" notion, Christ tells the people to give Caesar their tax money, to "turn the other cheek" when struck, as well as not to resist evil! "Render unto Caesar what is Caesar's?" (Mt 22:21) Is this really something a "political rebel" or "freedom fighter" would declare?

Jesus says he came not with peace but with a sword, but then he tells Peter to put away his sword, because "he who lives by the sword, dies by the sword." Which is it, a sword or no sword? This latter passage is odd also for the reason that no one but John (18:10)—held by most to be the latest of the gospels—*names* the person who used a sword to cut off the slave's ear. The other evangelists call the armed individual "one of those who were with Jesus" (Mt 26:51); "one of those who stood by" (Mk 14:47); and "one of them" (Lk 22:50). This lack of naming the person with the weapon is all the more strange in Mark, since he is presented traditionally as "Peter's interpreter" and would thus know if the individual in question *was* Peter, as was asserted by John. This fact confirms the unreal air of the gospels that indicates their having been written long after and far away from the purported events related in the story. Moreover, does it seem realistic that "Peter" could cut off the ear of the high priest's servant and not be arrested, especially since the authorities were looking for excuses to destroy Jesus and his following?

At Matthew 28:18, Jesus tells his disciples that he will be with them until the "end of the age/world"—or, *aion* in the original Greek, which also means "for ever." Earlier, in Matthew 26, Christ admonishes his followers not to worry about the cost of the ointment rubbed into his feet, saying that his disciples would always have the poor but would not always have him, their Lord. Aren't these two statements contradictory, that Christ will be with them forever but he would *not* be with them always? Geisler's apology for this apparent contradiction is that Jesus's admonition regarding him not being with his disciples refers to his physical presence, while his eternal presence is spiritual.[1] But, why doesn't Jesus just stay with us always, physically as well? Why this cat-and-mouse game where we have to guess whether Christ is really with us? Also, if Jesus is the omniscient and omnipotent Lord of the universe, knowing fully well about the poor, why doesn't he just put an end to poverty?

A number of other contradictions and inconsistencies appear within the gospels, including Jesus commanding his followers to bother not with the Gentiles, but only with the "lost sheep of Israel"; yet, at the end, after his resurrection, Christ exhorts his disciples to go to "all the nations." Throughout the gospels Jesus is quite adamant that he has only come for Israel—why is this mission altered suddenly and dramatically in the end? Did the omniscient Lord profoundly change the reason for his mission all of a sudden?

These factual discrepancies are not simply disagreements in doctrine or dogma that can be smoothed over by theology and philosophizing. These are incongruities in supposed *facts* of what purportedly happened historically on Earth. No other subject in history is treated in this haphazard and kid-gloves manner, which is to accept glaring contradictions and obvious errors of fact that would otherwise be corrected by studious historians finding an accurate path. Because there exists no such accurate path, historians remain left to create countless supplemental books trying to find the "real Jesus," nevertheless largely based on these diverging and flawed texts. Unfortunately, it does not serve a civilization well to function in this less-than-honest manner. In fact, a case

---

[1] Geisler, *WCA*, 359.

could be made showing that a problem of this magnitude is at the root of many of society's ills. Again, instead of engaging in mental gymnastics to reconcile the numerous problems, should we not simply ask whether or not the evangelists and later scribes made *mistakes*, because they were writing *fictionalized* accounts?

Errors in Time and Place

In addition to the many problems already noted are several others concerning anachronisms and erroneous gospel topography or geographical locations. Some of the towns mentioned in the New Testament have never been found to exist in the historical or archaeological record, and still others are evidently plucked from the Old Testament, such that their names are outdated and were not in use at the time the gospel drama supposedly took place.[1] Indeed, the gospel story is anachronistically set in a time that had been long gone by the beginning of the first century, depicting, for example, archaic agriculture, and giving an impression of a vast wilderness full of sheep and shepherds, when in fact much of the small, 90-mile-long area of Palestine in question was already well developed and densely urbanized in the first century of the common era. In fact, the population of Palestine overall during this period was an estimated 500,000 to 1.5 million. Moreover, it has been evinced that Mark in particular reveals an evident ignorance of the Palestinian topography and geography, indicating the evangelist did not live there and may have never even visited the nation he is writing about. Upon inspection, the same can be said about the other evangelists as well, although apologetics waves away this assertion by using some suspect arguments.

Quirinius's Census?

One specific instance of apparent biblical error in time and place has been pointed out many times: To wit, the excuse in Luke of the census to place the Holy Family in Bethlehem remains unprecedented, unhistorical and illogical, in that no Roman census required people to return to their

---

[1] See, e.g., Leidner.

cities of birth in order to register, which would be a very costly and nonsensical requirement. The date of the census is also questionable, as Luke claims Jesus was born during the reign of Herod; yet, according to Josephus, Quirinius's census would have occurred *after* Herod's death, around 6/7 AD/CE, when Quirinius served as governor of Syria. Apologetics contends either that there were two Quiriniuses or that the one Quirinius served an "earlier tour of duty" 11 years prior to his governorship of Syria and was somehow involved in Augustus's census of 8 BCE.[1] The evidence for such an assertion is sketchy at best and non-existent under scrutiny. Christian apologists also argue that an Egyptian papyrus discussing a purported census by Gaius Vibius Maximus in Egypt during the second century provides evidence that Luke's claims are true. However, the text's provenance is unknown, and the terminology cannot be truthfully interpreted to confirm that such a census required people to return to their homelands, if the text is even genuinely from the pertinent era. Even so, a census calling wandering shepherds and nomads to their homes for a head count might make sense, so such an enrollment under these circumstances is possible, but not as concerns people who are living in settled areas, which constitute the bulk of demographics in the pertinent areas of Palestine at the time. Moreover, a procedure that may have occurred in Egypt is not necessarily applicable to Judea/Palestine.

Regarding Quirinius—or *Kyrenios* in the Greek, frequently translated as "Cyrenius"—Dr. Crossan remarks:

> ...even if Augustus had ordained a complete census of the Roman world, and even if Quirinius had overseen its administration in Archelaus' territories, the Roman custom was to count you in the place of your domicile or work and not in that of your ancestry or birth. That is little more than common sense. Census was for taxation; to record people in their ancestral rather than their occupational locations would have constituted a bureaucratic nightmare.[2]

---

[1] Bucher.
[2] Crossan, *THJ*, 372.

Moreover, the passage in Josephus regarding Cyrenius/ Quirinius (*Antiquities*, XVIII, I, 1) indicates that the census or "taxation" under him occurred fairly recently after he was sent there by Caesar as *governor*—having, as Josephus says "supreme power over the Jews"[1]—and that the census/ taxation was a *new* thing at that time, reviled and resisted by the locals. Hence, it would be surprising if Quirinius had been involved in an earlier census, or even a later one, without Josephus mentioning it.

It would not have been too difficult to make such a mistake in the ancient world, so Luke cannot be severely faulted. However, claims of inerrancy for the New Testament truly seem to be more far reflective of stubborn conditioning rather than reality. Moreover, it is possible that Luke took his data from Justin Martyr, who, in his *First Apology* (34) mentioned the census of Quirinius:

> Now there is a village in the land of the Jews, thirty-five stadia from Jerusalem, in which Jesus Christ was born, as you can ascertain also from the registers of the taxing made under Cyrenius [Quirinius], your first procurator in Judæa.

In the first place, the title of procurator represents an anachronism, as officials in Judea were not deemed such until later in the first century. Secondly, if Martyr had Luke's gospel in front of him, it would be logical and in line with Justin's habit of citing scripture to mention the evangelist's work. Nevertheless, he does not, and we are left looking elsewhere for the origin of the double-census of Quirinius. Could it simply be that Luke made a mistake or based his reportage on someone else's erroneous work, such as Justin Martyr?

Abiathar or Ahimelech?

In another example of an evident error in the New Testament, Mark 2:26 portrays Jesus as saying that the high priest during David's entry into the temple depicted at 1 Samuel 21 was *Abiathar*, whereas the Old Testament passage states that it was *Ahimelech*, Abiathar's father.

---

[1] Whitson, 376.

Hence, either Jesus is incorrect, which casts doubt on his claim to be the all-knowing Lord, or Mark is wrong, which, again, shows that the New Testament is *not* inerrant. The apology offered for this verse by Geisler is that Christ refers to the "days of Abiathar," which could include the time preceding his appointment as high priest.[1] In reality, the Greek for this scripture is *epi abiathar tou archiereos*. One of the pertinent words here is *epi*, a preposition that means "upon," "on" or "at," as in "at the time." The passage could be translated as "at the time of Abiathar the high priest," clearly indicating that Jesus meant to convey that *Abiathar was high priest at the time*, a logical conclusion. This sort of sophistry within apologetics is proffered on numerous occasions when the New Testament seems to be incorrect.

Gadarenes, Gerasenes or Gergesenes?

Moreover, the attempt to explain the discrepancies regarding the name of the people where the demoniac is cured, i.e., the Gadarenes, Gerasenes or the Gergesenes, does not account for the fact that in ancient manuscripts and in translations of the same gospel the name varies from one to the other. It seems there is a mistake here, by someone asserted to have been infallibly inspired by the Holy Ghost, as it would be difficult to believe that the Holy Ghost did not know which of the terms was correct for the name of these people. Indeed, the infallible Holy Spirit seems to be careless and disorganized, compared to the standards to which we hold our *human* scholars and scientists today.

The Baptist's Death

The beheading of John the Baptist presents a problem as well, as at Mark 6:17-29, concerning which Meier remarks, "The strongly legendary tone of the Marcan story as well as its differences with Josephus' account incline me to the view that the Marcan account contains little of historical worth, even with reference to the historical John."[2] Meier continues to state that there are "indications that not every word of Mark's narrative can be taken as historically accurate." He

---

[1] Geisler, *WGA*, 370.
[2] Meier, II, 171.

further explains that Mark's assertion that "Antipas' second wife, Herodias, had previously been the wife of Antipas' half-brother Philip" represents an "inaccurate statement" and is "simply incorrect, as we know from Josephus's *Jewish Antiquities*."[1] Meier also calls this mistake a "glaring historical error," remarking that the efforts by Christian fundamentalists to reconcile this *error* include an attempt at "salvation by conflation," combining two characters into one named "Herod Philip," whom Meier deems a "Herodian poltergeist" who "never existed outside of the minds of conservative exegetes."[2] Msgr. Meier further states:

> Similarly, to maintain that Josephus is somehow wrong or confused would be a gratuitous assumption made to rescue Mark's accuracy at any cost. Josephus shows a much greater knowledge of Herodian genealogy than does Mark.... Indeed, Mark may have made more than one genealogical mistake in this story.... *if Mark can be so wrong about the basic familial relationships that are the driving engine of the plot of his story about John's execution, why should we credit the rest of his story as historical?*[3]

In discussing the "precise place of John's execution," about which Mark and Josephus diverge, Meier remarks that there is no reason to doubt Josephus, and he concludes that *"once again Mark is wrong in his presentation."*[4]

Such remarks as Professor Meier's, found in an 1100-page scholarly work that few laymen will ever read, provide evidence that the patent *errancy* of the gospels is known and accepted by some within the hallowed halls of higher academia. Additionally, in his commentary about Mark's presentation of John's death, Meier raises the issue of the evangelist's apparent reliance upon not a historical account but on Old Testament narratives of other "persecuted and martyred prophets," such as Elijah and "the folkloric motifs in the Book of Esther." In discussing the influence of these earlier scenarios upon Mark's narrative, Meier states:

---

[1] Meier, II, 172.
[2] Meier, II, 172.
[3] Meier, II, 172. (Emph. added.)
[4] Meier, II, 173. (Emph. added.)

These folkloric motifs find parallels in Greco-Roman stories of love, revenge, rash oaths, and women asking for what kings would rather not give, all in the context of royal banquets.[1]

This last comment suggests that Mark's account is not based on "historical fact" but on a *folkloric motif*: To wit, the death of John the Baptist as presented by Mark is *fictional* or *fictionalized* at best. Meier further remarks:

> As we have seen, *the story in Mark 6:17-29 is erroneous in key historical matters* (i.e., the marital problem that set off the conflict with John, the place of John's imprisonment and execution, and perhaps the identity of the daughter) and is suffused with legendary and folkloric traits. Moreover, the links between the accounts of Mark and Josephus exist largely in the mind of the modern exegete.[2]

In other words, Mark is *wrong* in several important instances, and those who opine Mark and Josephus to be connected are fantasizing. These remarks rank as a stunning commentary from a biblical scholar and ex-Catholic priest, serving to illustrate: 1. Mark's history, like his geography, is not entirely accurate; 2. Mark is wrong, therefore his gospel is not "inerrant; 3. Mark's gospel is also therefore suspect as to its historical value; and 4. The other synoptics, if based on Mark's narrative, cannot likewise possibly be deemed "inerrant," and are likewise suspect as to their historical value.

Mosaic Authorship?

Over the centuries, numerous scholars have put forth intelligent, rational and scientific arguments that the Pentateuch or first five books of the Bible could not have been written by Moses, as the Bible asserts. Yet, at Luke 5:46 Jesus is depicted as asserting as fact this untenable and evidently erroneous idea of Mosaic authorship—if Christ was truly the omniscient Lord, would he not know that Moses could not possibly have written the Pentateuch? Prior

---

[1] Meier, II, 170.
[2] Meier, II, 174-5. (Emph. added.)

to the creation of Christianity only pious Jews would believe in the Mosaic authorship of the Pentateuch. Could this entire story largely represent the product of pious Jews attempting to create a messiah?

The Pre-Crucifixion Church?

At Matthew 16:18, Jesus says he will build his "church" (Greek *ekklesia*) upon the "rock" of Peter. Just a short while later, at Matthew 18:17, Jesus speaks of "the church" as if it already were an established entity. An honest assessment of the situation suggests these verses were written long after the facts, when there *was* an established church, such that the reader would understand the reference. Such being the case, can we really trust that Matthew 18:17 records an actual verbatim remark made by Jesus, since, according to the gospel story, *there was no church at that time*?

Judas's Blood Money

Another anachronism occurs in the depiction of Judas receiving his blood money of silver pieces that were "weighed out." It is claimed that at the time of the gospel story, silver pieces had been out of circulation for some 300 years![1] Moreover, currency at that time was not "weighed out." Would it not be sensible to ask whether this passage reflects not an actual, historical event but a pericope fabricated in order to "fulfill prophecy," specifically that of Zechariah 11:12-13? In fact, when at Matthew 27:9 the evangelist claims to be quoting Jeremiah, he appears to be conflating verses from Zechariah (11:12-13) and Jeremiah (32:6-9; 18:2-3), possibly because the evangelist used the Septuagint as the source for his quote and there is in the Septuagint no corresponding scripture to Jeremiah 32:6-10; whereas, these verses at Zechariah 11:12-13 *do* appear in the Septuagint. In any event, Matthew's quote is incorrect, as concerns the Old Testament texts as we have them.

The same sort of scriptural conflation occurs at Mark 1:2 and was evidently recognized in ancient times to be an error. In that scripture, Mark conflates verses at Exodus 23:20 and Malachi 3:1 with Isaiah 40:3, which altogether the evangelist

---

[1] See, e.g., Carlson.

quotes as being from "the prophet Isaiah." In later versions, however, sharp-eyed scribes removed the words "Isaiah" and left the verse at Mark 1:2 as "it is written in the prophets," in general, rather than Isaiah in specific.

As a further example of an error in the New Testament portrayal of the alleged time of Jesus's advent, the evangelists make the assertion that it was a custom to release a prisoner at the Passover, but there is no evidence that there existed any such custom, Jewish or Gentile, at any time.

A number of other specifics are also evidently incorrect, including the depiction of two robbers being crucified with Jesus—robbery was apparently not an offense that called for crucifixion—and Jesus's family and friends conversing with him while he was on the cross, as the Roman authorities did not allow people to approach the crucifixion victims.

These and other inconsistencies cast doubt as to whether or not the evangelists actually knew the area and culture they were writing about and had ever lived there at any point, much less the era in question. Knowing all these facts, it would appear to the reasonable and rational mind that the matter is settled as to the obvious *errancy* of the Bible, and that claims to the contrary are less than honest and scientific.

Chronological Problems

As we have seen, there are many places where the gospels do not agree with each other on the chronology of events in Jesus's life. In fact, there exist numerous chronological discrepancies in the gospels that become reconciled only by the most extreme stretches of logic, and, instead of admitting that the evangelists or subsequent copyists may have made mistakes, terms like "dislocations" are used and other excuses are given, in a seemingly deceptive manner.

As another example of a chronological problem, the baptism of Jesus by John—an illogical act, since Christ is sinless—is pivotal to the tale, particularly in the gospel of John. It is in this moment that John the Baptist and others present are astounded to see and hear the indescribable wonders that reveal Jesus not only as the messiah but also as the Son of God, with God's own voice booming from the heavens and identifying Christ as such. Yet, not only does Luke gloss over this entire extraordinary episode with a brief two-sentence mention (Lk 3:21-22), he places the baptism *after* John has been imprisoned (Lk 3:20), giving the impression that John did not baptize Jesus at all.

In addition, Jesus's temptation is depicted in different manners: At Matthew 4:5-8, for instance, the devil is portrayed as taking Christ first to the "pinnacle of the temple and then to the "very high mountain." Luke (4:5-9), on the other hand, has the devil taking him "up" (to the mountain) first and then to the pinnacle of the temple. Which order was it, and who was there to report it? Christian apologist Dr. Geisler attempts to reconcile this problem with the justification that Matthew "describes these temptations *chronologically* while Luke lists them *climatically,* that is, topically."[1] This assertion seems to contradict the claim by Luke that he was carefully putting the events in the narrative *in order*—in his prologue in fact, Luke uses two different terms to emphasize that his narrative is "in order." Could a simpler answer not be that one or the other evangelist made a mistake? Perhaps one evangelist's account is a correction of the other, or maybe both are based on a patently mythical event?

Matthew and Luke also disagree as to the order of the healing of the demoniacs and the meeting of Matthew/Levi. In Matthew (8:32), Christ drives the demons into the swine and then calls Matthew (9:9); whereas, in Luke (5:27), Jesus meets "Levi" much *earlier* in the story than the healing of the demoniacs (8:33). Mark too is out of sync with the calling of Matthew, as at 2:14 he places it *before* Christ calms the storm (4:39), while Matthew depicts himself as being called by Jesus *after* calming the tempest (8:26). Luke and Mark also switch the order of the arrest of John the Baptist, as Luke (3:19-20) places it *before* the storm is quieted, while Mark puts John's arrest (6:17-18) *after* the tempest miracle.

One more instance of how the apologies for such problems seem deceptive occurs in the pericope of the

---

[1] Geisler, *WCA*, 329.

cleansing of the temple, depicted at the beginning in John and at the end in the synoptics. The apologetic reasoning for this dichotomy is that Christ committed the aggressive act twice, with F.F. Bruce, for example, placing the first act of aggression some two years earlier than the second![1] It is difficult to believe that Jesus overturned the moneychangers' tables even *once*, much less twice, since this momentous occurrence turns up nowhere in the historical record. There is no indication anywhere in the synoptic gospels that Jesus had previously cleared the temple—which one would think would have been a highly noteworthy event—no recollection by an evangelist, no bitter or critical commentary by any Jewish authorities, who surely would have been incensed by Christ's behavior. This earlier act of violence is never brought up as a reason for the authorities, Jewish or Roman, to be angry with Jesus and to justify their harsh treatment of him. Nor is there any mention of this wild and highly noticeable behavior in any non-biblical document—one would think that the opposing Jews would have recorded such an event, especially since they were so very fanatical about the temple, and would have offered Jesus's *vandalism* as a reason for persecuting him early on in the gospel story, if it had happened at that point. That there were *two* cleansings of the temple, during both of which Christ overturned the tables of the moneychangers, seems impossible to believe. While the efforts may be sincere for those who refuse to doubt the inerrancy of the Bible, this type of conclusion appears sophistic and disingenuous to many people.

Nevertheless, this episode in the gospel story has convinced countless people that there *had* to be a person behind all of the fairytales they think were added to his biography, because this act of aggression does not seem to be something someone would make up. On the contrary, when Old Testament scripture is studied, it becomes evident that this part about the temple being cleared of moneychangers is a reflection of the earlier scripture at Zechariah 14:21: "...And there shall no longer be a trader in the house of the Lord of hosts on that day." This book, Zechariah, is the penultimate before the New Testament, followed only by

---

[1] Bruce, *NTD*, 190.

Malachi. It is evident that this pericope was included in the gospel story in order to make it seem that Jesus had "fulfilled prophecy," which would explain it erroneously being depicted at different times in the various gospels. Apologists use such "embarrassing" moments in the gospels as to argue that the story is historical, since such episodes would not be included otherwise, as they make Christ and/or his disciples "look bad." A number of these "scriptural embarrassments," however, can be explained in like manner, with such episodes reflecting the use of the Old Testament as a blueprint, rather than depicting real events.

To continue with the chronological discrepancies, in Mark (3:22), after naming the disciples, Jesus "goes home, but the crowd is too great." Christ's "friends" grab him, and scribes from Jerusalem claim he's possessed by demons, because he can cast out demons. This last pericope of casting devils out appears earlier in Matthew, at 9:34, *before* Christ gives the disciples their missions.

Yet another chronological problem between the gospels occurs with the depiction of the Last Supper. In the synoptics, the Last Supper coincides with the Passover meal; in John, Passover begins *after* Jesus has already been crucified. Moreover, the events of the Last Supper become less gripping when it is realized that this type of sacred meal occurred in other legends and myths. Concerning the eucharist, the Catholic Encyclopedia states that "the idea of a sacred banquet is as old as the human race and existed at all ages and amongst all peoples."[1] Moreover, the sayings supposedly uttered by Jesus at the Last Supper are depicted differently by all of the synoptists.

The reconciliation of the gospel narratives as concerns the crucifixion and resurrection is so problematic that some people have issued an "Easter challenge" to put the events in a proper and logical order.[2] How can we claim, then, that we know the order of the events of Christ's Passion? Or even that it really happened? Again, is it not possible that, instead of an account based on a factual resurrection, the

---

[1] *CE*, "Mithraism."
[2] See, e.g. Barker.

evangelists were reworking such "prophecies" as found at Isaiah 26:19, Daniel 12:2 and others?

As an example of the difficulties in the Passion account, in Mark (15:25) Jesus is depicted as being crucified during the "third hour," while in John (19:14), it is around the "sixth hour." Which is it? The apology for this discrepancy is that "John follows the *Roman* time system while Mark follows the *Jewish* time system."[1] There is no evidence for this extraordinary claim, however, and a more logical assessment may be that one or the other of the evangelists made an error, particularly in consideration of the other facts regarding the genesis of the gospel story and the seemingly fictional nature of many elements therein, including and especially the passion narrative.

Moreover, early manuscripts of Matthew 27:49-50 depict Jesus as having a spear stuck in his side *before* he dies; whereas, in John (19:33-34) Christ is already dead when he is side-wounded. The phrase regarding the spear and the water and blood in Matthew is omitted from the RSV and other editions. Could there be a political reason for its inclusion?

In Matthew, Jesus says he will be dead for three days; yet, he dies on Friday afternoon and rises on Sunday morning, constituting fewer than *two* days. The apologist argument that Friday, Saturday and Sunday can be counted as whole days does not account for the "sign of Jonah," which puts the messiah in the tomb for three *nights* as well. Clearly, Christ was not in the tomb for three *nights*. (Jonah 1:17; Mt 12:40) Nevertheless, the apologists feel the need to provide a highly convoluted and illogical argument in order to demonstrate that Christ *did* in fact remain for three nights in the tomb, despite what the texts state.[2]

Based on all these factors, it is reasonable to suggest that the gospels are not chronologically accurate because their writers were not infallibly inspired, and that the Bible is not the inerrant Word of God or a reliable "history book" but, rather, significantly consists of traditions, fables and myths.

---

[1] Geisler, *WCA*, 370.
[2] See, e.g., Geisler, *WCA*, 343-344.

Translation Errors and Language Problems

The fact that some passages are omitted in certain versions and translations of the New Testament demonstrates that the book has been interpolated and altered, again leading to the reasonable and scientific conclusion that the Bible as we have it could not possibly be the inerrant Word of God infallibly recorded by inspired scribes. One apologetic solution to this dilemma is to assert that all individuals involved in the construction and preservation of the New Testament texts were "filled and guided by the Holy Spirit." According to this belief, even the translators—modern day included—have been working under the guidance of the Holy Spirit. As Orthodox Christian Bishop Alexander remarks: "And since the ultimate author of Sacred Scripture is the Holy Spirit, the translator needs His illumination and inspiration to correctly convey His message."

Because such a position appears untenable, many Christian scholars and apologists today no longer adhere to this notion that translations themselves are inspired, claiming instead that only the "originals" are inspired. The rank-and-file believers, however, still frequently maintain—as they have been taught—that the King James translation, for one, *is* inerrant and its translators inspired. Regardless of whether or not trained apologists believe this claim anymore, the average Christian may not be aware of the debate regarding various translations and may indeed receive the impression that the Bible favored in his or her church *is* inerrant. In the words of evangelical Christian Gary Amirault:

> At an early point in my walk with Jesus, I was strongly under the influence of men and women who believed in the "Inerrant Bible" doctrine. They believed the King James Bible was the only one Christians should use because it was inspired of God and without errors. They believed other translations were inspired of Satan, the "Alexandrian cult," and the Roman Catholic Church.[1]

---

[1] Amirault, "The King James Bible is 'Inerrant?'"

The reality is that even today many pastors continue to promote the purported inerrancy of the King James Bible. In fact, there remain ministries fervently dedicated to "defending and promoting the KJV." Within these organizations, the King James Bible continues to be held up as "inerrant," despite the scholarship that has revealed the Textus Receptus at its basis to be flawed. One fundamentalist KJV defender, Brandon Staggs, comments on the debate thus:

> Almost every "fundamental" statement of faith reads that God's word is perfect and inspired in the *original autographs*.
>
> But isn't that a statement of unbelief? What good is God's word if it only exists in manuscripts which no longer exist? Why would God inspire Scripture just to let it wither to dust?
>
> Many modern scholars believe that the real ending of the Gospel of Mark has been lost and that we can not be certain how Mark concluded his Gospel. And yet these same scholars will boldly declare belief in God's preservation of Scripture.[1]

Evangelicals like David Sorenson, in fact, go so far as to deem "apostates" those who follow the "critical text," such as the RSV, as opposed to those who maintain the inerrancy of the "Received Text," i.e., the basis for the KJV.[2] Continuing with his apology for the KJV, Staggs states:

> It is my belief that the King James Bible, originally known as the Authorized Version, first published in the year 1611, is God's word in the English language without admixture of error.

Despite this indoctrination of inerrancy, an investigation of the translations of the New Testament into English reveals much as to whether or not they could possibly be considered "inerrant" works by "infallibly" inspired scribes.

---

[1] Staggs, "King James Bible and other versions: why does it matter?"
[2] Sorenson, "Erasmus, King James, and His Translators."

The Kings James Bible

Prior to the discovery of the most complete, ancient Greek manuscripts of the New Testament—the Codices Sinaiticus, Alexandrinus and Vaticanus—we possessed only much later copies in Greek. One of the most important translations of the Bible, the King James Version, was based not on these earliest manuscripts but on the later Greek texts, as well as on the preceding English editions such as the Tyndale, Great, Geneva and Catholic Bibles, the latter of which was in turn founded upon Jerome's Latin Vulgate.

Claimed by many Christian fundamentalists to be the only inspired and inerrant translation of the Bible into English, the King James Version, also called the "Authorized Version," possesses an interesting history, in that it was composed over several years from 1604 to 1609 by six groups comprising upwards of 40 translators. Each translator's section was edited by the other members of the group, then passed around to the other groups, and so on, until a finalized version was accepted and was subsequently published in 1611. This complex history provokes several questions, including why the Holy Spirit needed so many minds and hands to work on God's Word. Wouldn't it have been much faster and less fraught with the chance for error if only one person infallibly inspired by the Holy Spirit had translated the texts? *Common sense indicates that only if the individuals involved were relying on their own intellectual faculties and erudition would there need to be a committee of the sort used in the translation of the King James Bible.*

Concerning the KJV, Dr. Ehrman remarks:

...The King James Version is filled with places in which the translators rendered a Greek text derived ultimately from Erasmus's edition, which was based on a single twelfth-century manuscript that is one of the worst of the manuscripts that we now have available to us!...

...The King James was not given by God but was a translation by a group of scholars in the early seventeenth century who based their rendition on a faulty Greek text.[1]

Centuries after the KJV became the "noblest monument of English prose," in fact, there arose a clear need for a new, updated translation. As the "Preface" to the Revised Standard Version relates:

> ...the King James Version has grave defects. By the middle of the nineteenth century, the development of Biblical studies and the discovery of many manuscripts more ancient than those upon which the King James Version was based, made it manifest that these defects are so many and so serious as to call for revision of the English translation....[2]

Hence, despite the esteem by evangelical Christians, it is understood by various scholars that the King James Bible was not "given by God" and possesses "grave defects." In fact, the Greek text that the KJV largely followed is now considered a seriously flawed composition, "hastily compiled" by Dutch theologian Desiderius Erasmus (c. 1466-1536), who pieced it together using a single Greek text from the 12th century and a few other manuscript portions, producing the "Textus Receptus" or "Received Text." Not finding the last six verses of the New Testament, from the book of Revelation, Erasmus used the Latin Vulgate to translate the pertinent verses back into Greek. Hence, these particular scriptures were not rendered from the original or even early Greek texts but are the retranslations from a Latin translation of a Greek copy of the New Testament. It is upon *this* defective translation that the King James Bible is based in large part, further demonstrating the tenuousness and frailty of maintaining that the KJV was infallibly inspired by the Holy Spirit.

Moreover, the translation of the KJV was not confined to the Greek texts but also used previous English translations, including the Tyndale Bible. One of the earliest translators of the Bible into English, William Tyndale (d. 1536), was burned at the stake for "heresy." Yet, Tyndale's translation

---

[1] Ehrman, *MJ*, 209.
[2] RSV, iii.

has been used in the creation of every significant English rendition of the Bible since his time, including the King James Version.[1] Was Tyndale inspired? If so, why would God let him be hideously killed? If he was not inspired, how can the English translations such as the KJV, based in considerable part on his work, themselves be considered inspired?

As one example of where the differences between ancient manuscripts/authorities have led to some "grave defects" in the translation, in Mark 9, verses 44 and 46 are omitted from the RSV, which says they are likewise omitted from "the best ancient authorities." RSV gives its reason for excluding these verses as the fact that they are "identical with verse 48." These three identical verses are reproduced three times in the King James Version as: "Where their worm dieth not, and the fire is not quenched." Hence, some of these ancient *authorities* carelessly reproduced verses in the same paragraph, which was not very difficult in consideration of the run-on Greek text they were originally using. Or, if these repetitions were originally intended, how could the editors of the RSV (and others) remove these verses? One or both of these editions must not be correct.

Regarding the KJV, the RSV continues:

> The King James Version of the New Testament was based upon a Greek text that was marred by mistakes, containing the accumulated errors of fourteen centuries of manuscript copying. It was essentially the Greek text of the New Testament as edited by Beza, 1589, who closely followed that published by Erasmus, 1516-1535, which was based upon a few medieval manuscripts....

> We now possess many more ancient manuscripts of the New Testament, and are far better equipped to seek to recover the original wording of the Greek text...[2]

One result of this need for revision is the Revised Standard Version itself, which bases its translation upon the King James Bible and "the most ancient authorities," i.e., the

---

[1] Tenney, 420.
[2] RSV, v.

Greek codices. Yet, how do we know which of the Greek texts is correct, as they differ significantly? If the Holy Spirit was inspiring the translators of the KJV, why weren't they shown the most ancient Greek manuscripts instead, if these are more correct and closer to the originals of God's Word? In fact, why would the Holy Spirit allow the originals or autographs to be destroyed in the first place? Why don't we possess the pristinely and miraculously preserved texts written by the very hands of the evangelists themselves?

If these most ancient Greek texts are not more correct than the later ones, why are more modern translations based on them? It is well known that the most ancient manuscripts "contain scribal errors of all sorts." In fact, one of the oldest MS fragments, P46, contains the "largest percentage of blunders on record!" Under these circumstances, it is surprising that anything in the New Testament can be known concretely and that definitive statements concerning biblical inerrancy can be logically and honestly made.

Moreover, the numerous Latin translations were so varied and unreliable that St. Jerome was commissioned to create an authoritative Latin text (Vulgate) from reputable Greek manuscripts.[1] Again, the KJV was *also* based in part on the Latin Vulgate, which few Christian evangelicals or fundamentalists would claim was inspired.

Even with the KJV revealing itself to be a large mess, fundamentalist proponents of it contradictorily claim that it does indeed represent the "originals" or autographs of the biblical texts.[2] One wonders if these individuals who make such definitive declarations—expressing their own *opinions*, in fact—are themselves inspired such that we should take their word on it?

The King James fundamentalists also argue that the 17th-century English of the KJV is "not archaic" and that changing it constitutes an "assault" on God's Word![3] What about translations into other languages, if even other English renditions are no good? Or, do all the rest of the people in the world need to learn King James English in order to be

---

[1] Tenney, 417.
[2] Gipp, Sam, *The Answer Book*, reproduced in Staggs's "Shouldn't we value the original autographs above any mere translation?"
[3] Staggs, "Aren't archaic words in the KJV in need of updating?"

saved? Why would God make the salvation of millions of people's souls so difficult, if not impossible? It seems a rather cruel thing to do to the millions who will *never* learn English or who are illiterate in *any* language. If only the King James English translation is inspired, why bother translating the Bible into any other language? Are all the missionaries who create and pass out Bibles in hundreds of different languages completely wasting their time? Are these missionaries not sincere Christians, believing as they do in the translations they are sharing? The arrogance expressed in the KJV fundamentalist response to this quandary ranks up there with Lucifer's quest to take over heaven: "God has always given His word to one people in one language to do one job—convert the world.... Thus in choosing English in which to combine His two Testaments, God chose the only language which the world would know."[1]

After scientifically analyzing the manuscript tradition and the creation of the King James Bible, it seems incredible and egregious that someone could maintain the following sentiment expressed by a KJV fundamentalist writer:

> The manuscripts represented by the King James Bible have texts of the highest quality. So we see that the best manuscripts are those used by the King James translators.[2]

This position strikes one as obstinate, unscientific and unreasonable, but is little different from the maintenance by other fundamentalist Christians that the Bible as a whole is inerrant, that the gospel tale is 100% factually accurate, and that Christianity is the "only true religion."

In addition, the argument maintaining "inspired originals" is not very appealing, for the reason proffered by Dr. Ehrman that we do not possess the originals. Regarding the doctrine of "inspired originals," KJV fundamentalist and evangelical Christian Daryl Coats asks:

> If the Bible were inspired only in the original manuscripts, no one today has an inspired Bible. If

---

[1] Gipp, *The Answer Book*, reproduced in Staggs's "If we have a perfect Bible in English, don't we need one in every other language?"

[2] Gipp, *The Answer Book*, reproduced in Staggs's "Aren't modern translations based on better manuscripts?"

that is true, what makes your religion any different from that of the Buddhist, or Hindu, or Moslem, or Mormon?[1]

Indeed, is it truly honest and righteous for any one culture to insist that its "holy book" alone is the "Word of God?" In reality, none of these texts can be scientifically proved to be the "inerrant Word of God."

Born of a Virgin?

An exegesis of the texts reveals that despite the claims of inerrancy, there were problems with the translation of the Bible even before it was rendered into English. For example, the assertion that Jesus's mother, Mary, was a "virgin" when she gave birth ranks, of course, as one of those miracles that less credulous people have difficulty accepting. When the scripture cited as "prophecy fulfilled" in Jesus's nativity is examined, however, it seems that Mary's virginity may be a contrivance based on an erroneous or loose translation, not on a historical fact. In the original Hebrew "prophecy" at Isaiah 7:14 to describe the individual who would conceive the son named Immanuel, the term used is *almah*, which means a "young woman" but not necessarily a virgin. The apology for this problem is that the word *almah* in the Bible invariably refers to an "unmarried woman," which automatically means she is a "virgin." Granted that in some places in ancient times the chances of that situation may have been more likely, the fact will remain that a "maiden" is *not* necessarily a "virgin." If *almah* can or should be translated every time as "virgin," why is there a separate word in Hebrew for "virgin," i.e., *bethulah*? According to Strong's Concordance, "virgin" is the *only* definition for *bethulah* (H1330), whereas *almah* (H5959) is defined as:

1) virgin, young woman
   a) of marriageable age
   b) maid or newly married

From this definition, it would seem inaccurate to state that an *almah* is *only* an "unmarried woman" and/or a virgin, as is asserted by Christian apologists. In this instance, the

---

[1] Coats, "The Two Lies."

KJV translates *almah* as "virgin," while the RSV renders it "young woman." The three other instances in the KJV where the word *almah* is translated as "virgin" occur in one peculiar place regarding the mundane activity of drawing water, as in "when the virgin cometh forth to draw" (Gen 24:43), and in the very sensual Song of Songs (Sgs 1:3, 6:8). Other examples of *almah* are translated in the KJV as "maid" (Ex 2:8; Pro 30:19) or "damsel" (Ps 68:25). Where the term *bethulah* is used in the Hebrew, emphasis often is given to make certain it is understood that the individual in question had "not known man by lying with him." No such clarification is given for *almah*, and it appears unreasonable and unscientific to insist that it be translated as "virgin" in all instances, especially in the case of a pregnant female! Moreover, in all other uses in Isaiah (23:12; 37:22; 47:1; 62:5), the author utilizes the term *bethulah* to describe a "virgin"—if at verse 7:14 he also meant "virgin," why use the term *almah* and not *bethulah*?

The Greek translation of the Old Testament, the Septuagint, does in fact render the word *almah* as *parthenos*, which means "virgin."[1] As we have seen, many of the scriptures cited or quoted in the gospels came from the Septuagint, from which the evangelists evidently got their ideas, not from a factual state of virginity in a historical Mary. Moreover, the fact that the Septuagint had been in existence for at least two centuries prior to the Christian era demonstrates that the virgin-birth motif preceded Christ's purported advent. It may be that the translators of the Septuagint and those who used the Greek rendering of Isaiah 7:14 in the New Testament were attempting to compete with the claimants of virgin or divine births of other gods, kings and heroes around the Mediterranean and

---

[1] The word *parthenos* occurs 17 times in the Septuagint (or "LXX"), appropriately corresponding to the Hebrew word *bethulah* at Judges 19:25, for example. Oddly enough, the KJV translates this term *bethulah* in Judges as "maid." At Genesis 24:14, the LXX translates as *parthenos* the Hebrew word *naarah* (H5291), which is odd in consideration of the fact that in Genesis 24:16, both the words *naarah* and *bethulah* are used, both rendered *parthenos* in the LXX. The LXX also renders the *almah* at the well (Gen 24:43) as *parthenos*, and so on. Thus, the LXX indiscriminately translates *three* different Hebrew terms as *parthenos*, rendering their distinction meaningless and their intention of chastity suspect.

elsewhere.[1] Rather than assuming that a Jewish virgin became pregnant without intercourse and gave birth to the Almighty Lord of the cosmos, would it not be more logical and plausible to suggest that this passage was used as part of the *messianic blueprint* by the creators of the gospel texts?

Indeed, we could likewise aver that the meaning in Matthew is not necessarily reflective of that in Isaiah: To wit, Matthew insists that a virginal Mary conceived and gave birth without intercourse, while, in fact, the original Isaiah says no such thing but simply that a virgin will conceive, which is quite possible. It does not say "without intercourse" or that she remained a virgin and still gave birth. Matthew's interpretation is not wholly influenced by Isaiah's scripture but appears to incorporate the tales of virgin births in other myths and legends.

"Children," "Deeds" or "Results?"

Another translation oddity occurs at Matthew 11:19, concerning the Greek term *teknon*, which the RSV translates as "children." Different versions render *teknon* variously as "children," "deeds," "results," "actions" and "works." The same pericope is related at Luke 7:35, using the same word *teknon*; yet, the translators uniformly render it as "children." Why, if the Holy Spirit was inspiring the translators, would the translations of the same term not be uniform, conveying the precise, same meaning, instead of leaving us to guess? If the Holy Spirit is looking over the shoulders of the translators, would not each know what word the others had used? This is but one of numerous instances where the terms chosen by translators vary—why would God or the Holy Spirit induce such discrepancies?

Jesus the Carpenter?

One more translation example reveals how a story element previously determined to be part of a "biography" of a real person called Jesus Christ is in fact questionable as to whether or not it was a true characteristic of his life. To wit,

---

[1] For more information on the subject of virgin or divine births, see *Suns of God*.

when the texts are examined closely it is clear that characterizing Jesus as a "carpenter"—a widely held belief—has very little basis in the literary record, and *none* in the historical or archaeological records. In the first place, the Greek word commonly translated as "carpenter"—*tekton*—could refer to an artisan or worker in other trades as well, such as a smith, builder or mason. Per Strong's (G5045), *tekton* means the following:

1) a worker in wood, a carpenter, joiner, builder
a) a ship's carpenter or builder
2) any craftsman, or workman
a) the art of poetry, maker of songs
3) a planner, contriver, plotter
a) an author

We have no description in the New Testament of Jesus sawing wood or doing any other carpentry work specifically. In fact, this designation of Christ as a *tekton* can be found in the Bible *only once*, at Mark 6:3, in the pericope where Jesus returns home to astound the people he grew up with. Firstly, we would need to ask why, if some of these people were around when Jesus was born, surrounded by prodigies and wonders, including a clear designation as the messiah, they would be astonished by him as an adult. Secondly, in this same pericope Matthew (13:55) has the crowd calling Jesus the "*son* of the tekton," which, again, could be a carpenter, a smith, a mason or another type of worker. Luke portrays the folks as labeling Jesus simply the "son of Joseph." Furthermore, there is evidence—from the early church father Origen in the third century, for one—that this scripture about the tekton in Mark was not present in the original text. In *Contra Celsus* (VI, 36), Origen remarks that "in none of the Gospels current in the Churches is Jesus Himself ever described as being a carpenter." Confirming Origen's assertion, this term *tekton* as an appellation of Jesus does not appear in the earliest manuscript of Mark (P45), dating from Origen's era.[1] In that manuscript, Christ is called the "*son* of the carpenter," as he is in Matthew.

In any event, all of our ideas that Jesus was a humble carpenter—vividly brought to life in so many books and

---

[1] Ehrman, *MJ*, 203.

movies—may in fact be based on a later scribe's interpolated phrase or an erroneous translation, but not on the genuine biography of a real person. As the scriptures are examined in this manner, and the layers are peeled away, we find a number of characteristics attributed to Jesus that are evidently false or, at best, later additions that may or may not be true but certainly were not included in the originals. A picture develops of an artificial, patchwork "biography" put together piecemeal over time of the "most important man who ever lived." This idea of patching together over a period of decades and centuries what was supposed to be a biography provided by eyewitnesses of the time is perturbing to our quest in determining who Jesus really was, because we have so little to go on and so much appears to have been fictitious.

A Camel or Rope?

Another difficulty in our analysis of the biblical texts presents itself in the nonsensical passage at Matthew 19:24 concerning the "camel" passing through the eye of a needle. It is theorized that the word was originally *gamla* in Aramaic, which evidently means both "camel" and "rope," as in a thick cable made of camel's hair. It is logical to suggest that the original word is meant to convey not "camel" but "cable rope," and that the original translators of this saying got it wrong. However, one argument avers that the term "eye of a needle" refers to a particular gate in a town or city, which would be more sensible than the eye of a real needle, as a camel *can* pass through a city gate.

"The End of the Age?"

At Matthew 28:18, Jesus says, "I am with you always, to the close of the age." What does that mean? Some translations state "world," rather than "age." If Jesus is with us until the end of the world or age, what happens after that? The word used for "age" or "world" is the Greek term αιων—*aion*—for which Strong's Concordance gives the meaning as:

1) for ever, an unbroken age, perpetuity of time, eternity

2) the worlds, universe
3) period of time, age

Again, Jesus is first depicted as saying that he will only be with his disciples a short while, whereas later he states he will be with them for eternity. The difference, apologetics claims, is one of the physical versus the spiritual, although if Jesus is the Alpha and Omega, and has always been with us, it is difficult to surmise he was never "felt in anyone's heart" until after his incarnation. It is interesting to note that the word "aion" or "aeon" is a "cult" term used within Gnosticism, once a commonly accepted form of Christianity that later became "heresy." Instances of Gnostic terminology and thought can be found in a number of places in the New Testament, including and especially in some of the oldest layers of the Pauline epistles.[1]

Originals or Not?

To reiterate, there are many places where the evangelists do not agree with each other verbatim about what Jesus said. Ancient manuscripts of the same gospel also record Jesus's words differently from one to the next. Not all of these versions can be correct; therefore, some of them are wrong. How can we be certain that we are in possession of Christ's precious, original words? The KJV fundamentalist argument is that God simply didn't care about the originals and let them be destroyed. If God is so careless about the originals, why should we care about them? In fact, why should we care about the Bible at all, with such a blasé attitude as God holds towards it? Since the originals have simply been destroyed, we must take the word of mere *human beings* that the King James translators of Erasmus's hastily compiled Received Text is inerrant—why should we believe *them*? Like King Jehoiakim and the prophet Jeremiah, who are depicted in the book of Jeremiah (36:23, 51:63) as destroying the originals of that text twice, why don't we just toss out the whole Bible?

Moreover, we cannot even look towards the *original languages* for an inspired Bible, say the KJV fundamentalists: "If the Bible is inspired only in the 'original languages,' it is

---

[1] See e.g., Doherty, *JP*.

barbaric," goes the argument![1] Based on 1 Corinthians
14:11, in which Paul discusses the difficulties of dealing in
different languages, it is reasoned that a tongue foreign to
one's own constitutes a "barbarian" language. So, what
about for those of us who *do* know Greek and/or Hebrew? Is
King James English the only language that is *not* barbaric?
Would English not also be barbaric to those who do not know
it?

Also, why would the Holy Spirit, who is supposedly
guiding the efforts of the evangelists, have them record
Jesus's sayings in their own peculiar styles, rather than
verbatim in proper and correct Greek? Even if Christ spoke in
Aramaic, why wouldn't the Holy Spirit—who *is* Jesus and
would therefore know exactly what he said—inspire the
evangelists to translate his words all the same? Moreover, if
Jesus is the omniscient Lord, who knows all languages
perfectly, why would he speak Aramaic and not Greek—did
Christ only come for the relatively small and isolated
population of Aramaic-speaking Jews? Yet, at the end the
Lord changes his mission to include Gentiles, many of whom
spoke Greek, the lingua franca of the time. Wouldn't an all-
knowing God realize that to reach a Gentile audience,
Aramaic would be inappropriate and unhelpful? By the
argument using 1 Corinthians, wouldn't Aramaic also be
barbaric?

Furthermore, why is each gospel so obviously unique in
style and grammar? Could it be that these are mere human
beings writing these texts, without the inspiration of the Holy
Spirit? The claim of "divine inspiration" begs the question as
to why the Holy Spirit did not correct the various translation
problems and errors, among so many other mistakes.
Logically and rationally, of course, we may simply suggest
that the copyists and translators were fallible humans who
made mistakes.

Also, those who chose the books of the canon, such as
Church father Irenaeus, declaring these and no others to be
"inspired" and canonical, must themselves have been
inspired by the infallible Holy Spirit. Otherwise, mistakes
could have been made, and books that were not inspired

---

[1] Coats, "The Two Lies."

may have been incorporated into the canon, and vice versa. The idea that the selectors of the NT books must also have been inspired opens up certain difficulties, including the fact that the final canonization required a couple centuries of raucous and violent infighting, with doubt cast upon every currently canonical text. This fact begs the question of why God as the Holy Spirit would require so many individuals and so much time to iron out all these differences. This scenario would most logically and scientifically be viewed as a *human* endeavor and concerted effort by many individuals who were simply acting under their own power and motivation.

In addressing the concerns raised once it is determined that no translation can be considered "inerrant," Christian apologetics sometime claims that what we do have is "good enough." But are these translations "good enough?" If there are errors in them, how can we accept that everything they say is correct and accurate? If the omnipotent God/Jesus is so concerned with the salvation of our souls, why not once and for all present us with the inspired and inerrant originals, which he could easily manifest, even if they were destroyed?

What all this analysis means is that it would be highly questionable to assert that *any* translation is inerrant and that its translators were infallibly inspired by God as the Holy Spirit. Therefore, by reading any translation in English or other language one cannot attain an entirely inerrant understanding of what the original authors meant to convey. As we have seen, we do not possess the originals— apparently gleefully destroyed by God—so we are in a double bind as to why we should believe.

Illogic and Irrationality

In the name of integrity and honesty, the rational person needs to ask why we must suspend logic and scientific methodology when it comes to religious texts and traditions. It seems unconscionable for God to force believers into abandoning their critical, logical and rational minds, but this suspension is precisely what the believer is asked to do, repeatedly—indeed, not thus suspending logic and reason

may constitute an "antisupernatural bias!"[1] Several
examples of where we must abandon logic in order to
believe the gospel story as historical fact have already been
provided. Even from the beginning of the tale, we encounter
strange occurrences, as we read in the gospel story about
the wise men following a star to find Jesus; yet, after
tracking the star for many miles the strangers from the East
become so lost that they must stop at the house of Herod in
order to inquire where the new "king" has been born!
Bizarrely, Herod shows them the way, but he too is so
confused that he seems to have forgotten completely his
own instructions and must slaughter all the children under
the age of two in the village, instead of simply finding Jesus
using the same directions he gave to the magi.

Not only does this heinous episode not appear in the
historical or archaeological record, as there is not a word
about *any* of the sensational events surrounding Jesus's birth
in the works of any Jewish or Roman historian, but it also
seems illogical and artificial. In reality, it is impossible to
believe that no Jewish scribe would have recorded such an
offensive mass murder of children, but we are left with not a
mention of this hideous crime outside of the gospel of
Matthew. The quandary this fact raises as to the authenticity
of the account is further underscored by the presence of
similar infant-slaughtering themes in other legends and
myths, such as in the story of Moses. The apologist
argument for this omission from history is that Bethlehem
had a very small population at the time, so Herod killed
"only" a couple of dozen babies at most. This apology begs
the question of why, if Bethlehem was so tiny, both Herod
and the wise men couldn't find the baby Jesus in the first
place, especially with a brilliant spotlight in heaven shining
above his birthplace.

Furthermore, it would be very surprising if the people of
Bethlehem had forgotten all about the slaughter of their
children that attended Jesus's birth, even if there were only
a couple of dozen babies killed! Surely, the townsfolk would
have been aware all along that Christ had been the child
honored as the Lord God and future king of the Jews,

---

[1] Geisler, *CA*, 313.

constituting such a threat to Herod that he became the cause of this abomination. Yet, when Jesus is an adult, no one acknowledges the awful circumstances of his birth, and this infanticide is never again referred to, as if it never happened. Moreover, why would the all-powerful and all-seeing Lord, taking birth as his own Son in Jesus, allow Herod to mercilessly kill all of these innocent children, while he himself fled to Egypt? Did the omniscient Lord not see this horror coming? Could the omnipotent God not stop it? In addition, this Herodian infanticide was not "prophesied" by the Old Testament Jeremiah, as asserted by Matthew: The OT scripture quoted refers to the "Babylonian Exile," not the slaughter of infants six centuries later. This type of twisting of scriptures to fit purported "prophecies" has occurred more commonly than fathomed.

Crazy or Fiction?

According to the story, an angel informed Joseph and/or Mary that she would be bringing forth the Lord Himself, via a miraculous conception and virgin birth produced by the Holy Spirit, and that this child—again, the Lord God Almighty—would "save his people from their sins." (Mt 1:21) This divine being would be called "Son of the Most High" of whose kingdom "there will be no end" and who the Holy Spirit further called "the Son of God." *How, then, could Christ's family and friends later doubt his sanity*, trying to seize him against his will in order to stop him, as they are depicted at Mark 3:21? The scripture at Mark relates, "And when his friends heard it, they went out to seize him, for they said, 'He is beside himself.'" (The term for "beside himself" also means "out of his mind" or "insane.") In the original Greek, the word translated as "friends" in the KJV and RSV is *para*, a "preposition indicating close proximity," which could also be used to designate *family members* and *relatives* (i.e., "those close to him" or "his own"), as well as friends. In this regard, other translations do render the term *para* to mean "family," "own people," "relatives," etc. How could *Christ's own family* ever doubt him, if the circumstances of his divine birth were true, as well as other prodigies, such as the astonishing teaching in the temple at the age of 12? (Lk

2:38-42) Even the fetal John the Baptist knew who the Lord was—surely the rest did too!

Jesus's Siblings?

In addition, while the dubious "carpenter" aspect of Jesus has been much publicized, other purported, germane aspects of Christ's life have been completely ignored, including references to his family members. For instance, at Mark 6:3 the evangelist writes:

> "Is not this the carpenter, the son of Mary and brother of James and Joses and Judas and Simon, and are not his sisters here with us?" And they took offense at him.

What are we to make of this verse and the one at Matthew 13:55? If it is brought up to fervent believers, they too may take offense! Yet, it is a significant remark that warrants further commentary, such as who *are* Jesus's brothers and sisters? Is Mary also their mother? How did she remain a "perpetual virgin?" Christians have claimed over the centuries that Christ's brother and sisters were *Joseph's* children from a previous marriage, but there is no evidence for this assertion, other than this brief mention that Jesus even had brothers and sisters. The Catholic Encyclopedia, of course, argues for Mary's perpetual virginity and that she never bore any other children, explaining these "brothers and sisters" as "cousins" whose mother is Mary's sister, Mary.

Protestant apologists such as Geisler, however, see no problem in accepting that these brothers and sisters are really Christ's siblings, born to Mary, who does not remain a "perpetual virgin."[1] If Jesus had so many brothers and sisters, why do we never hear about them again? Is it not reasonable and realistic to suggest that some of Jesus's siblings would be involved in the development of Christianity? Except for "James, the brother of Jesus," we hear nothing about these siblings. Christ has at least four brothers and two sisters—what happened to the other five besides James? Why is James's role in the gospel story so

---

[1] Geisler, *WCA*, 346.

non-existent, even though he is later depicted as head of the Jerusalem Church? Nevertheless, there is not a word about him in the gospels, other than identifying him as one of the four brothers. The Catholic Encyclopedia argues that "James the brother of the Lord" is in fact the same as James, son of Alphaeus, and "James the Lesser," and is *not* a biological brother of Jesus but, again, his cousin, as a son of Christ's aunt, also named Mary.[1] Since we are not even certain whether or not Jesus had biological brothers, or if these were "cousins," or if they were simply members of the congregation, how can we paint an accurate biography of Jesus? In addition, if this dynasty of rabble-rousers were running amok all over Judea, how could it escape the notice of the authorities and historians? Like so much else about the gospel story, this part comes across with an air of unreality and fabrication.

Moreover, if all of Judea was aware of Jesus's birth, with *astrologers*[2] from afar following a star to honor the divine babe, recognizing him as the Son of God along with all the other wonders, why at Matthew 13:54-57 would the people

---

[1] *CE*, "The Brethren of the Lord."

[2] The word for the "wise men" in the biblical Greek is μαγοι—*magoi* or *maji*—which, per Strong's Concordance (G3097), means: "1b) the oriental wise men (*astrologers*) who, having discovered by the rising of a remarkable star that the Messiah had just been born, came to Jerusalem to worship him." (Emph. added) Oddly enough considering the pivotal role in the gospel story, in the Old Testament God *proscribes* astrologers (Is 47:14). Apologists such as Norman Geisler attempts to clarify this purported event of the astrologers following a star at Jesus's birth by asserting that this situation does not constitute "astrology" because it is not using the stars to *foretell* Jesus's birth: "The star guiding the Magi was not used to *predict*, but to *proclaim* the birth of Christ." (Geisler, *WCA*, 326) It nonetheless remains inexplicable why God would use members of a foreign priesthood of a religion that was largely *astrological* or *astrotheological* in nature to serve as pivotal figures in the birth of his own Son/himself, unless in order to emphasize specifically the astrological nature of the stellar event surrounding his birth. Moreover, in his *Stromata* (I, 15), Clement Alexandrinus specifically states that the Persian Magi "foretold the Saviour's birth." In other words, the reality is that the ancient magi were priest-*astrologers* who did in fact *foretell* births, and it would be difficult to explain why God would use them to follow a star if there were no astrological meaning attached to the act. Moreover, adding to the evident air of fiction about this tale, it is likely that the evangelist was using an old pre-Christian motif in order to usurp the Pagan priesthood of the astrological Zoroastrian religion.

of Jesus's "own country" later be astonished by his miracles and ask whether or not he was the "son of the tekton," in actuality being offended by him (Gr. *skandalizo*)? Why is the Lord Jesus depicted at first laboring unknown and later rejected, as if he were a common scoundrel or worse?

It is odd that the Jews as a whole were desperately waiting and agitating for the messiah; yet, when Christ came, with all the attendant signs and wonders, and fulfilling numerous messianic prophecies, practically no one noticed. This bizarre lack of notice is all the more peculiar considering the circumstances of Jesus's life, including as a 12-year-old flabbergasting the temple elders. After all these events, would the Jews just go about their business for a decade or two, forgetting all about Jesus, to the point where, when Christ finally began his ministry, no one knew who he was? Why did no one record Jesus's earlier life? Did the messiah—known throughout the country, presumably, because of the miraculous circumstances of his birth and other wonders—just drop out of sight, with no one asking him anything or having any interest in his life? And, if the Messiah's people were so sorely and desperately suffering under the yoke of the foreign occupation—and many Jewish rebels and rabblerousers certainly felt that way—why would he wait for decades before he acted to save them?

Continuing with the illogic in the gospel story, why would the devil offer God/Jesus the control over all the kingdoms of the world? Is God/Jesus not omnipotent and already in control of the earthly kingdoms? Isn't the Lord also in control of Satan? If not, how can God be considered all-powerful? If God *is* in control of Satan, why does he make Satan tempt him?

If Jesus is somehow separate from God, such that he needs to verify that he *is* God by having himself tempted, how can we claim that Christ possesses all of God's powers and is thus God himself? This argument is tautological, and the tale is illogical, as is the premise of the gospel story itself.

Indeed, why would God need to fix the creation that he made badly in the first place—man—by coming to Earth as his own Son and being brutally scourged and murdered? Is this a plan that we ourselves would think to use in fixing something we created badly?

Additionally, does it not seem a harsh and irrational punishment for someone who utters, "You fool!" to be "liable to the hell of fire," as Jesus is depicted as stating at Matthew 5:22? Do you really believe this frightening fate will happen to everyone who says, "You fool?" In an evident contradiction, Jesus himself is later portrayed as calling the scribes, Pharisees and his followers, "You fools!" a number of times.[1]

Christ further states at Matthew 5:37 that anything we say more than "yes" or "no" is "evil"—does that make any sense? How could we conduct our lives if all we could ever say is "yes" or "no?"

At Matthew 5:39, Jesus tells his followers, "Do not resist one who is evil. But if any one strikes you on the right cheek, turn to him the other also..." Does this command make sense? Are Christians supposed to allow evil to run rampant and to let themselves be beaten up? Should Christians allow Satan to overcome them? Why, then, in a very important episode verifying that Jesus is God, does Christ himself resist Satan's temptations in the desert?

If we are "perfect" like our Father in heaven, why does Jesus call us "evil" and "sinners" for whom he has come? And, if God is our Father, the same as Jesus, why do we need an intermediary between us and God, i.e. Jesus or a priest, minister, etc.? At Galatians 3:20, Paul says that an intermediary implies more than one but that *God is one*. If God is one, how can he also be three, as in the Trinity of the Father, Son and Holy Ghost? If God is omnipresent, wouldn't that mean that everything is God, including us? The significance of this last assertion cannot be understated: If God is everywhere present, then we are "him," and "he" is us. God is everything, and *everything is God*—doesn't that sound like pantheism as well? The word "pantheism" comes from the Greek, "pan" meaning "all," and "theism" pertaining to God/divinity. Can something be monotheistic and pantheistic at the same time? If not, how do we separate out the omnipresent God?

---

[1] Matthew 23:17, 19; Lk 11:40, 24:25.

If God is all good, how can he lead us into temptation? If he doesn't lead us into temptation, why are we to pray to him in the Lord's Prayer specifically *not* to lead us into temptation? In fact, later in the Bible this prayer is seemingly abrogated when it is claimed contradictorily that God himself "tempts no one." (Jas 1:13) Nevertheless, why does God make the righteous and sin-free path so narrow and difficult to follow, by putting so many *temptations* in our path? Would a *human* father be considered a good and moral individual if he were to throw all sorts of temptations and roadblocks in the path of his children?

Other of Jesus's sayings are illogical and absurd, such as the scripture about the lamp and the eye at Matthew 6:22-23:

> "The eye is the lamp of the body. So, if your eye is sound, your whole body will be full of light; but if your eye is not sound, your whole body will be full of darkness. If then the light in you is darkness, how great is the darkness!"

Luke repeats this strange saying and appends to it additional confounding language. Is this statement to be taken literally? What about the blind, whose eyes are not "sound?" How can the "light in you" be darkness? The explanations for this saying rely on mysticism—do Christians believe in these mystical explanations? In fact, Christian apologists *do* assert that this odd parable is *not* to be taken literally. If not everything in the Bible is to be taken literally, where do we draw the line as to what is literal, historical and factual, and what is metaphorical, allegorical and mythical? Since there's no solid and valid scientific evidence of even Jesus's existence, much less what he said or did, could not the entire story of Christ be deemed a figurative "exemplary teaching," not to be taken literally?

The idea that the Bible is not always to be take literally is confirmed by the apology proffered by Josh McDowell:

> The Bible claims that God used human personalities
> to receive and communicate eternal truths. Therefore,
> expressions of speech (such as when Jesus used

exaggeration) should not always be taken literally, then pitted against another portion of Scripture.[1]

In other words, where the Bible is inconvenient to the facts, it need not be taken literally. May we not, then, deem any portion of the Bible as "exaggeration" or, perhaps, "hyperbole," and not take it literally?

As another instance of unreal oddities in the New Testament, since the cross supposedly only gained spiritual significance *after* Christ died on it, what is Jesus referring to when he instructs his disciples to "take up the cross?" (Mt 10:38, 16:24; Mk 8:34, Mk 10:21; Lk 9:23, 14:27) Again, is this unusual request meant to be taken literally? Or, as previously noted, a reflection of pre-Christian veneration of the cross, as found on Jewish ossuaries.

In addition, Matthew 11:12 says, "From the days of John the Baptist until now the kingdom of heaven has suffered violence..." The RSV notes that other ancient authorities state that "the kingdom of heaven *has been coming violently*." Why the difference, and which is the original? Is it logical to assert that heaven can "suffer violence?" Can heaven be "coming violently?" How could it be considered *heaven* then?

Also, at Matthew 16:19, Jesus gives Peter the "keys of the kingdom of heaven," and says that whatever he—Peter—"binds on earth" will be "bound in heaven" and whatever he "looses on earth" will be "loosed in heaven." What does this mean? The Greek word for "bind," *deo*, also means "forbid" or "prohibit." The Greek word for "loose," *luo*, also means "declare unlawful." Does Peter have the same authority as God in creating prohibitions and legal declarations? If so, and if Peter is the basis of the Roman Catholic Church, as tradition holds, should we not *all* be Catholics and follow the Catholic Church's "laws" or doctrines to the letter? Or did God change his mind many centuries later when Martin Luther caused the Protestant Reformation? Is Peter—the rock upon whom Jesus built his church—no longer in charge of creating prohibitions and legal declarations on Earth?

Furthermore, Jesus is portrayed as being God the Father himself, saying, "I and the Father are One" (Jn 10:30),

---

[1] McDowell, 49.

among other depictions. Yet, at certain points, such as at Matthew 20:23 or when he's basically praying to himself in the garden of Gethsemane, Christ is separate from whom he calls "my Father" but who in reality is *himself*! The very premise of this story of a giant, invisible man in the sky splitting himself up into not two but three individuals, in order to act out this strange drama, seems to be extremely bizarre and certainly no more historical or factual than the *myths* of other cultures.

Another instance of illogic occurs with the apologist argument regarding the diverging chronology for the pericope of Jesus's anointment by a woman in the house of Simon. This reasoning holds that since Christ's ministry was at least one to three years long—that number being unclear in the gospels as well—he would have been anointed in houses *many* times. However, all that anointing would be surprising, not only since there is no precedent for it but especially since the disciples fiercely objected to such a costly ritual even *once*, and they did not suggest that it had ever happened before. Moreover, of all these possible anointments, why would the evangelists hit on two Simons? Were all these anointments *only* in the houses of people named Simon? The more logical response is that one or both of the evangelists got the facts wrong.

During the Passover celebration, Jesus acknowledges that one of his disciples would betray him, saying that it would be better for this man "if he had not been born." If God sent his only begotten Son to be crucified for the sins of mankind, then in turning Jesus over to the authorities, Judas would be doing God's will, so why should he be punished? Judas serves an important role in God's plan for salvation, which is presumably under God's own control. Hence, it would seem that Judas should be *rewarded* for thoroughly obeying God's will. In fact, as the Gospel of Judas and other Christian writings reveal, Judas *was* esteemed in certain sects as an obedient servant of God.

At Matthew 26:50, Judas approaches to identify Jesus, who asks why he is there. Why would Christ do that, when he already knew Judas would betray him that very night? Furthermore, why does Judas need to kiss Jesus to identify him, considering that Christ had become widely known during the preceding weeks? Other ancient authorities, RSV notes, have Christ also tell Judas to "do that for which you have come." It seems that in ancient times others noticed the same illogicality of Jesus asking why Judas was there, and attempted to correct the error by adding this phrase. Obviously, the ancient authorities felt they had the right to change what Christ supposedly said, *essentially fabricating a quote*. Under these circumstances, are we not justified in wondering *how much else of the gospel story is fabricated*?

How could Peter, after witnessing Jesus's many miracles—even walking on water himself!—and seeing Christ transfigured on the mountain, deny him later? And why would Jesus, knowing that Peter would deny him, make the disloyal apostle the "rock" of his church? Peter, who had witnessed the Lord in all His glory, surrounded by Moses and Elijah, and pronounced the Son of the Father by the latter's own voice declaring, "This is my son, in whom I am well pleased"—yet, the "faithful apostle" goes on to deny Jesus, cowardly running off when confronted! Despite this treacherous behavior, Peter is nonetheless given the keys to the kingdom of heaven and has Christ's church built upon him, becoming the first pope. Would this sort of activity not set a precedent that regardless of our disbelief in or denial of Jesus, we need not fear punishment but could reasonably expect to be rewarded?

The irrationalities continue: Why would the Jewish crowd, who had been following Jesus around and many of whom had been healed by him, shouting "Hosannas" upon his triumphal entry into Jerusalem, nevertheless ask for an infamous criminal, Barabbas, to be released, and for Christ to be put to death?

If Jesus *is* God, why would he cry out, "My God, my God, why hast thou forsaken me?" How can God forsake himself? Moreover, why are there different accounts of what Jesus/ God said while on the cross? Couldn't God/Jesus as the Holy Spirit infallibly inspire the evangelists to recall his exact words?

Also, why do Matthew, Mark and Luke make no mention of Jesus as the remover of sin? Matthew only mentions the word "sin" in two places, while the term never appears in Mark and Luke. Only John records Christ's role as the remover of sin—and John uses the word 15 times. If Jesus is the remover of sin—the whole reason Christ supposedly came to earth!—how could the synoptists omit this detail, if this story is factual?

At the end of John (Jn 20:31, 21:25), the evangelist writes that Christ's deeds were so many that the "world itself could not contain the books that would be written" about them. Concerning this statement, Dr. Blomberg remarks that "John's gospel ends by saying, somewhat hyperbolically, that the whole world couldn't contain all the information that could have been written about Jesus..."[1] If it is acknowledged even by Christian apologists that there is "exaggeration" and "hyperbole" in the Bible, how can we be sure that other incredible claims made therein do not also represent a bunch of hype? As can be seen, there exist enough hyperbole, illogic and irrationality to cause one to question the purported historicity of the gospel story itself.

Jesus's Character

Regardless of whether or not they believe in Christ's miracles, countless people follow Jesus because they suppose he set a great moral example. But, did he really? If we all acted like Jesus, would the world truly be a better place? There are a number of instances that make Christ's character seem less than stellar. To reiterate one important example, if Jesus is the all-powerful God who could change the world with ease, why does he flee from the petty thane Herod, leaving behind innocent infants to be murdered hideously in his place? As the omnipotent God, Jesus could easily stop this horrible slaughter, but he does not, choosing to run away and hide instead.

Many people who read the gospels are bothered by Jesus saying he came to bring not peace but a sword. (Mt 10:34) Jesus not only speaks about coming with a sword but also makes many pronouncements that the world will be in violent chaos—these concepts are objectionable to peace-loving people, and, again, since Christ is the omnipotent Lord of the cosmos, he is in charge of these events and could prevent them from happening, if he wished. Hence,

---

[1] Strobel, 64.

since apparently Jesus does not wish to thwart these horrifying events and their appalling loss of limb and life, how could he be considered "all good?" Is it "good" to allow—or *cause*, if you are the omnipotent God—your children to flounder, suffer and die?

Moreover, when Christ tells people to *hate* their mothers and fathers, and to leave them behind in order to follow him, he sounds very much like a cult leader. The same can be said when Jesus denies his mother and brothers (and sisters), appearing callous and uncaring towards them. Christ also seems to encourage people to die for him, or suffer martyrdom, by telling his followers that "he who loses his life for my sake will find it." (Mt 10:39) Jesus further informs his disciples that they will be rewarded a "hundredfold" if they leave their family and nation in his name. At Luke 14:33, Jesus instructs his followers that only those who renounce all that they have can be his disciples. In addition, in the book of the Acts of the Apostles (5:5, 10), Christ's "rock," Peter, essentially causes the deaths of two people who did not give him enough money! These teachings seem to be very objectionable and the marks of a cult leader. How many people do these things demanded by Christ, abandoning family and home, and giving up all their possessions, for his sake? Can we pick and choose what makes us perfected Christians destined for heaven?

Christ also predicts that his disciples will be hated for his sake and will suffer and be put to death—why, if Jesus is the omnipotent Lord and could easily prevent this horror? Why the fixation with suffering and death? In fact, if Jesus is God, and God is all-powerful, Christ could easily change the entire world and not have *anyone* suffer in his name or at all.

Continuing in an aggressive vein, at Matthew 13:41-42 Jesus evokes some frightening imagery: "The Son of man will send his angels, and they will gather out of his kingdom all causes of sin and all evildoers, and throw them into the furnace of fire; there men will weep and gnash their teeth." The "Son of man" is Christ himself, who is basically stating that he will send angels to burn "evildoers." At John 15:6, Jesus says, "If a man does not abide in me, he is cast forth as a branch and withers; and the branches are gathered, thrown into the fire and burned." These passages have been used over the centuries to justify witch-burnings and assorted other tortures of non-believers. Was it really a good idea for the omnipotent Lord to make such violent threats, which incited his fanatic followers to seize thousands of innocent people in order to torture and/or murder them? Instead of burning "evildoers" in this horrible manner, why can't the all-powerful God simply change them? And if Christ has been with us for 2,000 years—or for eternity, as Christian doctrine dictates—then wasn't *he* in charge of the world during this sickening period of horrific violence? *Especially* as concerns the Church in his very name? If not, where *was* Christ, who is eternal and omnipresent, during this time when there were endless horrors in his name? Why didn't Jesus stop this terror immediately? And what about life on Earth today, with all its horrors—why can't the omnipotent God/Jesus end such atrocities? Could the answer be that the figure in the New Testament named "Jesus Christ" was not who he was purported to be?

Jesus's violent side surfaces yet again at Luke 19:27, where Christ tells a strange parable about a king, in which he has the king say, "But as for these enemies of mine, who did not want me to reign over them, bring them here and slay them before me." If this passage does not refer to Christ and the kingdom of God, why does Jesus tell this parable? And if it *does* refer to Christ and the kingdom, as is widely accepted, doesn't it indicate a very aggressive, violent and dangerous character?

Also, being the omniscient Lord, why didn't Jesus know beforehand that his beloved cousin John the Baptist was about to be gruesomely murdered? Being omnipotent, why didn't he prevent this hideous crime of beheading a holy man? And not just any holy man, but the very one who recognized Jesus as the messiah, being Christ's forerunner! In addition, in the story Jesus does not seem to be particularly disturbed by John's awful death.

Furthermore, some people object to Jesus equating the Canaanite/Palestinian woman with a "dog," making Christ appear uncompassionate and bigoted. In repeatedly stating that he came not for the Gentiles, and in making a remark that an offending brother is like a "Gentile and a tax collector," Jesus again seems to be bigoted against non-Jews.

When Peter objects to Jesus being killed, he is expressing concern about his Lord; yet, Jesus snarls at his apostle and calls him "Satan." Why would Christ be so hostile and attack Peter so viciously simply because his apostle did not want him to die?

Jesus also seems very violent not only when he attacks the moneychangers in the temple but also when he curses the fig tree. If Jesus is God, and God created the fig tree, why would Jesus/God make it barren of fruit in the first place, such that he would have to curse and destroy the poor tree later? If Christ is the omnipotent Lord, could he not just snap his fingers and make the fruit materialize? Is the angry and violent attack on the tree really a sign of a godly character? Also, why does Jesus—the Almighty God Himself—need food in the first place? Can't Christ just blink his eyes and make the food appear or his hunger disappear?

Dr. Geisler's apology for this difficult passage includes the reasoning that Christ knew the fig tree was supposed to have fruit, but he needed to approach it in order to see that it really did (Mk 11:13) and, seeing that it had foliage, he assumed it would bear fruit as well: "It was the foliage that drew Jesus to the tree in hope of finding fruit."[1] This excuse begs the question as to why the omniscient Lord of the cosmos needed to draw near physically to the fig tree to discover whether or not it had fruit. Moreover, Geisler's argument that, being the omnipotent Lord, Jesus "can curse a fig tree for reasons unknown to us" could be deemed a flimsy "copout," with other interpretations appearing equally weak.

Furthermore, it seems to be highly arrogant and presumptuous of Jesus to assume that he could just take someone's ass and foal, simply by declaring that he is the Lord of the universe! Why would Jesus not manifest his own ass, rather than borrowing someone else's, without even telling them? Wouldn't this act ordinarily constitute theft? What kind of example does Jesus set here?

---

[1] Geisler, *WCA*, 565.

At a number of points (Mt 3:7, 12:34, 23:33), Jesus calls Jews "vipers," and at John 8:44 he attacks the Jewish authorities, saying they are of their father "the devil." These remarks seem very harsh, essentially stating that the Jewish authorities are evil and the spawn of Satan. Christ is thus abusive of pious Jews, calling them all sorts of names, and then he threatens to destroy the temple. Is this proper behavior? How would we react to this behavior if someone threatened to destroy a temple today? Unfortunately, the anti-Jewish sentiment in John has been utilized over the centuries for nefarious ends. As the omnipotent Lord, shouldn't Jesus have seen these violent confrontations coming and presented himself more temperately in order to avoid them?

In addition, Jesus predicts that Judea will be destroyed, which many people logically believe is simply reportage after the fact by the biblical scribes. Nevertheless, even if Christ did predict this occurrence, since he is omnipotent, why didn't he stop it? Since he is God, he must have caused it in the first place. Where is Christ's compassion and understanding?

If God/Jesus is compassionate, why does he have a planned tribulation for the entire world, during which millions of people, including innocent men, women and children, are going to suffer and die horribly?

As we have already seen, Jesus also shows a lack of character when he discusses the poor, evidently not at all wishing to help them but simply accepting that they exist—and declaring that they will *always* exist, despite the fact that, as the all-powerful God, he could snap his fingers and end poverty immediately. In consideration of what huge problems poverty and slavery represented within the Roman Empire—with an estimated 1 to 1.5 million slaves in Italy alone—the failure to address and condemn these major social ills becomes all the more egregious. Adding insult to injury is the fact that Jesus Christ is purported to be the all-powerful Lord of the cosmos, who, presumably, could end slavery, poverty and all suffering instantly. Instead, one of Christ's most important followers and arguably the major establisher of Christian doctrine besides Christ, Paul, actually *encourages* slavery in his letters to the Ephesians, Colossians and Titus:

Slaves, be obedient to those who are your earthly masters, with fear and trembling, in singleness of heart, as to Christ... (Eph 6:5)

Slaves, obey in everything those who are your earthly masters, not with eyeservice, as men-pleasers, but in singleness of heart, fearing the Lord. (Col 3:22)

Bid slaves to be submissive to their masters and to give satisfaction in every respect; they are not to be refractory... (Tts 2:9)

The word for "slaves" in the Greek is *douloi*, from the singular δουλος, which is often rendered "servant" in the various versions of the Bible, in order to soften the impression. The fact will remain, however, that slavery and poverty were rampant in the Roman Empire and beyond, and, despite claiming to be the savior of the world, Christ made no condemnation of, or attempt to end, either problem. Indeed, Rome was *full* of suffering people; yet, the omniscient and omnipotent Lord of the universe who came to Earth to alleviate people of their sins oddly felt fit to make his appearance in a tiny backwater section of the Roman Empire far away from this suffering!

Moreover, some of Jesus's words and deeds were so absurd and repulsive to the locals that they claimed he was possessed by demons and "mad." (Mk 3:21-22; Jn 10:20) The issue of Christ's seeming megalomania and arrogance— exhibiting "delusional psychosis" and "grandiose beliefs"— has been profound enough for apologists to craft arguments in defense of Jesus's sanity. Jesus's megalomaniacal and arrogant jargon includes: "I am the Alpha and Omega" (Rev 1:18, 1:11, 21:6, 22:13); and, "I am the way, and the truth, and the life; no one comes to the Father, but by me." (Jn 14:6)

These numerous examples constitute objections regarding the character displayed by Jesus throughout the gospels. There are people who, even if they believe there was a man called Jesus who did some of the things in the gospel, do not think he was a particularly good man, much less a god. Christ often comes across as arrogant, as well as angry, and he continually speaks down to people in a very haughty and conceited manner. He is self-absorbed and obsessed with issues that are seemingly not very important, such as whether a fig tree bears fruit for him or his head will be anointed, whereas real problems, such as slavery and poverty, remain unexamined and unchallenged by him.

Repellant Deeds, Sayings and Doctrines

In addition to the abundant character flaws are a number of peculiar and repugnant teachings by Christ and within Christianity as a whole. For instance, at Matthew 5:40-42, Jesus tells us that, should anyone sue us for our coat, we should just give him our "cloak" as well! Should we really follow that command? How many Christians have done so? And what happens to those who do not? Christ also exhorts that "if any one forces you to go one mile, go with him two miles." Are we supposed to surrender ourselves to people who would force us to do things, essentially constituting slavery? Jesus further instructs us to give to anyone who begs or borrows from us. Can we really do that and live a decent life? What about our children—should we not save and prepare for them? In his apology for the scripture encouraging Christ's followers to give to anyone who asks of them, Geisler proffers a highly speculative justification, saying that "Jesus no more expected His listeners to take, without qualification, the command to 'give to him who asks you' than He intended them to literally cut off their hands and pluck out their eyes if they offended them...!"[1] There is, in reality, no substantiation for this conjecture of what Christ *expected* or *intended* as concerns these particular verses, and this apology leaves us with the impression that Jesus's remarks are meaningless and pointless. If Christ did not intend for us to understand these comments literally, why even say them, as there is no sensible figurative way in which to comprehend them?

Furthermore, at Matthew 6:25, Jesus advises us not to worry about the future, not even about what we will eat and drink—is this a practical teaching? Why, then, if God knows we need food and drink, do people die from thirst and starvation every day? And if God knows our needs, why

---

[1] Geisler, *WCA*, 333.

must we pray to him for bread on a daily basis, as in the Lord's Prayer?

At Matthew 7:11, Jesus tells his followers that they are "evil." Who exactly is evil—*all* of us? Why would God make us evil? If we are made in God's image, how can we be evil, unless God is evil?

Christ's pronouncements regarding marriage, divorce and adultery appear to be very harsh and uncompassionate. Does it sound like a good idea to consider an "adulteress" a woman divorced for reasons other than unchastity, including, perhaps, domestic violence and abuse? Is not a woman who has been "unchaste" or committed infidelity an adulteress anyway? Doesn't this declaration mean that *all* divorced women would be considered adulteresses, regardless of whether or not they were faithful? Should we also deem a man who marries such a woman an "adulterer?" The penalty for adultery in Old Testament times often was death, by stoning or otherwise (Deut 22:22; Lev 20:10). Christ said he did not come to abolish the Mosaic Law but to fulfill it— should we therefore stone adulterers, as defined by Jesus?

Christ tells his followers that they should cut off their hands and feet, and pluck out their eyes, but should anyone really do that? Should we cut off people's hands if they steal? Amputations of this kind have been common in various cultures since ancient times, so it was already a custom and understood as *literal*, not something "figurative" that Jesus was exhorting. Are these gruesome concepts something "good" to which we should expose the innocent and impressionable minds of children?

What about becoming an eunuch for heaven by being castrated? Apologists may say that it is better to be castrated than to forfeit heaven, but some people might respond that heaven is not a proven place, so castration is quite a risk to take. Apologists also claim that the phrase "receive this" in the "eunuchs for the kingdom" scripture refers not to the castration but to acquiring an understanding of Jesus's purported "parable" here. In the original Greek of the verse there is no way to determine whether the word for "receive it"—χωρειτω or *khoreito*—refers to actual castration or the statement itself. This fact has not prevented translators of recent Bible editions from rendering the phrase "accept this *statement*." (New Living Translation) This rendering remains an *interpretation* of what the editors thought Jesus may have *meant*. If the New Testament represents the literal Word of God, it is puzzling why God/Jesus would go to the trouble of putting forth such remarks and then not make them clear, such that they constantly require interpretation.

Moreover, even if the "it" does refer to the *statement*, what *is* Jesus trying to impart here? If he is speaking in a parable, in effect winking at his listeners, is Christ not likely conveying nevertheless that he condones or *encourages* men to become eunuchs for heaven? The fact will remain that early Christians such as Church father Origen and others perceived Jesus's words as meaning that *they should become castrated*—and they followed through with what they considered a commandment from their Master. Indeed, this verse has traditionally been interpreted to mean that Jesus's disciples should abstain from sexuality, such that it is clear that Christians from the earliest times onward believed Christ was encouraging them to be "eunuchs for the kingdom of heaven." As a later example, in 1871 biblical commentators Jamieson, Fausset and Brown rendered the word "eunuch" thus: "persons constitutionally either incapable of or indisposed to marriage." As concerns the last phrase regarding "receiving it," Jf and B comment, "He who feels this to be his proper vocation, let him embrace it." Regardless of any other possible interpretation of this scripture, segments of Christendom over the centuries, including various sects such as the Russian "Skoptsi," have viewed this scripture as an inducement to castration at worst and abstinence at best.

When Christ says that families will be handing over their members to be killed, including children having their parents put to death, as at Matthew 10:21-23, he is in effect creating a blueprint for his disciples to follow. Why would the God of the universe bring about such a horrible creation, when, being all-powerful, he could manifest anything he wants?

Another strange teaching appears at Matthew 18:21-22, where Jesus tells Peter that the latter must forgive his brother's sins against him not seven but "seventy times seven." Is that really wise? Is it possible? Should we really just forgive people over and over again, no matter what they do? Even if they are murderers or rapists? How are we to forgive them? Should we not punish them and not let them do it again?

In pressing his point, at Matthew 18:34-35, Jesus tells Peter that *everyone who does not forgive his brother "from his heart" will be tortured in prison by the Lord God*. In this pericope, Jesus relates the story of a slaveholder who delivers one of his unforgiving slaves to torturers, and then says that God will do the same to all of us for not forgiving our brothers' sins.

It should be noted that many translations of this Matthaean verse cloak the term "slave"—*doulos* in the Greek—behind the word "servant," while the term for those who tortured the slave—*basanistes* in the singular—is translated as "jailers" and "tormentors." Strong's defines this word *basanistes* (G930) as:

1) one who elicits the truth by the use of the rack
a) an inquisitor, torturer also used of a jailer doubtless because the business of torturing was also assigned to him

Hence, the term is more appropriately translated as "torturer." What happens to those of us who do not follow these exhortations to forgive our brother? Will we all forfeit the Kingdom of Heaven and be cast into hell to be tortured by God? If it's not God who is to torture us, then who—Satan? If the torture is God's punishment for not forgiving our brother's sins, then is Satan God's instrument? Is all of this logical and sensible? Should an all-good and merciful God be torturing people?

At Matthew 23:8, Jesus tells us to "call no man your father on earth, for you have one Father, who is in heaven." Does this mean we can't call our own fathers "father?" If so, doesn't that seem harsh? What about priests? Is the Catholic practice of calling priests "father" against God? Why does no one literally follow this command of Jesus? If we can overlook this scripture, can we not ignore others as well, including those that tell us to believe the incredible claims regarding Jesus in the first place? In the next breath, Christ tells us that he is our Master—should we ignore that scripture as well? Jesus follows this overbearing declaration of his dominion over us with a lecture on humility—doesn't that seem hypocritical?

In the pericope of the "widow's mite" at Luke 21:1-4, Jesus seems to be encouraging poor people to give away all their belongings to the temple/church. Is this a good policy? Why does the omnipotent Lord need the money of poor people or *any* people at all? Doesn't this sort of behavior set a dangerous precedent for people to prey on the poor, old and gullible?

In Matthew 24, Jesus tells two long parables about "wise and foolish maidens" and about money, so that he can impart the following lesson:

> "For to every one who has will more be given, and he will have abundance; but from him who has not, even what he has will be taken away."

Does this teaching sound right? Doesn't it seem to be lacking in compassion?

At John 12:25, Jesus says, "He who loves his life loses it, and he who hates his life in this world will keep it for eternal life." This scripture has been repeated many times and is fairly well known, but does it sound very good? Isn't Christ encouraging people to be miserable and even suicidal about being alive? Isn't Jesus essentially saying, "If you love life, you have to die. But if you hate life, you have to stay alive forever." Could such a remark not be construed as very cruel? If God gave us this life, why should we "hate" it? Did God give us very bad lives? Why would an all-good, all-powerful and merciful God do such a thing?

At the Last Supper/eucharist, when Jesus tells his disciples that they should eat the bread and drink the wine because these are Christ's body and blood, doesn't that sound like barbaric cannibalism and vampirism? When you first heard about the eucharist, perhaps as a child, how did you feel about it? Were you not repulsed by the notion of drinking some guy's blood and eating his body? Are these barbaric, cannibalistic concepts really something we should be exposing our children to?

The bloodiness continues, as at Matthew 27:25 the Jews are depicted as saying, "His blood be upon us and our children." Why would the Jews make such a statement? If it is because they want to be washed in the "blood of the lamb," wouldn't that absolve them of their sins? If Christ gave his life in atonement for sins, why would being bathed in his blood be a bad thing? Why were the Jews labeled "Christ-killers" and persecuted repeatedly over many centuries, when they were evidently asking for the salvific baptism in the blood of the Lamb? In any event, the whole concept of blood atonement in the first place ranks as repulsive and barbaric—and unnecessary for an all-powerful and loving God.

Is it logical to vilify Jews as committers of deicide, when it was by all pious accounts *God's own plan* to take birth as a human and *sacrifice himself* on the cross? Jesus himself is depicted as saying he will be crucified, long before he is found guilty of anything remotely meriting capital punishment—and that in itself is another issue, because Jesus's alleged misdeeds did not warrant the death penalty. Christ's sacrifice was salvific, not expiatory, meaning it was for our salvation, rather than as a punishment for any crimes he committed. Indeed, it is a matter of Christian doctrine that God so loved the world that he gave his only begotten son. (Jn 3:16) In such a case, it would appear to be blasphemy to demonize the people who served as crucial participants in God's highest plan for the salvation of mankind!

As we have seen, various factions attempted to place the onus of Christ's death on either the Romans or the Jews, for political reasons. Whether Romans or Jews, they were evidently under divine guidance in sacrificing Jesus; therefore, they could not be found culpable of "deicide," unless God—whose plan it was in the first place—himself is guilty of deicide. How can anyone be guilty of "deicide" since it is impossible to kill the immortal God? What all this rumination means is that *an atrocious amount of people have been hideously tortured and murdered for no good reason whatsoever*.

Moreover, it is beyond shameful that anyone would destroy others centuries later for the supposed "sins of their fathers." Also, why would the all-powerful and loving God the Father allow his children—i.e., Christians—to go on rampages and kill millions of God's other children, including Christians, as well as God's chosen people, the Jews?

Moreover, if Jesus is God, and God's plan is good, why does he ask himself to stop the coming torment and suffering of his Passion? Why is this God's plan to fix his own creation? Indeed, according to Christian doctrine, Jesus the man is created specifically for the reason of coming to Earth and dying for our sins—again, isn't this a bizarre way for God to mend things? Does an architect whose building turns out badly jump off the edifice in order to fix it?

Furthermore, many people believe that teaching young, innocent and impressionable children that they are "born in sin" is abusive and harmful. There are numerous other repellant and scary sentiments expressed in the Bible, which includes many depictions of extreme violence and bloodshed on a massive scale.

All in all, the numerous instances of questionable sayings, deeds and actions in the gospels and New Testament as a whole are quite distinct and noticeable. This issue constitutes a very important one that should not be taken lightly and dismissed with a variety of trivial and unsophisticated excuses. It is further perplexing that so many intelligent and erudite individuals have engaged themselves in the study of biblical texts without these questions and objections being raised in their minds. Such a scenario is reflective not of the all-encompassing "truth" of the New Testament but of the intoxicating power of religious conditioning.

Apology Accepted?

"Men often run into gross mistakes by understanding that literally which the scripture speaks figuratively."

Rev. Matthew Henry, "Commentary on John 2"

"Early Christians certainly read scripture allegorically, understanding it to refer to some kind of so-called higher realities that weren't really present in the text itself."

Dr. Harold W. Attridge, "From Jesus to Christ"

The field of Christian apologetics provides responses for any number of the quandaries and objections concerning the difficulties and problems of the gospels, as illustrated by several examples already provided. To some people, however, many of these answers appear to be illogical and contrived, leaving us to continue wondering about any solid data upon which to base or judge anything concretely about the New Testament. Several of these responses and excuses also seem dishonest and lacking in integrity, such as the "principle of harmonization" that essentially constitutes a waving away of the hand indicating the gospel writers were not interested in accuracy. Other apologies come across as desperate and sophistic attempts to rationalize and harmonize issues that do not make sense and that do not follow natural laws or even appear realistic.

In addition to the apologies already explored are a number of other themes within the field of apologetics. For example, one more justification for the many discrepancies and difficulties in the gospel texts points out that the biographies of *other* people also reveal differences in what supposedly happened in the subjects' lives. However, here we are not discussing the biographies of "any old people" but *the inerrant portrayal of the Lord God himself*, allegedly infallibly recorded by scribes inspired by the Holy Spirit! The standard for judging the gospels needs to be *much* higher, since God himself is purported to have written them. Additionally, these texts were not composed by four unrelated individuals as is the case with the biographies of other people: The canonical gospels are the result of a concerted effort purportedly to depict *accurately* the life of the most important person ever to walk the face of the earth. The gospels simply cannot be so casually and carelessly handled as to justify various apologies, such as: The times were different; people saw things differently; the evangelists didn't care about accurate representation, etc. *Surely, the Lord God Almighty—the purported true author of the gospels—is not just "one of the people" who abides by the sloppy and disinterested rules of the day!*

"It Doesn't Matter?"

Indeed, at some point the reconciliation or harmonization of the many contradictions and differences in the gospels has apparently become so overwhelming that apologists have thrown their arms up into the air, proffering the excuse—essentially the first principle of harmonization—that the gospel writers and others simply did not care about the details and/or were affected by an "it doesn't matter" syndrome. This excuse begs the question as to why God would entrust his all-important appearance on Earth to people to whom "it doesn't matter." Why not choose individuals to whom it mattered greatly? And, would this "don't bother me with the details" attitude be appropriate in a modern workplace, for instance? Are these "ethics" that we would like to emulate?

As we have seen, this apology for admitted inconsistencies— for, there would be no need to excuse the ancients for a disinterest in details, if there were no such problems in the first place—is refuted by the author of Luke's gospel himself when he states that many before him had made attempts at portraying the story "in order." One word Luke uses to describe what these others have done before him is αναταξασθαι— *anataxasthai*—from the verb meaning, per Strong's (G392):

1) to put together in order, arrange, compose

Moreover, in Luke's passage appears the word ακριβως— *akribos*—which clearly means that Luke is striving for *accuracy*. Per Strong's the definition of *akribos* (G199) is:

1) exactly, accurately, diligently

Hence, it is obvious from Luke's painstaking choice of words that he was very much interested in *order* and *accuracy*. As Christian scholar Dr. Blomberg asserts, "...Luke is clearly saying he intended to write *accurately* about the things he investigated and found to be well-supported by witnesses."[1] Moreover, Luke's alleged accuracy is emphasized and relied upon within Christian apologetics, to demonstrate the gospel story's historicity. Expressing the same assessment, F.F. Bruce remarks, "Luke's record entitles him to be regarded as a writer of habitual accuracy."[2] In *The New Evidence that Demands a Verdict*, Christian apologist Josh McDowell includes a section entitled, "The Incredible Accuracy of Luke," complete with the much-publicized quote of Sir William Ramsay concerning Luke being a "historian of first rank," etc. Thus, the contradictory tactics within apologetics to preserve inerrancy include, on the one hand, putting forth the first principle of harmonization claiming that the ancients were not interested in details and accuracy, while, on the other hand, holding up Luke as an extremely accurate historian!

Then again, it has also been asserted that Luke is not very accurate at all. As we have seen, in addition to relying on the accounts of others for the events of the gospels, Luke has been posited by a number of scholars to have used the works of Josephus as one basis for his own historical data, a claim that makes sense if we logically and scientifically assign a late date to the gospel. Nevertheless, Luke's version fails to depict events precisely the same as Josephus, leaving us to wonder who is correct and accurate.

Again, the apologist claim that the evangelists did not care about accuracy means that God/Holy Spirit/Jesus was also not concerned with accuracy. In fact, to suggest that the Lord himself—as the real author—composed the gospels in the "it doesn't matter" manner is to attribute sloppiness and slovenliness to the perfect, all-knowing and infallible God of the cosmos! Yet, in infallibly inspiring the scribes to write his own biography in the gospel story, the Lord seems singularly disinterested in presenting it in a cohesive, rational and logical manner. Why would the omnipotent

---

[1] Strobel, 50. (Emph. added.)
[2] Bruce, *NTD*, ch. VII.

intelligent designer of the cosmos be incapable of coordinating four short books?

As to the apology that people back then "saw things differently," did the Lord too *evolve* in the last couple of thousand years such that his ability to portray events accurately and scientifically is now finally up to par with our own, since it is *he*, not "people back then," who supposedly authored the gospels? Or must we go back to blaming all this New Testament messiness on the *human* authors, conveniently speaking out of both sides of the mouth in our assertions regarding the true authorship of the gospels?

"The Bible is a Human Book."

Indeed, another apology contends that, while the Bible represents the inerrant Word of God, when discrepancies are noted one of the principles becomes that "the Bible is a human book with human characteristics." In fact, one of the first and most obvious concepts that strike us when we hear the apologetics for the diverging gospel accounts, is that, while believers claim these texts constitute the inspired and inerrant Word of God—understood to mean that God himself wrote them—apologists must continually invoke the *fallible human authors* in order to explain discrepancies, contradictions, oddities and errors. Laying the responsibility upon the evangelists themselves leaves God and his alleged inspiration out of the picture and wholly unaccountable, even though the very selling point of the biblical texts is that they are different from all other documents *because they are infallibly inspired by God*. With such a dichotomy of portraying the Bible as both the "Word of God" and a "human book," Christian apologetics appears to employ "sleight of hand" in its attempts at solving the myriad problems, activity that makes less credulous people skeptical, if not suspicious.

Even if the evident *disharmony* that requires so much harmonization can be explained in terms of the Bible being a "human book," the question needs to be asked why it was so difficult to create an orderly account, particularly if the texts were infallibly inspired by the Holy Spirit. Indeed, if the gospel writers and copyists were trying to depict actual historical events, it simply should not have been so difficult to get it right, concisely, linearly and so on. The events in

Jesus's life depicted in the gospels supposedly took place over a period of a few years at most—although, again, these events are compressed into a timeframe that could have been just a couple of weeks or less. In reality, the gospels do not even agree on the length of Jesus's ministry before he died. While it is clear that biographers of people who lived decades or centuries previously are not going to be entirely accurate—in fact, they will likely make a number of mistakes—the evangelists were allegedly reporting shortly after the events happened, a belief fervently adhered to by Christian fundamentalists. Two of these reporters—Matthew and John—were supposed to have been eyewitnesses to the events; yet, they garble them up so badly it has taken two millennia to disentangle them even to this extent.

Four Camera Angles

In fact, one apology sometimes submitted for the disparities between gospels is that Matthew *was* an eyewitness, so where the texts diverge, it is likely his version that is more accurate. Such an assertion, of course, would tend to impugn the other gospels as being *inaccurate* and, therefore, *wrong*. Thus, we come across another common apology for the problems and difficulties found in the gospels positing that they represent "four different camera angles." The camera-style argument goes as follows:

> The Gospels were written by different authors with varying styles. Each gives a different view of the action, emphasizing certain people and events while ignoring others.[1]

This reasoning—essentially the same as the biography and carelessness arguments above, in that it places the NT authorship upon its *human* writers—would be viable, if it too did not contradict the doctrine that God/Jesus as the Holy Spirit represents the true author of the gospels.

To reiterate, according to fundamentalist Christian doctrine, the Bible is the Word of God, and it was composed by the Lord himself, via the Holy Spirit. Hence, all four "camera angles" would nonetheless be those of God. If this

---

[1] "A Harmonization Chronology of the Resurrection."

assertion of divine authorship is true, wouldn't it make more sense for the four canonical gospels to be named "The Gospel According to *God*?" And, considering that Christianity is monotheistic, would it not make even greater sense for there to be only *one* Gospel according to God? What is the need for *four* gospels, if God is the author of them all? It is only by a serious bending of logic that an answer can be set forth for this paradox of insisting that fallible human beings are responsible for the difficulties, incongruities, inconsistencies and general disharmony of the Bible, which is nevertheless held up as inerrant because it was infallibly inspired by God!

Moreover, it is admitted by the author of Luke that he was not an eyewitness to the events; hence, he himself would not represent a "camera angle" at all. Mark too is purportedly recording Peter's experiences, not his own, so he too is no camera angle. Furthermore, the synoptics used a large amount of the same material, which records only *one* camera angle. In consideration of these facts, it seems odd that the Lord would entrust the telling of his all-important tale to those who had not witnessed his advent, particularly when there were allegedly *so many eyewitnesses*. Hence, in the gospel accounts we do not possess the testimony of four different eyewitnesses, as asserted by those who claim the gospel story represents "reliable history" because we *do* have the testimony of four different evangelists.

Even so, if these texts constitute the inerrant and inspired Word of God, it doesn't matter whether or not the writer was present as an eyewitness—he *must* have it right. As we have seen throughout this book, such contentions cannot be upheld, as the gospels are clearly full of difficulties and disparities that strongly suggest they are not inerrant.

Does The Bible Stack Up?

Amid claims that "it doesn't matter" emerges another common apology that, when stacked up against other texts, the New Testament is a "remarkably accurate source book." This argument also presupposes the first principle of harmonization that the ancients were not interested in, and were incapable of, accuracy and correct details in their records. This sweeping statement is false, of course, as many ancient writers have proved themselves very competent and accurate—and they did not have the benefit of a quorum of people who could peer-review their texts, as happened with the biblical texts and translations. Nor, according to Christian doctrine, did these authors have the benefit of the Holy Spirit as their ghostwriter. These ancient writers included Herodotus (464 BCE-447 BCE) and Thucydides (c. 471? BCE—c. 400? BCE), centuries prior to the common era, as well as Pausanias (2nd cent. AD/CE), all of whom have been found to be surprisingly accurate in their comparatively large amount of detail encompassing a significant period of history. There is thus little reality to the generalization that the ancients as a whole were not interested in or capable of accuracy and detailed accounts. Even Homer's *The Iliad* and *The Odyssey* demonstrate enough factual material as to be confirmable to a degree by science. According to the lax standards by which the Bible is judged, these texts could be deemed "historical," and it could be argued in an apologetics manner that the Iliad and Odyssey "prove" the existence of the Greek gods Hercules, Achilles and Ares, to name a few. Does the discovery of the site of Troy prove Homer's Trojan War to be factual? In more modern times, *Gulliver's Travels* is set in a specific time and place—does this fact mean Gulliver and the Lilliputians were real people? In reality, the gospels appear to be more of this fantastic genre than of the historical type.

What Jesus Felt or Thought

A number of the apologies for biblical difficulties outlined herein include discussions of what Jesus "thought," "expected," "intended," "meant" or "felt," as if the apologist knows the mind and heart of Christ. While they may be sincere in attempting to smooth out several sticky wickets, these efforts at determining what Jesus intended or meant often remain unsatisfactory and speculative, dependent on what the apologist values most and considers to be ethical. Such interpretations by apologists frequently represent their own psyches, rather than what Christ may have really thought or felt.

For example, all sorts of twisted logic and wishful thinking are applied to Jesus's disturbing remark that he came not with peace but with a sword (Mt 10:34), a prediction unfortunately borne out by the bloody history of the Christian church. In his defense of this saying, Dr. Geisler posits that what Christ "really meant" was that he came with peace but that violence would erupt around him:

> We must distinguish between the *purpose* of Christ's coming to earth and the *result* of it. His *design* was to bring peace—peace with God for unbelievers...and eventually, the peace of God for believers.... However, the immediate consequences of Christ's coming was to divide those who were for Him and those who were against Him—the children of God from the children of this world. But, just as the *goal* of an amputation is to relieve pain, so the immediate *effect* is to inflict pain. Likewise, Christ's ultimate mission is to bring peace, both to the human heart and to earth. Nonetheless, the immediate effect of His message was to divide those in the kingdom of God from those in the kingdom of Satan.[1]

In the first place, the presumption that those who have not been "for Christ" are therefore satanic and need to be "amputated" represents an extremely arrogant and judgmental position, reflecting megalomania and tyranny on the part of Jesus. Furthermore, it is not honest or logical to interpret Christ's words as the opposite of what he said—"I have *not* come to bring peace"—especially since Jesus is alleged to be the omniscient Lord of the universe who ostensibly knew exactly what he was doing in his plan for delivering the "good news" and salvation to mankind. Being all-powerful, Christ could thus have come up with a better plan whereby peace was immediately implemented merely by his presence, rather than bringing with him a massive, millennia-long trail of death and destruction. If Jesus's advent brings with it such violence, how could we call his coming "good news?" And why the heck would we want his *Second* Coming? In such a scenario, what is the difference between the reign of Christ and that of an earthly despot?

As another example of apologist impracticality, in the pericope in Matthew where Christ admonishes us not to pray in public, Geisler's apology depends on what he himself

---

[1] Geisler, *WCA*, 340.

believes Christ *intended* or *felt*, asserting that Jesus *meant* to convey an objection to "*ostentatious* prayer," rather than simply public prayer in general. Geisler even goes so far as to say, "He was not opposed to people praying in *appropriate* public places, but in *conspicuous* ones."[1] Unfortunately, this contention of what Jesus did or did not *oppose* remains based on *speculation* of Christ's character and intentions. Indeed, this type of apology ranks as highly speculative and relies on the *interpretation* of the reader for the many difficulties found in the Bible. As we have seen, some of these interpretations are definitely *not* literal.

In other speculative attempts at explaining oddities and inconsistencies, in their speculations apologists seem to reduce Christ to a rather petty and puerile character. As one more instance, in the apparent contradiction that occurs between Matthew and Mark regarding whether or not the disciples should take with them a staff, Geisler claims that Jesus was advising them not to take an *extra* staff with them, because at Matthew, where Jesus says to take "no staffs," he is not saying not to take "*a* staff."[2] This excuse seems to be sophistic and indicts Christ with a peculiar and eccentric way of expressing himself. Is it not more logical to conclude that one or the other evangelists is depicting the event incorrectly? Or that, perhaps, the story is fictional, which readily explains all of the discrepancies and difficulties?

Regarding the attempts at determining what Jesus thought or felt, in "What Would Jesus Think or Do?" conservative Christian scholar Dr. James Porter Moreland concludes:

> People, myself included, tend to distort things to agree with their own predilections, and nowhere is this more obvious or dangerous, than in representing Jesus' views.[3]

Indeed, as noted, many of the apologies proffered for the disharmony and other problems of the Bible represent little more than speculative interpretation of the apologist, based

---

[1] Geisler, *WCA*, 334.
[2] Geisler, *WCA*, 339.
[3] Moreland, "WWJTD."

on his or her own morals, values and education, or lack thereof. The same must be said of the efforts in determining who Jesus was.

The argument is further made that God's mind is not man's mind, so we cannot expect him to behave in the same way, i.e., "God works in mysterious ways." According to the ideology, however, "God made man in his own image," so our minds should function the same. Moreover, if we can't know God's mind, and Jesus is God, how can we pretend to know what Jesus thought, intended, meant or felt?

Literal or Figurative?

At certain times when confronted with bizarre and grotesque Christian doctrines such as the cannibalistic eucharist, or the sharing of Jesus's body and blood, in order to maintain the belief that the Bible is meant to be taken literally, apologists must come up with schemes which play so fast and loose with terms that they begin to lose all meaning. For example, concerning the repulsive ritual of the eucharist, Dr. Geisler remarks (412):

> The literal (i.e., actual) meaning of a text is the correct one, but the literal meaning does not mean that everything should be taken literally....

> There are many indications in John 6 that Jesus literally meant that the command to "eat His flesh" should be taken in a figurative way.[1]

Even if we accept this sophistic explanation that this pericope is "literally to be taken figuratively," what does it mean? Why is Christ comparing his body and blood to something we should eat and drink? Why is empathetic spirituality being couched in terms of barbaric cannibalism?

In discussing whether or not Jesus meant the bread of the communion as his literal body (Lk 22:19), Geisler also states:

> ...*common sense* is opposed to taking this literally. God created the senses, and all of life depends on our trusting the information they give us about the world. But those who believe in transubstantiation admit

---

[1] Geisler, *WCA*, 412-413.

that the consecrated bread (host) looks, smells, and tastes like real bread. Why then would God call on us to distrust the very senses that He created and asks us to trust continually for our very life.[1]

As has been evidenced throughout this book, numerous instances in the gospel story ask us to suspend our common sense; hence, Geisler's question could likewise be applied to the entire tale itself. Why indeed would God ask us to suspend our senses in accepting the bulk of the gospel story of Jesus Christ in the first place?

If, as proclaimed by conservative Christian scholar and minister Matthew Henry, we err grossly "by understanding that literally which the scripture speaks figuratively," how are we to know when to take something literally and when to understand it figuratively? In the New Testament, Jesus is depicted as a lamb, lion, vine, door or cornerstone—should we take these designations literally in order to satisfy the literalist dogma? No, we should not, as they are meant figuratively.

Hence, it is clear that there exists figurative speech in the Bible and that *not all of the Bible is meant to be taken literally*. In this regard, we may ask just how much of the New Testament story is figurative and how much literal? Could it not be that the whole tale is meant *figuratively* and *allegorically*?

While reading certain apologies and apologetics texts, one may frequently receive the impression of desperation to reconcile and harmonize at any and all costs, because fundamentalists are compelled through conditioning to believe in the evidently irrational and indefensible position that the gospels represent the inerrant and literal Word of God. Once we discard this indefensible position, however, we may be able to make more sense of the Bible as a "human book," i.e., *manmade* and containing *allegory*, rather than serving as literal and inerrant Holy Writ.

---

[1] Geisler, *WCA*, 394.

History or Propaganda?

"The works of Greek, Roman and Jewish historians all probably influenced the New Testament writers."

Dr. J.P. Moreland, *The New Evidence that Demands a Verdict* (556)

Instead of formulating illogical and incredible excuses for the many variant readings, dislocations, disparities, oddities and errors in the biblical books and manuscript copies, shouldn't we as seekers of truth at least *entertain* the notion that a number of these discrepancies and peculiarities constitute either mistakes or deliberate contrivances for specific purposes, because the Bible may not be the inerrant Word of God and the gospels may not in fact represent reliable and credible "history?"

To begin with, we may look at the fact that, whereas once there was a clamor to find the "original words" of the evangelist authors of the gospels, there is now a movement within textual criticism to determine exactly *why* there were such massive "variant readings"—or *changes*—made to the Holy Bible over the centuries. Why indeed did there emerge so many alterations and variations by a bewildering variety of writers, scribes, copyists and translators? Could it be, as suggested by the "new" push within the field of NT scholarship, that there were *political* reasons for many of the differences and problems found in variant readings between manuscript copies? According to the scholarship—widely embraced outside of the narrow confines of fundamentalism, which, despite its claims, in no way owns the field of NT scholarship—there were indeed *political* purposes for many of these changes. Moreover, couldn't this type of analysis also be applied to the discrepancies and inconsistencies between the four canonical gospels themselves as well?

A close examination does indeed reveal that the numerous inconsistencies and divergences of the canonical gospels and the ancient copies often *were* founded upon political, sectarian or doctrinal differences, which means that these texts are not necessarily recording "historical" events that had occurred decades or centuries earlier. In this regard, "holy writ" becomes not a historical record but a matter of political expediency. It is unquestionable that what has become accepted by some true believers as dogma, i.e., the "gospel truth," is asserted by other factions to be *human error*. This disparity, in fact, is at the root of the many fractures within Christ's church: For example, Protestant versus Catholic, as well as the countless sub-sects within each major break—all have determined that *their* doctrine is more accurate and authentic than the others, essentially impugning *error* upon the others. Such being the case, it seems impossible to make any honest claims of "inerrancy" within *any* of these factions. In addition to an inspection of textual difficulties with an eye to detecting propaganda moves, we need to look at the nature of purported "errors" charged by one faction upon another as well, and vice versa. Such an analysis, in fact, will reveal a significant latent fingerprint of the Christ.

While a number of the difficulties and discrepancies either between the gospels or in the various copies are insignificant as concerns content—though, in the case of peculiarities and variations between the "original" gospels, not as concerns claims of *inerrancy*—there remain many instances where the differences between the verses in the ancient texts are profound and significant, indicating whatever the scribe or faction thought appropriate to his or their time and place. What we often discover, therefore, in the examination of these discrepancies, interpolations, omissions and oddities is a view of the *politics* among the factions in charge of the biblical texts, as well as the evident *competition* with non-Christian or non-Orthodox priesthoods expressed in the voluminous writings of the early Church fathers.

A Uniquely Divine Birth?

As we have seen, various *translations* likewise have been rendered in order to accommodate "political" sentiments of the day. The controversial virgin-birth periope, for example, seems to have been included to compete with the miraculous birth stories of other individuals in the Pagan world. This suggestion of the virgin birth being not historical but a mythical motif added to the gospel tale would explain its absence from Mark (or "Ur-Markus"), widely considered to be the earliest of the gospels.

The divine-birth motif in the myths, traditions and legends of Pagan cultures was addressed by Catholic Church doctor and saint Jerome in his defense of the Christian virgin birth against the "heretic" Jovinianus (393 AD/CE):

> To come to the Gymnosophists of India, the opinion is authoritatively handed down that *Budda, the founder of their religion, had his birth through the side of a virgin*. And we need not wonder at this in the case of Barbarians when cultured Greece supposed that Minerva [Athena] at her birth sprang from the head of Jove [Zeus], and Father Bacchus [Dionysus] from his thigh. Speusippus also, Plato's nephew, and Clearchus in his eulogy of Plato, and Anaxelides in the second book of his philosophy, relates that Perictione, the mother of Plato, was violated by an apparition of Apollo, and they agree in thinking that *the prince of wisdom [Plato] was born of a virgin*…. And mighty Rome cannot taunt us as though we had invented the story of the birth of our Lord and Saviour from a virgin; for the Romans believe that the founders of their city and race were the offspring of the virgin Ilia and of Mars.

> Let these allusions to the virgins of the world, brief and hastily gathered from many histories, now suffice…[1]

Although Jerome wrote in the fourth century, a number of these virgin-birth legends and myths from "*many histories*"—the word "history" indicating a passage of time— such as those concerning Plato and the Roman founders Romulus and Remus, preceded the common era by centuries. Moreover, in asserting the story of the Indian savior Buddha's virgin birth as "authoritatively handed down,"

---

[1] Jerome, *AJ*, I, 42-43. (Emph. added.) In his *Stromata* (I, 15), Church father Clement of Alexandria (202 AD/CE) discussed "Boutta" as being worshipped by the Indians as divine, demonstrating a relatively early awareness of Buddhism in the Roman Empire and within the Christian church.

Jerome is apparently attributing some degree of antiquity to this mythical motif as well. Hence, it is reasonable and logical to suggest that, rather than representing implausible "history," the inclusion of the virgin birth—which by the evidence was an afterthought to the gospel story—serves as a move to compete with the divine births of these many other gods and heroes in the Roman Empire and beyond. Could these and other such "histories" be those of the Jewish, Greek and Roman writers that Christian apologist Dr. J.P. Moreland declared as influencing the evangelists?

Regarding the Christian virgin birth, in *Who Is Jesus?* Dr. Crossan remarks:

> The stories of Jesus' birth are religious fiction, or parable, if you prefer....[1]

Dr. Crossan further discusses the divine-birth motif found in the Roman world, in the story of Caesar Augustus (63 BCE-14 AD/CE), who was said to have been the son of the Greek sun god Apollo:

> ...On the night of his conception, Augustus' mother, Atia, fell asleep in the Temple of Apollo and was impregnated by the god in the form of a snake. Meanwhile, back at home, Augustus' father, Octavius, dreamt that the sun was arising from his wife's womb. Augustus, in other words, was conceived of a divine father and a human mother. And if you think that such stories had no political or social implications but were just imperial propaganda, look at this ancient decree of calendar change in the Roman province of Asia. It is found on marble stelae in all the Asian temples dedicated to Rome and Augustus.
>
> > *Whereas Providence...has...adorned our lives with the highest good: Augustus...and has in her beneficence granted us and those who will come after us [a Savior] who has made war to cease and who shall put everything in [peaceful] order...with the result that the birthday of our God signalled the*

---

[1] Crossan and Watts, *WIJ*, 10.

*beginning of Good News for the world because
of him... therefore...*

and it goes on to decree that the new year shall begin
for all the Asian cities on the birthday of Caesar
Augustus.[1]

As we can see, in the story of "our God" Augustus we
possess an undeniably pre-Christian divine-birth story that
was taken quite seriously. In this pre-Christian inscription,
we also have a widespread declaration of a "*Savior*" who
brought "*Good News*" to the world. Moreover, as Crossan
remarks, the Christian birth stories constitute "religious
fiction."

Even if it could be demonstrated that Jesus really existed
and was born at some point, there is no consensus as to
when that birth took place, as the day, month and year are
not identified. It is well known that Christ's December 25th
birthday is based not on an actual date of birth but on the
traditional winter-solstice nativity of the sun god(s). Even
the year as put forth in the gospels is undecided, as
scholarship determines that, per Matthew's gospel, the year
would be 4 BCE, whereas Luke appears to place Christ's birth
in the year 6 AD/CE. The fact that Jesus Christ was *not* born
on December 25th in the year 1 AD may not be widely
understood but should be made known, as this erroneous
date is proselytized around the globe.

Salvation is from the Jews?

Another instance of translation based on a political move
occurs in a Syriac rendition of Matthew 1:21, which typically
states that Christ will save "his people"—meaning Jews—
from their sins but which is changed in the Syriac to read
that Jesus will save "the world" from its sins.[2] The same
change happens at John 4:22, where it is literally asserted
that "salvation is from the Jews." Regarding this passage,
Ehrman relates that some Syriac and Latin editions render
the original Greek as "Judea," rather than "the Jews." Hence,
salvation emanates out of the land of Judea but not
necessarily out of the Jewish people, who were not the

---

[1] Crossan & Walls, *WIJ*, 19-20.
[2] Ehrman, *MJ*, 194.

target audience of these translations. On the contrary, it was likely that in such locations they were not particularly well liked enough to be considered the bringers of salvation or exclusively God/Jesus's people. Moreover, it is obvious that, as Christianity began to be spread among the Gentiles, the focus of Christ's mission was changed to encompass the world as a whole.

Son of Joseph?

One more political alteration between various ancient copies occurs at Luke 2:33, in the pericope of the proclamations by the righteous Simeon about Jesus's messiahhood. At some point the phrase "his father and his mother" (as it is rendered in the RSV) was changed to "Joseph and his mother" (KJV). It is clear that the phrase "his father" was offensive to those who believed Christ to have been the virgin-born Son of God; hence, Joseph could not have been his father. The same difference between manuscripts occurs at Luke 2:43, with some texts saying "his parents" (RSV) and others "Joseph and his mother" (KJV).

Massacre or Myth?

Furthermore, the Herodian massacre of the infants has never been demonstrated to be historical. The fact that this strange but pivotal episode receives mention *only* in Matthew is revealing, in that the author of Mark—again, commonly believed to have been the first of the canonical gospels—did not see fit to include this auspicious beginning. Nor did John mention the massacre, even though, in his quest to depict Christ as a divine being and the incarnate Word of God, he surely would have played up such an episode, had he known about it. Although Luke's gospel is the longest, he too seems oblivious to this horrid crime that finds no place in history. In reality, this grisly theme appears to have been included in order to compete with the stories of other gods and heroes circulating at the time, including other "saviors" such as Moses and the Indian god Krishna, who was pursued by the tyrant King Kamsa.[1] Hence, rather than representing history, the New Testament massacre of infants was evidently taken from pre-Christian myth.

Son of God?

Yet one more scribal modification that would appear to be blasphemy but that reflects a power play and casts doubt upon the historicity of the episode occurs with the disparate versions of Luke 3:22, in which God's voice pronounces Christ his beloved Son. The majority of ancient manuscripts and modern translations end this verse as "with thee I am well pleased." However, the earliest version, as verified by its appearance in the works of many Church fathers, was likely "today I have begotten thee," based on the supposed prophecy at Psalms 2:7: "You are my son, today I have begotten you." The evangelist was thus evidently aware that this quote came not from God's voice but from the OT psalm. In reality, this scripture in Psalms does *not* represent prophecy at all but applies to King David, the purported author of that book. This phrase may have been replaced by the other ending in order to remove the impression held by certain Christian sects that Jesus was not God's Son from birth. This doctrine is called "adoptionism," which contends that Christ was born human and became divine later.[2] It would be difficult otherwise to explain such a change, in consideration of the fact that the original (Ps 2:7) was a scriptural "messianic prophecy" that clearly was used as a blueprint for the verse at Luke 3:22.

In the same manner, it is asserted that in early manuscripts the phrase "Son of God" at John 1:34 and Mark

---

[1] According to the Indian sacred text the Vishnu Purana, at the birth of Krishna, King Kamsa remarked, "Let therefore active search be made for whatever young children there may be upon earth, and let every boy in whom there are signs of unusual vigour be slain without remorse." (Wilson, *Vishnu Purana*, V, 4) Extant Indian texts are late; however, the tradition of Kamsa's massacre is considered to be at least 2,300 years old, with a relevant depiction on the walls of a temple-cave on the Indian island of Elephanta evidently dating to three centuries prior to the Christian era. That elements of the Krishna tale were known to the West centuries before the Christian era is attested in the writings of the Greek geographer Megasthenes (c. 350 c. 290 BCE).

[2] See, e.g., Ehrman, *MJ*, 159.

1:1 is missing. Hence, this designation—and *characteristic* of Jesus, it could be argued—constitutes a later addition to the gospel story. Naturally, many other heroes and gods, such as Hercules, Dionysus and other "sons of Jove," were called "Son of God," which would, of course, give a political reason for Christ to be crowned with the title: competing with Pagan religions.

Demonstrating another alteration made in the story in order to improve upon Christ's character, in the passage at Mark 1:41 conveying the pericope of Jesus healing a leper, one of the oldest manuscripts, the Codex Bezae, portrays Jesus not as "moved with compassion" but as *becoming angry*. Going against the trend of attempting to get back to the originals, most translations choose to use the former phrase from later Greek manuscripts so as to depict Christ in a softer light. Even so, at verse 1:43, Mark has Jesus wagging his finger at the healed leper and driving him away, making the savior appear harsh in his treatment of a suffering person.

Another discrepancy between the gospel accounts themselves that may be the result of "politics" or sectarian doctrinal differences occurs in the pericope of the hemorrhagic woman healed after touching the hem of Christ's garment. In Mark (5:24-34), the woman is depicted as coming up behind Jesus and touching his cloak, instantly being healed. In Matthew (9:22), however, the woman is not cured until Jesus turns around and tells her that *it is her faith in him that has healed her*, rather than simply grabbing his cloak. In this manner the Christian doctrine could be strengthened which claims *it is faith in Jesus that heals*, not his physical presence or any artifacts or relics of his, such that, long after he was gone from Earth, people could continue to be cured miraculously by him, as the living Christ—and such that, priesthoods intent on healing through Jesus would not need any (bogus) relics of Jesus's.

One more instance of interpolation based on political reasons may be evident at Matthew 10:23 and Luke 9:1, which concern Christ's "Second Coming"—or *parousia* (Strong's G3952), the term used in several places in the gospels, as at Matthew 24:3, etc.[1] In specific, Dr. Meier deems the "prophecy" of Jesus's coming at Matthew 10:23 to be "artificial" and "composite."[2] In other words, rather than representing a verbatim quote from Jesus's mouth, this passage is evidently strung together from other quotes, such as are found in the Old Testament and assorted pre-Christian texts.

Another glaring example stands out at Mark 3:32, where the crowd is telling Jesus that his mother and brothers are outside. Some ancient authorities include "and your sisters" after "brothers." Which is it? It is a shock enough to discover that Jesus had brothers—as we have seen, a whole debate in itself—but *sisters* as well? Why would the Holy Spirit have some authorities reveal that Christ had sisters, while causing other authorities not to mention them? It would seem that the omission of the "sisters of the Lord" may exist specifically to emphasize a bias against women, a prejudice present in other parts of the Bible as well and quite common throughout much of history.

In a related subject, the teachings on divorce (Mt 19; Mk 10) also changed from manuscript to manuscript over the years, with the details of adultery, for example, clarified and re-clarified to fit the era and sentiments of the ruling party of the time.[3]

The Resurrection of Lazarus?

The raising of Lazarus at John 11:1-44 presents us with another interesting conundrum that likely reflects not history but propaganda—and that represents another of the clearest fingerprints of the Christ. As discussed, this pericope appears *only* in John's gospel, leaving one to wonder why the others would omit such a stunning display of Christ's divinity. It is possible that the reason Lazarus's resurrection

---

[1] The only gospel in which this term *parousia* can be found is Matthew, in four verses in the 24th chapter. *Parousia* does not appear again in the New Testament until Paul's First Epistle to the Corinthians, after which point the concept is developed in 19 other verses within the rest of the NT. In none of these instances is the word translated as the "*Second* Coming" but merely "the coming"; nor does the word always apply to Christ. (1 Cor 16:17; 2 Cor 7:6, etc.)

[2] Meier, II, 341.

[3] See, e.g., Carr.

was not included in the synoptics is because, as suggested earlier, it constitutes not a historical episode but a retelling of an ancient mythological theme found in other cultures.

Regarding the important subject of correspondences between the non-Christian and Christian religions, such as the divine births elucidated by Jerome, New Testament scholar, minister and contributor to the Revised Standard Version of the Bible, Dr. Bruce M. Metzger, remarks:

> That there *are* parallels between the Mysteries and Christianity has been observed since the early centuries of the Church, when both Christian and non-Christian alike commented upon certain similarities.[1]

As a confessing Christian, however, Dr. Metzger proceeds to clarify, reduce and dismiss a number of these purported parallels, in an effort that, while reflective of immense and impressive erudition, does not satisfactorily incorporate the fact of numerous previous instances of "borrowing" within both pre-Christian Judaism and so-called Paganism. When it comes to Christianity, there seems to be some difficulty in mainstream scholarship to accept into its analysis the basic human nature of absorbing from others interesting and significant ideas that may be beneficial to the individual or group in question. That such borrowing and absorption did occur widely remains a fact that must be included into any honest and scientific discussion of the origin of religion in general and Christianity in specific.

In his dismissal and clarification of the correspondences between these religions, Metzger adds, "Even when parallels are genealogical, it must not be uncritically assumed that the Mysteries always influenced Christianity, for it is not only possible but probable that in certain cases the influence moved in the opposite direction."[2] By "genealogical," Metzger evidently means following a linear progression of one parallel begetting another. Although he then claims that Christianity may have influenced Paganism, because the Pagan priesthood was attempting to keep its flock from fleeing to a more desirable Christian faith, the word "always" in Metzger's commentary implies that there *are* influences of

---

[1] Metzger, *HLS*, 8.
[2] Metzger, *HLS*, 11.

the Pagan mysteries upon Christianity, as does the clarification "certain cases." Moreover, on p. 18 of his apology, Metzger further attempts to delineate the differences between Paganism and Christianity:

> ...The motif of a dying and rising savior-god has been frequently supposed to be related to the account of the saving efficacy of the death and resurrection of Jesus Christ. The formal resemblance between the two, however, must not be allowed to obscure the great differences in content.
>
> ...In all the Mysteries which tell of a dying deity, the god dies by compulsion and not by choice, sometimes in bitterness and despair, never in a self-giving love. But according to the New Testament, God's purpose of redeeming-love was the free divine motive for the death of Jesus, who accepted with equal freedom that motive as his own.

In the first place, unlike many apologists, here at least Metzger does not deny the motif of the dying-and-rising savior-god that has been contended to have existed within Pagan religion long prior to the Christian era. Metzger even goes so far as to declare the parallel a "formal resemblance," although splitting hairs in order to create distance between the two. Secondly, Metzger disingenuously depicts the non-Christian dying gods unfavorably, while ignoring the wretched state of Jesus upon his own pending agony and death: For example, in the Garden of Gethsemane Jesus *begs* his Father *not* to *compel* him to undergo the coming torment! Quoting Metzger's own RSV:

> Then he said to them, "My soul is very sorrowful, even to death; remain here, and watch with me." And going a little farther he fell on his face and prayed, "My Father, if it be possible, let this cup pass from me; nevertheless, not as I will, but as thou wilt."... Again, for the second time, he went away and prayed, "My Father, if this cannot pass unless I drink it, thy will be done."... So, leaving them again, he went away and prayed for the third time, saying the same words. (Mt 26:38-44)

It is obvious that Jesus went very reluctantly to the cross, dramatically if not hysterically "falling on his face," and agitatedly asking God *three times* not to do this thing to him. Like other apologists, Metzger attempts to differentiate between the tales of non-Christian dying-and-rising gods and that of Jesus by saying that these gods' passions were caused by others, while Jesus's was not. However, the fact remains that Jesus's death was likewise caused by others, including not only Jews and Romans but also God the Father, as is obvious from this episode in Gethsemane.

Furthermore, while on the cross, the pitiful Christ is made to cry out, "Eli, eli, lama sabachthani!" (Mt 27:46) This *bitter* and *desperate* wail has universally been translated into English as, "My God! My God, why have you forsaken me?!" Therefore, what exactly are the meaningful differences between the deaths and resurrections of the pre-Christian gods and that of Jesus?

Indeed, when Christ is resurrected, he cautions Mary Magdalene not to touch him, because he has not yet "ascended to the Father" (Jn 20:17). Is not Jesus implying that God has not yet entirely acted upon him? Did not the all-powerful *God* resurrect his own Son? Wasn't this resurrection *by God* one of the major points of Jesus's advent? Moreover, at the end of the gospel of John, Jesus makes a long, drawn-out speech using the word "Father" 10 times over the span of 23 verses. In using the word "Father" 134 times in 111 verses overall in his gospel, it seems to be one of John's purposes to emphasize the Fatherhood aspect of God—*and* the Father's reigning role in Christ's life.[1] Also, if Christ specifically asks Mary not to touch him because he has not ascended yet to the Father, why does he later allow

---

[1] In comparison, Matthew uses the word "father" 61 times across 55 verses in all; Mark 19 times in 18 verses; and Luke 48 times in 40 verses overall. Several of the instances of "father" in the synoptics concern not God but other males. John's gospel repeatedly discusses *the* "Father," as in God, specifically with this meaning 122 times, or 92 percent of the time that he uses the word "father." By contrast, Matthew's use of "Father" with this meaning occurs only 73 percent of the time, while Luke intends "Father" 44 percent of the time. Mark's gospel uses the godly meaning of "Father" only 27 percent of the time, the other 73 percent in regard to earthly fathers. It is obvious from these facts that the Fatherhood of God was increasingly developed or emphasized as time passed.

Doubting Thomas to handle him, *before* he has ascended to the Father? (Jn 20:27) This story seems bizarre, illogical and artificial.

As another example of a Jewish writer who evidently influenced Christianity—as one of those, perhaps, whom Dr. Moreland cites—there appears in the works of the Hellenized Jewish philosopher and historian Philo of Alexandria (20 BCE-50 AD/CE) a "trial of a mock-king," or *passion*, which oddly resembles that of Christ. Philo lived at the precise time and wrote about the same area as that of Christ's alleged advent but made no mention of the "Word made flesh" or his followers, even though Philo was well known for his Judeo-Hellenistic development of the *Logos* concept. If we factor in the many other evidences, it seems that the gospel passion was based significantly on the passion account found in Philo as concerns a man named "Karabbas," who was dressed up in a mock crown and purple robe, given a fake "scepter," and paraded about in the same manner as Christ.[1] Regarding the Jewish philosopher and the New Testament, Friedlander remarks, "Philo has been a valuable mine whence the writers of the New Testament have drawn some of their best treasures."[2] He then names several of them, including the famed concept of the Logos, which, again, Philo developed intricately long before it showed up within Christianity.

In reality, the correspondences between Jesus and the gods of the religions of the Roman Empire at the time rank as well known enough within the scholarly world that the believing Christian Tenney observed:

> The cult of Cybele, the Great Mother, came from Asia; that of Isis and Osiris or Serapis, from Egypt; Mithraism originated in Persia. While all of them

---

[1] Philo, *Flaccus*, 36-40. It has been widely hypothesized that the name "Karabbas" originally was "Barabbas," or "Son of the Father," a term used to describe the violent prisoner released by the mob at Jesus's trial. In Hebrew, the letter "K" or *kaph* is almost identical with the "B" or *beth*, and it would be an easy substitution of "Karabbas" for "Barabbas." It has further been theorized that Jesus and Barabbas are the same entity, as in some ancient copies of Matthew the criminal is called "Jesus Barabbas"—*Jesus, Son of the Father*. Interestingly, purple robes were also worn by the *sun god* Helios, who was likewise depicted with "dazzling beams that crowned his head." (Ovid, *Metamorphoses*, II)
[2] Friedlander, xl.

differed from each other in origin and detail, all were alike in certain broad characteristics. *Each was centered about a god who had died and who was resuscitated.* Each had a ritual of formulas and lustrations, of symbol and of secret dramatic representations of the experience of the god, by which the initiate was inducted into that experience, and so presumably rendered a candidate for immortality.[1]

Both Metzger and Tenney's conclusion that there do in fact exist significant parallels between Christ and other gods is well founded, because, as Metzger remarked, from the earliest centuries both non-Christian and Christian alike commented on these correspondences.

As one extremely important example of an early Christian comparison of Jesus with other gods, in his defense of the "new superstition" of Christianity, Church father Justin Martyr (c. 150 AD/CE) felt compelled to provide analogies to Christ's story from previous non-Christian mythology and legend, remarking:

And when we say also that the Word, who is the first-birth of God, was produced without sexual union, and that He, Jesus Christ, our Teacher, was crucified and died, and rose again, and ascended into heaven, *we propound nothing different from what you believe regarding those whom you esteem sons of Jupiter.* For you know how many sons your esteemed writers ascribed to Jupiter: Mercury, the interpreting word and teacher of all; Æsculapius, who, though he was a great physician, was struck by a thunderbolt, and so *ascended to heaven*; and Bacchus too, after he had been torn limb from limb; and Hercules, when he had committed himself to the flames to escape his toils; and the sons of Leda, and Dioscuri; and Perseus, son of Danae; and Bellerophon, who, though sprung from mortals, *rose to heaven* on the horse Pegasus. For what shall I say of Ariadne, and those who, like her, have been declared to be set among the stars? And what of the emperors who die among yourselves,

---

[1] Tenney, 68. (Emph. added.)

whom you deem worthy of deification, and in whose behalf you produce some one who swears he has seen the burning Cæsar *rise to heaven* from the funeral pyre?[1]

Thus, Martyr's apology contains the utterly astonishing admission by an early Church father that there existed in the stories of other gods the themes of the virgin birth, the crucifixion, the death and resurrection, and the ascension.[2] The divine subjects of the commentaries by Martyr and other early Church fathers, in fact, could be viewed as the "DNA of the Christ." Again, Martyr is undoubtedly one of those Christian sources raised by Dr. Metzger in his concurrence that there *are* parallels between the story of Jesus Christ and pre-Christian tales.

Even though in his apology comparing Jesus to other characters of pre-Christian myth and legend Justin Martyr does not specifically mention any *Egyptian* gods, the Christian father *does* discuss the "Greek" god Bacchus or Dionysus, who, like the Egyptian god Osiris, was torn to pieces but who is also immortal and eternal, which essentially means that he too rose from the dead, as Martyr appears to be confirming. Although perceived as a *Greek* god, Dionysus possessed a long association with Egypt, in particular with the highly popular Osiris.

In his *Exhortation to the Heathen* (IV), Church father Clement of Alexandria (died c. 215) shows a familiarity—although contemptuously, as is typical of the early Christian apologists towards other religions—with the myth of Osiris, as well as the Greco-Egyptian god Serapis, a hybrid of Osiris and the Egyptian god Apis, which, per Clement, "together make Osirapis." Serapis himself was associated with the Greek god Asclepius,[3] who, as can be seen from Justin's

---

[1] Martyr, *The First Apology*, XXI. (Emph. added.)

[2] It should be noted that, based on valid scientific examination, it becomes evident that Justin Martyr's writings emerge in the historical and literary record *before* the canonical gospels. Although he does discuss what appears to be a *single* text called "Memoirs of the Apostles" (like the single, canonical book "Acts of the Apostles"), Justin never mentions *any* of the canonical gospels, and purported "allusions" to the gospels found in Martyr's work can be explained otherwise upon close inspection. See *Suns of God* for an in-depth discussion of Justin Martyr.

[3] Murphy-O'Connor, 31.

remarks, was also killed and raised to heaven. The god Serapis/Asclepius is important for a couple of reasons: 1. The Emperor Hadrian is quoted as saying that the Christians of his time worshipped *Serapis*;[1] and 2. There was a Serapis/Asclepius sanctuary built at Jerusalem during Hadrian's reign, c. 135 AD/CE, prior to the clear emergence of the canonical gospels in the literary record.

Depicted as a man wearing white robes and sporting long, dark hair and a beard, the healing god Asclepius was called "Soter"—*Savior*—centuries before the Christian era, as were other pre-Christian gods, including the father god Zeus/Jove and various other "sons of Jove."[2] Oddly enough, John's gospel (5:1-13) depicts Jesus as curing a man at the "Pool of Bethesda," the precise location of "the miraculous medicinal baths where clients of the god Serapis (Asclepius) gathered in hope of healing."[3] Interestingly, John (5:2) describes the pool as having "five porticoes," and the only building at the site with five porches apparently was the sanctuary of Serapis/Aesclepius, built in honor of the healing god's five daughters. According to Dr. James Charlesworth, no one besides John had mentioned this large structure with five porches at Jerusalem:

> ...in John 5:2 the author describes a monumental pool with "five porticoes" inside the Sheep Gate of Jerusalem where the sick came to be healed: the pool, we are told, is called Bethesda. No other ancient writer—no author or editor of the Old Testament, the Pseudepigrapha, not even Josephus—mentions such a significant pool in Jerusalem. Moreover, no known

---

[1] Regarding the Hadrian quote, Dr. Metzger relates: "Cf. the following statement in a letter which Flavius Vopiscus attributes to Hadrian: 'The land of Egypt... I have found to be wholly light-minded, unstable, and blown about by every breath of rumour. There those who worship Serapis are, in fact, Christians, and those who call themselves bishops of Christ are, in fact, devotees of Serapis... Even the patriarch himself, when he comes to Egypt, is forced by some to worship Serapis, by others to worship Christ.'..." (*HJS*, 4fn) Metzger declares the letter an "obvious forgery," but the grounds upon which this assertion is made are unclear and may be based on the *a priori* assumption that the gospel story and mainstream church history are true. Upon inspection, however, the opposite claim could also be made that the Hadrian quote is genuine in whole or in significant part.
[2] MacMullen, 48, 84, 167.
[3] Murphy-O'Connor, 28.

ancient building was a pentagon, which was apparently
what John was describing with five porticoes. It
seemed that the author of John could not have been
a Jew who knew Jerusalem. Archaeologists, however,
decided to dig precisely where the author of John
claimed a pool was set aside for healing. Their
excavations revealed an ancient pool with porticoes
(open areas with large columns) and with shrines
dedicated to the Greek god of healing, Asclepius...
The author of John knew more about Jerusalem than
we thought.[1]

John may have known more about Jerusalem than
previously thought—too much, in reality, for Christian
apologetics to handle, even though this fact of John's
accuracy would certainly bolster the case that the gospels
represent "reliable history." The problem is, of course, that
the evidence suggests the evangelist was anachronistically
describing a *post-Hadrianic Jerusalem*, sometime after 135
CE, when this pentagonal building was purportedly constructed!
In other words, John's gospel must have been written
sometime after 135 CE.

Since the Pool of Bethesda episode is not found in the
synoptic gospels, and since the emergence of John cannot be
scientifically dated to earlier than the last quarter of the
second century, it is possible, if not probable, that this pool
pericope was included not because it is "historical" but in
order to appropriate the followers of Serapis at Jerusalem.
Hence, we have a strong gospel connection to the sanctuary
of a god, Serapis-Asclepius, who was asserted by Justin to
have died and resurrected.

In reality, *any* god who was "killed" yet maintained
immortality/ascended to heaven could be said to have been
"resurrected." The applicable definition of the word
"resurrection" means, "The act of rising from the dead or
returning to life."[2] "Resurrection" is not a strictly *Christian*
term; nor does it apply in some peculiar way *only* to Jesus.
As we see from Justin Martyr, the idea of a god dying and
rising is abundant enough within pre-Christian religion and

[1] Charlesworth, "Reinterpreting John," *Bible Review*, 2/93.
[2] *American Heritage Dictionary*, Houghton Mifflin, 2006.

mythology—these aspects of Pagan religion, in fact, represent part of what are called "the mysteries," as discussed by Dr. Metzger and Dr. Tenney.

Moreover, even the Old Testament contains a hint of the important dying-and-rising-god mystery, in the scripture at Ezekiel 8:14 concerning the Jewish women's mourning for the Sumero-Syro-Babylonian god Tammuz:

> Then he brought me to the entrance of the north gate of the house of the LORD; and behold, there sat women weeping for Tammuz.

The word "Tammuz" is defined by Strong's (H8542) as "sprout of life" and as referring to "a Sumerian deity of food or vegetation." From these facts of the "sprout of life" being mourned for his death, it is clear that Tammuz represents a very old dying-and-rising god in the precise area where the gospel tale supposedly took place centuries later. Regarding this scripture about the mourning for Tammuz, conservative Christian authority Matthew Henry remarks:

> An abominable thing indeed, that any should choose rather to serve an idol in tears than to serve the true God with joyfulness and gladness of heart! Yet such absurdities as these are those guilty of who follow after lying vanities and forsake their own mercies. Some think it was for Adonis, an idol among the Greeks, others for Osiris, an idol of the Egyptians, that they shed these tears. The image, they say, was made to weep, and then the worshippers wept with it. *They bewailed the death of this Tammuz, and anon rejoiced in its returning to life again.*[1]

Thus, the resurrecting god Tammuz was evidently associated with the Egyptian god Osiris, whose ancient presence in Israel, in fact, has been indicated by certain intriguing archaeological discoveries, such as a stele from Hazor with the name of Osiris on it and an apparent Egyptian temple at Jerusalem.[2]

Concerning the Tammuz verse in Ezekiel, Christian commentators Jamieson, Fausset and Brown also state:

---

[1] *BLB*, "Commentary on Ezekiel 8." (Emph. added.)
[2] Acharya/Murdock, *SOG*, 88.

Tammuz (the Syrian for Adonis), the paramour of Venus, and of the same name as the river flowing from Lebanon; killed by a wild boar, and, according to the fable, permitted to spend half the year on earth, and obliged to spend the other half in the lower world. An annual feast was celebrated to him in June (hence called Tammuz in the Jewish calendar) at Byblos, when the Syrian women, in wild grief, tore off their hair and yielded their persons to prostitution, consecrating the hire of their infamy to Venus; next followed days of rejoicing for his return to the earth; the former feast being called "the disappearance of Adonis," the latter, "the finding of Adonis." This Phoenician feast answered to the similar Egyptian one in honor of Osiris.[1]

It is clear from these facts as well that the concept of a dying-and-rising god was prominent in the ancient religions, including and especially in the myth of Osiris. In reality, within the Egyptian religion existed the long-held belief in the immortality of the soul and the resurrection of the dead, as evidenced not only in very ancient pre-Christian texts such as the Egyptian Book of the Dead (c. 1580–1350 BCE) but also in the practice of mummification. Indeed, the numerous mummies found all over Egypt clearly indicate an obsession with the *physical* resurrection of the dead, long pre-dating the Christian era. Upon close scrutiny, it seems that, rather than representing an implausible "historical" event, the biblical resurrection of Lazarus—in his wrappings, similar to a *mummy* (Jn 11:44)— may likewise constitute a motif from the *Egyptian* religion.

The Greek name "Lazarus" or "Lazaros" equals "Eleazar" in Hebrew and, per Strong's (G2976), means "whom God helps." It is a strange coincidence firstly that the person whom Jesus resurrects happens to be named "whom God helps," and secondly that "Eleazar"—or, breaking down its original components in Hebrew, *El-Azar*—closely resembles a combination of the Semitic word for God, "El," with the Egyptian name for Osiris, "Ausar." Interestingly, there exists an ancient Phoenician inscription called "the Carpentras" that does indeed identify Osiris with the Semitic god "El" or "Elohim," calling him "Osiris-Eloh."[2]

---

[1] *BLB*, "The Book of the Prophet Ezekiel."
[2] Heath, 92. Cf. Genesis 3:21, et al.

Deemed "*the god of the resurrection,*" Osiris himself was resurrected, as is evident from the myth in which he is torn to pieces, put together, and comes alive again, to attain to everlasting life. The association of Osiris with the resurrection is so abundant in ancient Egyptian texts it would be impossible to list all the references here.[1] As famed Christian Egyptologist E.A. Wallis Budge remarks:

> The story of Osiris is nowhere found in a connected form in Egyptian literature, but everywhere, and in texts of all periods, the life, sufferings, death and resurrection of Osiris are accepted as facts universally admitted.[2]

If the abundance of texts proves the factuality of a story, as is claimed within Christian apologetics regarding the New Testament manuscripts, Osiris would need to be recognized as what he is claimed to be in numerous very ancient Egyptian texts: The everlasting Lord of the Resurrection![3] This "argument of abundance," however, constitutes a logical fallacy and in reality does not prove historicity, as might be obvious from the immense popularity of *fiction* books today printed by the millions globally.

Nevertheless, in assessing this situation, we must rationally and logically ask whether or not the nascent Christianity could truly have made *any* inroads into Egypt, where this deeply revered god Osiris had been worshipped for thousands of years, without incorporating major tenets from the Egyptian religion into its own doctrines. Indeed, it would seem the height of naivete and a lack of education to insist otherwise.

In consideration of the facts that the gospel of John appears to contain blatantly Egyptian elements, that it was one of the earliest texts used by the Egyptian Christian congregation, and that the earliest extant fragment of a copy of it was discovered in Egypt, it is not unreasonable to suggest that, in addition to looking for the emergence of this gospel in the wrong century, its provenance is likewise sought in the wrong *country*. Could the Gospel of St. John in actuality have been composed at Alexandria in Egypt for an

---

[1] See, e.g., "The Egyptian Book of the Dead" and "The Pyramid Texts." See also *The Christ Conspiracy* and *Suns of God* for more on Osiris.
[2] Budge, *The Egyptian Book of the Dead*, xlix.
[3] Renouf, 30, 118.

Egyptian audience familiar with, or followers of, Egyptian religion?[1]

As we have seen previously in the instances of the water-to-wine miracle and the virgin-birth motif, this type of political maneuver within religion is well known and well practiced. Indeed, an in-depth analysis as found here reveals indications that *Christianity as a whole was created for political reasons*: Firstly, in order to usurp the gods of other cultures with a Jewish messiah; and secondly, to unify the Roman Empire under one state religion combining Judaism and Paganism.

In addition to these intriguing connections to ancient gods, the concept of the resurrection itself within Christianity has been altered and clarified in a variety of manners in order to satisfy evident political needs. Regarding the many doctrinal meanings of the resurrection, the Interpreter's Dictionary remarks, "This diversity of view is due to the fact that the doctrine was evolved in different philosophies to resolve different problems."[2] In other words, the variances in the resurrection doctrines are a result of sectarian interpretations that frequently contradicted each other and needed to be smoothed over.

The Naked Youth

Within our analysis of various elements of the NT that seem to serve as propaganda, there do emerge a couple of homey touches in the gospels that seemingly attach some historicity to the story. One such earthy example occurs in a pericope found *only* in Mark (14:51-52), regarding the "young man" in the garden of Gethsemane who followed Jesus as the latter was being arrested, and who was wearing nothing but a "linen cloth" that came off him as he was seized, thus causing him to run away naked. The commentary over the centuries on this strange episode centers on whether or not the naked young man was in fact *Mark*

---

[1] In his *Refutation of All Heresies* (X, 17), Church father Hippolytus (died c. 236) wrote that the Gnostic heretic Cerinthus learned his tenets from the Egyptians, an interesting assertion in light of the facts that John has strong Egyptian connections, and that Jerome and Irenaeus both claimed John was written in response to Cerinthus.
[2] *IDT*, 39.

himself, the assumed author of the gospel, who was trying to show that he was at the scene, but it was so disturbing even he had fled. In attempting to paint him in a better light, it has further been presumed that this young man "fled" in order to tell others what was happening. For various reasons, including Church father Papias's explicit statement that Mark was *not* one of the disciples who saw the Lord at any point, it cannot be argued for certain that this character *is* Mark.

This peculiar passage has led to much other speculation, rightfully asking why the youth was only wearing a flimsy linen cloth and was *naked* underneath, and why it was such an important issue to mention this naked boy running away. Biblical commentator Matthew Henry was adamant that this naked boy was "no disciple of Christ," i.e., Mark or any other, speculating instead that he was an adherent of a certain ascetic Jewish sect whose members went about wearing only a thin linen cloth in order to display their piety and mortification of the body. The pericope may have been included for political reasons to cast this particular sect in a bad light, as being cowardly.

In *The Pre-Nicene New Testament*, Dr. Robert Price evinces that the passage is borrowed from Amos 2:16: "'…and he who is stout of heart among the mighty shall flee away naked in that day,' says the LORD."[1] In other words, upon inspection this "homey touch" may not in fact add anything "historical" to the tale, but may represent either propaganda or yet another Old Testament scripture used as a *blueprint* to create a *fictionalized* patchwork "biography."

The "Twelve"

In still another example of a possible "political" motive, some ancient manuscripts and modern translations of Luke 22:14, depicting Christ sitting at the table with the disciples, omit the word "twelve," as it is not found in the earliest manuscript. In consideration of its importance in the Old Testament and in pre-Christian symbolism, the establishment of 12 disciples or apostles may not have been historical but may have served as part of a doctrinal and ritualistic formula

---

[1] Price, 106.

added later. That there is symbolism in the Bible is admitted even by the most fervent apologists, such as Norman Geisler, who refers to the patent symbolism in the book of Revelation.[1] In addition, according to Geisler we may also engage in "spiritual interpretation" of difficult passages;[2] hence, our metaphorical and symbolic explorations are not unwarranted in our quest to discover who Jesus was.

Regarding the number 12, in *Antiquities of the Jews* (III, VIII, 7), Jewish historian Josephus discusses in *astrological terms* Moses's setting of the tabernacle table and the 12 stones of the high priest's breastplate that correspond to the 12 Tribes of Israel:

> And when [Moses] ordered twelve loaves to be set on the table, he denoted the year, as distinguished into so many months. By branching out the candlestick into seventy parts, he secretly intimated the *Decani*, or seventy divisions of the planets; and as to the seven lamps upon the candlesticks, they referred to the course of the planets, of which that is the number... And for the twelve stones, whether we understand by them the the months, or whether we understand the like number of the signs of that circle which the Greeks call the *Zodiac*, we shall not be mistaken in their meaning.[3]

Thus, not only is the number 12 significant in antiquity, but so too is 70 or 72, representing the "dodecans" of the zodiac as well as the number of Christ's direct disciples.

Confirming Josephus's contention, Church father Clement of Alexandria (*Stromata* VI) describes the Jewish breastplate in the same manner:

> The twelve stones, set in four rows on the breast, describe for us the circle of the zodiac, in the four changes of the year.

Within pre-Christian mythology, "the Twelve" represent *gods*, as described by Greek historian Herodotus (440 BCE)

---

[1] Geisler, *WCA*, 551.
[2] Geisler, *WCA*, 553.
[3] Whitson, 75.

concerning the Egyptian pantheon,[1] or in the famed myths regarding the 12 Olympian gods, such as Zeus, Apollo, Poseidon, et al. In view of the commonality and significance of "the Twelve" in pre-Christian religion, it is possible that the Christian Twelve constitute part of the same symbolic formula.

The Sacred Meal

Continuing with the discrepancies between texts, conspicuously absent from the RSV are a phrase and verse at Luke 22:19-20, which appears in the KJV the scriptures as:

"And he took bread, and gave thanks, and brake [it], and gave unto them, saying, This is my body which is given for you: this do in remembrance of me. Likewise also the cup after supper, saying, This cup [is] the new testament in my blood, which is shed for you."

The RSV omits the phrase and sentence from "which is given for you" onward to the end, through the cup and blood, "which is shed for you." In other words, this section about the Eucharist was appended to the gospel sometime later, possibly centuries afterward. The political reason for this interpolation could be that the communion became more of a central focus, doctrine and ritual of the Catholic Church in later decades or centuries. Moreover, Ehrman asserts that the phrase "for you" was interpolated to emphasize Christ's salvific role, stating that "the verses appear not to have been part of Luke's Gospel" but were added to demonstrate Jesus's humanity.[2] As previously noted, this sort of sacred meal was common in the pre-Christian world as well, which may be another reason for its emphasis within Christianity, such that it could compete with the rituals of other religions.

---

[1] Herodotus, *The History*, II, 43-44: "...But the Egyptian Hercules is one of their ancient gods. Seventeen thousand years before the reign of Amasis, the twelve gods were, they affirm, produced from the eight: and of these twelve, Hercules is one...."
[2] Ehrman, *MJ*, 166-167.

The Bloody Sweat

In another evident political move to counter "heretics" such as the Docetists—a Gnostic-Christian sect who claimed Jesus manifested *only* as a "phantom"—or for some other reason to show Christ's humanity, two verses in Luke about the Lord sweating "great drops of blood" (Lk 22:44) do not appear in several early authorities, including the Codices Alexandrinus and Vaticanus.[1] This verse clearly breaks the narrative, and is an obvious interpolation into the original text. The presence of this bloody sweat motif in the work of Justin Martyr (*Dialogue with Trypho*, CIII) has been used to suggest that Justin was aware of Luke's gospel. However, a scientific analysis of all the evidence suggests that any copying likely occurred in the opposite direction.

The Trial and Crucifixion

One more instance of scripture possibly altered for political purposes may be found in the pericope of the purported custom of releasing a prisoner during Passover, which has never been shown to be historically accurate. This fact of non-existence for this alleged custom may have been noticed in ancient times, as at Luke 23:16, some "ancient authorities," RSV notes, add the line, "Now he was obliged to release one man to them at the festival," after the pericope with Pilate, Jesus and Barabbas. Why would some authorities include this important sentence, while others omitted it? And why would the translators feel that it was best omitted? Is it because someone at some point noted that such a claim was *factually inaccurate*? Such factual inaccuracy would indicate: a. The Bible is *not* the inerrant Word of God; and b. The gospel story was not being reported as it allegedly happened, casting doubt on parts of it, at least, as ever having taken place. The reality is that the gospels are riddled with so many such inconsistencies, inaccuracies, fallacies and contradictions as to bring into question the alleged historicity of the entire story.

As another example of how the politics of the day may have influenced the gospel writers or subsequent scribes, at Matthew 27:24 the word "righteous" is omitted from the

---

[1] Ehrman, *MJ*, 139-140.

phrase "righteous one's blood," as found in "other authorities" describing what Pontius Pilate said while he was washing his hands of Jesus's death. This disparity between manuscripts serves as a reflection, perhaps, of the ambiguous nature of Pilate, as he was perceived by different sects. As Pilate is viewed as alternately bad and good within the canonical gospels, the same debate was going on between early sects, with some actually esteeming the Roman ruler. Depicting him as calling Jesus "righteous" would make Pilate seem more sympathetic and virtuous himself. The interpolation of the term "righteous" would therefore constitute a political move, not an actual, direct quotation. The same could be stated concerning many sayings and quotations in the New Testament, in fact.

Moreover, the events of the passion have been disputed over the centuries by Jewish scholars who have argued that the representation of the Jews and the Romans in the gospels is inaccurate and unhistorical, particularly as concerns Jesus's trial and the involvement of Jewish authorities. Regarding Christ's condemnation, the *Universal Jewish Encyclopedia* remarks:

> The Gospel statements that Pilate was hesitant to put Jesus to death and did so only because of the fear of the people are contradicted by the contemporary historians (Josephus and Philo), who agree in representing the Roman governor as a cruel, inconsiderate and inflexible ruler, who did not hesitate to launch his cohorts against an unarmed crowd or to mingle the blood of the Galileans with their sacrifices (*Luke* 13:1) and by the account in Tacitus, which plainly states (*Annals* 15:44) that Jesus was executed *by* Pontius Pilate.[1]

As we have seen, in addition to those altering Pilate's role were other passages added or changed either to emphasize or to reduce the Jewish role in the gospel story in general but in Christ's death in particular. Another such instance of stressing Jewish involvement in Jesus's death may be found at Matthew 27:26, where some scribes, including those who worked on the Codex Sinaiticus,

---

[1] *UJE*, 84-85.

interpolated the words "to them" after the verse in which Pilate is depicted as handing over Christ to be crucified.[1]

At Luke 23:34, the first sentence is omitted in some early manuscripts: "And Jesus said, 'Father, forgive them; for they know not what they do.'" It is possible this act of forgiveness was interpolated in order to highlight a doctrine of the still-forming church or to increase tolerance and acceptance of Jews, who may have been perceived as "Christ-killers." Ehrman argues that the forgiveness prayer may have been original to Luke, in which case its deletion may serve as a sign of resentment towards Jews and towards the act itself of forgiving them. In either case, we would possess another example of a quote being manipulated for political reasons, casting doubt on its historicity.

In addition, the gospel account of the crucifixion was apparently designed to incorporate not only Old Testament "messianic prophecies" but also Pagan mythology, as reflected by early Christian apologist Justin Martyr, who contended that, in declaring Christ to have been crucified, *Christians were propounding nothing more than was said of the Pagan gods*. In fact, early Church father Minucius Felix (c. 250 AD/CE) made similar comparisons—unfavorably, of course—between Christianity and pre-Christian religion, specifically as concerns the cross and the image of a *man on a cross*, or *crucifix*. Addressing the Romans in his apology *Octavius*, Felix remarked:

> You, indeed, who consecrate gods of wood, adore wooden crosses perhaps as parts of your gods. For your very standards, as well as your banners; and flags of your camp, what else are they but crosses gilded and adorned? Your victorious trophies not only imitate the appearance of a simple cross, but also that of a man affixed to it.[2]

This astounding admission from an early Christian apologist regarding Roman crosses with a man on them emerges in the literary record centuries before Christ was ever likewise depicted as hanging on a cross. Indeed, the representation of Christ on a cross did not appear in art until

---

[1] Ehrman, *MJ*, 194.
[2] Felix, *Octavius*, ch. 29.

the 6th century.[1] In other words, the Romans bore images of a man affixed to a cross at least three centuries before the Christians created crucifixes of Jesus!

Also centuries before Christ himself was ever represented in art as crucified, Church father Tertullian (c. 160 to 230?) too discussed an image of a *crucified Roman god*:

> The body of your god is first consecrated on the gibbet...[2]

Again in his *Apology* (16), Tertullian raises the subject of Roman gods in the *shape* of a cross or in *cruciform*:

> We have shown before that your deities are derived from shapes modelled from the cross. But you also worship victories, for in your trophies the cross is the heart of the trophy. The camp religion of the Romans is all through a worship of the standards, a setting the standards above all gods. Well, as those images decking out the standards are ornaments of crosses. All those hangings of your standards and banners are robes of crosses.[3]

Hence, Tertullian attested that the Romans bore images of not only a man but also *gods* on crosses, that they additionally possessed gods themselves in cruciform and that these images were objects of *worship*.

Furthermore, nowhere does Tertullian contend that the Romans with their crosses, crucifixes and gods in cruciform copied the Christians, which he surely would have impugned most vociferously, had it been true. The facts indicate the opposite: To wit, the image of a god in cruciform—or a *crucifix*—appears in non-Christian religion centuries before it does within Christianity.[4]

---

[1] *CE*, "Ecclesiastical Art."

[2] *Apology*, 12. American Heritage defines gibbet as: "An upright post with a crosspiece, forming a T-shaped structure from which executed criminals were formerly hung for public viewing."

[3] Tertullian, *Apology*, 16; tr. Rev. S. Thelwall

[4] The astonishing admissions of the early Christian apologists are so abundant that another volume could be devoted to these alone, unraveling the Christ myth in this manner. The fact will also remain that, like Metzger and Tenney, many Christian scholars have been aware of these striking similarities between Christ and other gods.

The Sun of Righteousness

In this same chapter 16 of his *Apology*, Tertullian also makes the stunning contention that *Christians were said to be worshipping the sun*! In denying this charge, Tertullian responds:

> Others, again, certainly with more information and greater verisimilitude, believe that the sun is our god. We shall be counted Persians perhaps, though we do not worship the orb of day painted on a piece of linen cloth, having himself everywhere in his own disk. The idea no doubt has originated from our being known to turn to the east in prayer. But you, many of you, also under pretence sometimes of worshipping the heavenly bodies, move your lips in the direction of the sunrise. In the same way, if we devote Sun-day to rejoicing, from a far different reason than Sun-worship, we have some resemblance to those of you who devote the day of Saturn to ease and luxury, though they too go far away from Jewish ways, of which indeed they are ignorant.

In its article on Tertullian, the Catholic Encyclopedia paraphrases the pertinent parts of the Church father's work thus:

> ...your gods are images made on a cross framework, so you worship crosses. You say we worship the sun; so do you.[1]

Hence, an early Christian apologist not only felt compelled to address what appears to be a frequent contention that Christians were sun-worshippers and that Christ was the sun, but he also seems to be asserting that such a contention is more accurate than other observations about his religion!

These contentions of Christian sun worship persisted for centuries and remained prevalent enough by the time of St. Augustine (354-430 AD/CE) that he too was forced to protest them in his *Tractates on the Gospel of John* (XXXIV):

---

[1] *CE*, "Tertullian."

I think that what the Lord says, "I am the light of the world," is clear to those that have eyes, by which they are made partakers of this light: but they who have not eyes except in the flesh alone, wonder at what is said by the Lord Jesus Christ, "I am the light of the world." And perhaps there may not be wanting some one too who says with himself: *Whether perhaps the Lord Christ is that sun which by its rising and setting causes the day?* For there have not been wanting heretics who thought this. *The Manichæans have supposed that the Lord Christ is that sun which is visible to carnal eyes*, exposed and public to be seen, not only by men, but by the beasts. But the right faith of the Catholic Church rejects such a fiction, and perceives it to be a devilish doctrine: not only by believing acknowledges it to be such, but in the case of whom it can, proves it even by reasoning. Let us therefore reject this kind of error, which the Holy Church has anathematized from the beginning. *Let us not suppose that the Lord Jesus Christ is this sun which we see rising from the east, setting in the west; to whose course succeeds night, whose rays are obscured by a cloud, which removes from place to place by a set motion*: the Lord Christ is not such a thing as this. *The Lord Christ is not the sun that was made, but He by whom the sun was made*. For all things were made by Him, and without Him was nothing made." (Emphasis added.)

Thus, we have clear evidence that for centuries Christianity was perceived as sun worship and Christ as the sun. This fact represents a major clue as to who Jesus was, demonstrating the environment into which the gospel tale was introduced and the prevailing religious concepts against which his priesthood was competing.

The Sacred Spear and The Side-Wounding

Another related clue that may have been the result of a propaganda move occurs at Matthew 27:49, in which the RSV omits the phrase about the soldier taking a spear and piercing Jesus's side, with water and blood pouring out. Why was this scripture included or omitted in different versions, if the incident really happened? Like so much of the gospels, this part also seems to have been added for a specific purpose, rather than as a reflection of actual "history." In some of the cultures of the Roman Empire at the time, there evidently were other gods and sacrificial victims who were likewise portrayed as having been "side-wounded," including the Norse Father-God Odin, who was hung on a tree and wounded with a spear.[1] The political reasons for this interpolation, then, may include an attempt to integrate these other cultures of the empire into what would become the state religion.

The Empty Tomb Redux

We have already seen that in the raising of Lazarus we possess an old resurrection motif. In the verses concerning Christ's own resurrection, we find a plethora of alterations and interpolations between various copies of the gospels, evidently committed for a variety of doctrinal and political reasons. For example, missing from the RSV but present in other ancient texts is the phrase "of the Lord Jesus" appended to the end of Luke 24:3: "but when they went in they did not find the body." Leaving the phrase as is could give rise to the suspicion that the women had entered the wrong tomb, where there had never had a body in the first place, hence explaining the emptiness.

In the same vein, in the pericope at Luke 24:10-11 of Mary Magdalene and the other women telling the apostles about the empty tomb, the RSV ends with "but these words seemed to them an idle tale, and they did not believe them."

---

[1] Much like the Christian father-god incarnated in Christ, in the Norse mythology Father Odin is depicted as hanging on the "world-tree" in an act of sacrifice, while wounded by a spear. The old Norse text the Havamal, one of the Norse (prose) *Eddas*, contains a poem called the Runatal, stanza 138, in which Odin says: "I know that I hung, on a windy tree, for all of nine nights, *wounded with a spear*, and given to Óðinn, myself to myself, on that tree, which no man knows, from what roots it runs." (Thorgeirsson, emph. added.) Furthermore, the "All-Father" god Odin's invincible and beloved son, Balder, is pierced with a spear of mistletoe. Although Balder dies, in the time of the Ragnarok or Norse "apocalypse," he will be reborn or resurrected. This latter motif is similar to Christ's "Second Coming" depicted in Revelation. Moreover, as Jesus is the "Light of the World," so Balder is the "god of light." In this way, Balder is the savior of the world who brings peace. Like Jesus and the Twelve, Balder is also depicted with "12 knights."

Other ancient authorities append this verse with, "He is not here, but has risen," as if to emphasize that not only was the tomb empty but that Christ was resurrected, rather than having his body stolen, as was charged beginning in the second century.

Another verse found in "other ancient authorities" but absent from the RSV occurs at Luke 24:12, in the pericope of the Marys, et al., appearing at the empty tomb. The omitted verse has Peter running to the tomb, seeing empty cloths, and returning home wondering what had happened. Why does this verse appear in some ancient authorities but not others? And, if it actually reflected real history, how could Peter be unsure of what had transpired, since Christ had told him repeatedly that he would rise from the dead? Could Peter—who had witnessed so many miracles, including Christ's transfiguration—truly be so thickheaded as not to understand or accept what had occurred? If Peter is that dense, why would God/Jesus choose him as the "rock" upon which to build his kingdom of heaven? Perhaps this verse is a response to the charge that the disciples had stolen Jesus's body: If Peter is the ringleader of the church, chances are he would have been behind the plot to steal Christ's body. Hence, an interpolation causing the apostle to investigate and "wonder" at the empty tomb would make it seem as if he knew nothing about such a plot and certainly did not participate in it. The unique language in this verse, not found anywhere else in Luke-Acts but apparently copied from John or a source that John also used, validates the idea that this passage is an interpolation.

Indeed, the patent absurdity of Peter wondering what had happened occurs also at John 20:9, in which Peter and his companion disciple (John?) find the cloths in the empty tomb and are perplexed, "for as yet they did not know the scripture, that he must rise from the dead." This assertion that the disciples did not know the pertinent scripture (Hos 6:2) is ludicrous, in that Christ himself mentioned several times that he would rise again after his death, as at Matthew 16:21, 17:23 and 20:19. At Matthew 16:22, in fact, Peter himself is even portrayed as reacting to Jesus's prediction of his death and resurrection, so how could he possibly not know about it? The Pharisees too are portrayed at Matthew

27:63 as knowing that Christ claimed he would rise from the dead after three days—why wouldn't Jesus's closest disciples know this scripture? Rather than representing a "historical" event, it seems this illogical pericope concerning the empty tomb was added for one or more political purposes.

In this regard, in mocking so-called Pagan religion and comparing it to Christianity, apologist Minucius Felix declared the Egyptians also incorporated an empty tomb in their worship of the risen Osiris or Serapis. Said Felix:

> And you behold...and the tomb of your Serapis or Osiris empty....[1]

This comment refers to the myth of Osiris in which he is killed and dismembered, with his body parts "scattered about." Nevertheless, with the help of his wife, Isis, Osiris is restored to life for all eternity, again, as the Lord of the Resurrection. These facts suggest that the biblical empty tomb is no less mythical than that of Osiris/Serapis, and was inserted for a "political" reason, in order to incorporate this theme found within non-Christian religion.

Another "political" verse omitted from the RSV occurs at Luke 24:40, depicting the risen Christ as showing his hands and feet to the disciples, which may have been added in order to combat the Docetic heresy that Jesus existed only as a "phantom" and to emphasize that Christ did indeed undergo an actual physical resurrection.

The Ascension into Heaven

As discussed previously, the ascension of Christ is not mentioned by either of the two purported witnesses among the evangelists, Matthew and John, and the authenticity of the brief references in Mark and Luke is dubious. Rather than serving as a "historical" event, perhaps the ascension was added to the gospel tale also to testify against the Docetists that Christ did in fact possess a physical body. In addition, when we factor into the equation the words of Justin Martyr concerning the ascensions of *other* gods of the Roman Empire at the time, we possess scientific and logical reasons to suggest that Christ's story was no more historical and no

---

[1] Felix, *Octavius*, 21.

less mythical than theirs—and that their myths preceded the gospel tale.

As another example of the ascension to heaven in the tales of pre-Christian deities, Justin Martyr raises up certain "messianic prophecies" that he contends influenced the story of the god Bacchus/Dionysus:

> The prophet Moses, then, was, as we have already said, older than all writers; and by him, as we have also said before, it was thus predicted: "There shall not fail a prince from Judah, nor a lawgiver from between his feet, until He come for whom it is reserved; and He shall be the desire of the Gentiles, binding His foal to the vine, washing His robe in the blood of the grape." The devils, accordingly, when they heard these prophetic words, said that Bacchus was the son of Jupiter, and gave out that he was the discoverer of the vine, and they number wine [or, the ass] among his mysteries; and they taught that, having been torn in pieces, *he ascended into heaven.*[1]

In addition to the ascension, the vine, wine and ass also play prominent roles not only in the Dionysus myth but in Jesus's story as well, a fact that obviously did not escape Martyr's notice and that he felt compelled to address, in another stunning admission as to the unoriginality of the gospel tale. The fact cannot be denied that this theme of a divine Son of a heavenly Father whose emblems included the vine, wine, ass and ascension existed *before* the Christian era, for a variety of reasons, including the standard excuse given by the early Church fathers and many apologists today that the devil *anticipated* Christ's coming and imitated certain aspects of his life's story *before* his advent. Moreover, Martyr specifically associates the myth of Dionysus as having come from the "Mosaic prophecies" found at Genesis 49:10. Unlike various modern apologists, Justin does not *deny* that these correspondences between Jesus and Dionysus exist. Nor does he claim that the myth of Dionysus was based on that of Christ; he could not honestly do so, because *the Dionysian myth preceded the Christian*

---

[1] Martyr, *The First Apology*, LIV. (Emph. added.)

era. The same assertion can truthfully be made of the other correlations Martyr raised in his apology. Note that Martyr does not give a scriptural precedent here for Dionysus's ascension into heaven, which is nonetheless obviously pre-Christian.

Certain other apologists point to the Old Testament verses at Isaiah 14:12-14 in support of the notion that the ascensions of pre-Christian gods and heroes were based on the Jewish scriptures, rather than the other way around. Such a development would be very surprising, however, since the Jewish scriptures were zealously guarded from outsiders, who were not considered worthy of reading them. Nor is there any evidence of the Jewish stories being shared abundantly throughout the pre-Christian world, which was barely aware of the existence of Jews, Hebrews or Israelites until a few centuries prior to the Christian era. Moreover, today we know that Moses was not "older than all writers," as asserted by Justin. In fact, mainstream, scientific scholarship does not attribute the writing of Genesis to the Jewish lawgiver, and modern archaeology has proved that the writings of the Sumerians, for one, are far older than the alleged time of Moses. Additionally, in the Greek poet Homer's *Iliad*, composed beginning around 800 BCE, various gods are depicted with a number of the same characteristics as found in the much later Christianity, including the ascension of the immortal god Mars/Ares—*who had been wounded in the stomach with a spear*—into the "broad heavens," to reside with his father Jove/Zeus.[1] It is in regard to these "sons of Jove" that Justin Martyr also refers when he is admitting these all-important themes found within Christianity existed *prior to the Christian era*. In addition, this famous author, Homer, is likely among those to whom Dr. Moreland referred when he remarked that the New Testament writers utilized the works of the Jewish, Greek and Roman historians.

Instead of dismissing these pre-Christian themes or making irrational and unscientific excuses such as "the devil got there first," it would seem sensible to suggest that there is another reason for the ascension and other motifs in

---

[1] *The Iliad*, V, tr. Samuel Butler.

certain mythologies, based on visible natural phenomena, for example. The pertinent verses at Isaiah 14:12-14 that discuss ascending into heaven purport to represent the bragging of the character "Heylel," translated as *Lucifer*, the "Light-Bearer." Per Strong's (H1966), however, Heylel or Helel could also refer either to a king of Babylon *or* to the "morning star," i.e., the planet Venus. In fact, one of Venus's epithets in Greek was "Phosphoros," or "*Light bearer*." The RSV translates the term "Helel" at Isaiah 14:12 as, "O Day Star, son of Dawn!" In the Septuagint (3rd-1st cent. BCE), the word "Helel" is rendered as "(H)eosphoros," which just happens to be the name of a very old Greek god/titan who served as one aspect of the planet Venus. This god Eosphoros is mentioned in Homer's *Iliad* (23:226) and in Hesiod's *Theogony* (378), dating to the 9th and 8th centuries BCE, respectively. In determining the origins of the ascension in Isaiah, then, we may be compelled to seek a meaning beyond its appearance within the Old Testament, as the "morning star" was certainly known and visible to the ancient Gentiles aside and apart from the Jewish scriptures. In reality, it would appear that the Isaiah passage regarding Heylel or Helel was influenced by Greek mythology concerning the planet Venus, rather than the other way around.

Even if, against reason, we ignore the evidence from Homer, Justin Martyr and others of the ascension theme in pre-Christian cultures, we may surmise, particularly in consideration of the sloppy and haphazard manner in which the motif is introduced into the gospel story, that this pericope was adopted from the Old Testament, from the ascension into heaven not only of Heylel but also of Elijah (2 Kings 2:11), witnessed by his successor Elisha.[1] This assertion would once again demonstrate that the Old Testament was used as a *blueprint* in the creation of the gospel tale, with the authors simply cutting and pasting relevant passages, rather than recording actual historical events. Such an assumption ranks as far more logical than

---

[1] Like Elijah, the biblical characters Enoch (Gen 5:24) and Moses are said to have undergone "translations," which, although miraculous, do not constitute ascensions *per se*, where they are physically taken up into the air.

the improbability that Jesus's ascension represents a historical event.[1]

The Sayings of Jesus?

If the gospels truly represent the testimony of the advent of God on Earth, it would seem to be the epitome of blasphemy for a scribe decades and centuries later to change willfully not only the various pericopes but also the very words of the Lord Jesus Christ. If Jesus Christ really said these words, what business is it of the later scribes and copyists to change them? Yet, we find this type of blasphemous alteration to be the case in numerous instances, after some political or propagandistic purpose. How can this fact be explained? If the gospels were written by the people whose names are appended to them, under the direction and guidance of God himself, via the Holy Spirit, why did they need to be changed by "other ancient authorities?" Are all these later scribes likewise working under the infallible guidance of the Holy Spirit? And which version is correct? Did the Holy Spirit get it wrong the first time when inspiring the evangelists? But, if Jesus Christ *is* the Holy Spirit, why would he make mistakes in his words to begin with, such that he needed scribes down the road to alter or *fix* them?

Could all these seemingly sacrilegious and audacious alterations to Jesus's own words not be an indication that the story is *allegorical* and that the scribes were aware of this fact, such that they felt no fear or other factor that would prevent them from making such changes to "God's Word?"

We have already seen the several examples of verses and "prophecies" used in the creation of Christ's sayings and speeches, including the Sermon on the Mount. Indeed, as the *Universal Jewish Encyclopedia* states:

---

[1] Interestingly, evangelical Christian F.F. Bruce asserts that when the New Testament canon was finally drawn up, Luke-Acts, which had previously been one text, was divided into two, and the ending "and was carried up into heaven" was appended to Luke's gospel to "round out the narrative." (*NTD*, ch. III) Such a contention would also tend to verify that the ascension is a fictional afterthought.

...there is hardly a word which has been handed down as coming from Jesus which was not spoken or could not also have been spoken by Jewish teachers.[1]

The sayings of Christ have been boiled down by various scholars as representing the one place where we may find a "historical Jesus." Yet, as demonstrated, there is little new or original in Jesus's sayings that indicates a single individual about whom we can create a scientific biography. In other words, the rehashed, pieced-together sayings and speeches found in the New Testament are more reflective of the politics of the day than of a man named Jesus.

Over the centuries, there were many other changes in the gospel manuscripts based on doctrinal and political differences that developed within the church and its many branches, both orthodox and "heretical." For example, other verses tampered with to emphasize a political or doctrinal agenda include those which could be interpreted to indicate that Jesus was not always divine but had become "christed" through his baptism or other means. This perspective of a human Jesus becoming a divine Christ not at birth but later in life has been deemed "separationism."[2] Statements also seem to have been inserted in order to combat tendencies brought about by the apostle Paul, one such "anti-Pauline commentary" evidently appearing in the Sermon on the Mount, where Jesus is made to exhort his followers to adhere to the letter of the Mosaic Law, which Paul seems to abrogate on several occasions. The insistence of the immutability of the Mosaic Law at Matthew 5:19, for instance, seems to have been interpolated in order to combat Paul's laxity regarding the law.[3]

In consideration of all the various discrepancies, problems and patent proganda, it can be logically wondered whether the New Testament represents a "historical record" or "factual biography" of a stunningly miraculous life, or simply a propaganda tool for the priesthood to lay down its doctrines and dogma as they developed over the centuries. If the latter is true, even if the priesthood was under divine

---

[1] *UJE*, 85.
[2] Ehrman, *MJ*, 170, et seq.
[3] Friedlander, xviii.

guidance, could we honestly claim that the New Testament as it stands constitutes a reliable biography of the Lord and Savior Jesus Christ, who purportedly walked the Earth 2,000 years ago? At most, we could say that the NT represents an inaccurate portrayal based on the best or worst wishes of its composers. At the least, we would have to *entertain* the thought that the gospel story is *fictional*. Indeed, examining all these discrepancies, problems and errors in what is supposed to be an accurate and inerrant portrayal of actual historical events, one is prompted by honesty and logic to ask whether or not the evangelists and later scribes were just making it up as they went along!

Conclusion

"For we did not follow cleverly devised myths when we made known to you the power and coming of our Lord Jesus Christ, but we were eyewitnesses of his majesty."

2 Peter 1:16

There are many millions of people today who believe as they have been taught that the gospels are historical texts, infallibly inspired and inerrant, containing the sayings and deeds of the Son of God, who came to Earth 2,000 years ago in order to provide redemption and salvation. Because of the difficulties in believing all the miracles ascribed to Jesus, there are also many millions of people who do not believe Jesus is the Son of God who supernaturally confers anything upon anyone. This latter category of people usually perceives the gospel story as containing some history, including a general outline of the life of a man called Jesus, with the addition of a number of fables and fairytales. There is a third school of thought, however, that sees no evidence for either of the first two premises: In fact, this group apprehends that the story of Christ as recorded in the disparate and divergent gospels has so many difficulties, inconsistencies and fallacies that it cannot be taken literally. This faction avers that the gospels are works of fiction, much like *Gulliver's Travels* or any other clearly fictitious tale placed within a historical setting, and, shocking as it may sound, that no such historical person as Jesus Christ ever existed in the first place. This thesis evinces that the evidence shows most of the sayings, personality characteristics and biographical details found in the New Testament were cobbled together from earlier, pre-existing texts and traditions surrounding a variety of individuals, including both men and gods, both Jewish and Gentile, found widespread around the Roman Empire of the time.

Fingerprints of the Christ?

To begin with, while alike to the point where the synoptics largely constitute unoriginal copies of each other or common source-texts, the canonical gospels nevertheless diverge so widely in a variety of places, even in the same pericope, as to cast doubt upon the historicity of the tale and the inerrancy of the texts. In fact, so many problems and difficulties are presented by the four differing accounts— reflecting the obvious *disharmony* of the gospels—that a complex process of textual harmonization has been developed over a period of centuries. Hence, the gospels as they are represent a disharmonious mess that hardly appears to be "infallibly inspired" and "inerrant."

Moreover, the argument comparing the abundance of New Testament manuscripts with the relative lack thereof for other books of antiquity constitutes a logical fallacy. First, there was no concerted effort to proselytize these other books and to spread them around the world. Secondly, when Christians gained in power, they frequently destroyed whatever texts they could find, especially the writings of competing sects and religions. Thirdly, book industry statistics have demonstrated a tendency for *fiction* to vastly outsell non-fiction, meaning that the most abundantly printed texts have been *fictional*. If a concerted effort to publish a book and the abundance of its copies serve as indications of its veracity, then *The Da Vinci Code*—which contradicts the gospel story—would also need to be considered "true and historical fact." Moreover, there are thousands of ancient texts revolving around Egyptian religion as well, which would mean, by the abundance argument, that it too represented the "true religion." In reality, the abundance of manuscripts testifies to the power of religion but it does nothing to prove the veracity of the New Testament.

Furthermore, not only are the gospels anonymous but also the dates at which they unmistakably emerge in the historical record are far too late for them to serve as the writings of "eyewitnesses" or even companions to eyewitnesses. When scientifically scrutinized, the historical record clearly demonstrates the emergence of the gospels at the end of the second century.

Additionally, even though many times in the gospels Jesus was claimed to have been famed far and wide, not one historian of the era was aware of his existence, not even individuals who lived in, traveled around, or wrote about the relevant areas. The brief mentions of Christ, Christians or Christianity we possess from non-Christian sources are late and dubious as to their authenticity and/or value. Nor is there any valid scientific archaeological evidence demonstrating the gospel story to be true or even to support the existence of Jesus Christ. *Despite this utter lack of evidence, Christian apologists and authorities make erroneous and misleading claims that there are "considerable reports" and "a surprisingly large amount of detail" regarding the life of Jesus and early Christianity.*

Although it is widely believed that the character of Jesus Christ is unique and original, the fact is that many of the details of his life and virtually all of the sayings can be found in the Old Testament as concerns other "types of Christ" and assorted scenarios. In this manner, it can be logically suggested that the Old Testament served as a *blueprint* for the New. Indeed, even though apologists raise the issue of Old Testament prophecies as having been fulfilled in Jesus's life, what is more probable is that the writers of the New Testament constructed Christ's life precisely in order to follow these scriptures. It is a fact that the gospel writers refer repeatedly to certain events and sayings as "fulfillment of prophecy" found in one Old Testament book or another. It would be more rational to suggest that, rather than God descending on Earth to fulfill these supposed prophecies—and many of them certainly are *not* in reality prophecies at all—the authors of the gospels cut and paste the most germane scriptures that they considered to be characteristics of the coming messiah, weaving them together to *create* a *fictional* figure called "Jesus the Christ."

In addition, a scientific analysis and forensic investigation of the content of the gospels reveals a plethora of questions, impossibilities, difficulties, inconsistencies, illogic, fallacies, errors and repulsive doctrines. These numerous difficulties in turn cast doubt upon both the historicity and inerrancy of the New Testament. Moreover, the excuses proffered by apologists in maintaining biblical inerrancy at any cost frequently appear illogical and disreputable. For example, it is asserted that *only* the originals or autographs of the gospels were absolutely inerrant but that the copies are "adequate." In response to the query as to why the originals no longer exist, it is claimed that God destroyed the originals or autographs of the gospels in order not to tempt people to "tamper" with them. The fact remains, however, that the copies *were* tampered with, so destroying the originals made no difference, which the omniscient God surely would have known. In reality, the earliest extant manuscripts of the New Testament constitute some of the *most* flawed, riddled with errors—how could this be, and why would God allow such a development? Logically, honestly and with an eye to integrity, perhaps a better suggestion would be that the autographs were destroyed because they would prove *not* to be the inerrant products of infallibly inspired apostles and eyewitnesses to Christ's alleged advent. *The main problem with the doctrine of inerrancy is that in order for it to work, we must constantly avoid serious issues that strongly suggest it to be false*—and these confidence-destroying instances are not inconsequential. They are, in fact, numerous and significant.

After investigating this subject thoroughly, it becomes surprising that scholars and others can study biblical criticism yet still resolutely cling to their beliefs, which are frequently founded upon highly tenuous premises, as we have seen throughout this present work. The less "conservative" scholars will incorporate more of the logical and scientific criticisms into their assessment, while the conservatives obstinately defend the indefensible, including nonsensical tales, obvious inconsistencies, and puerile and deleterious interpretations of reality. This phenomenon can be explained not as a result of rational, scientific thought but by euphoria and childlike glee at the idea of miracles and magic: Blind believers become giddy with the supernatural and lose their natural sense.

To emphasize, the compulsion to view the gospels as inerrant and every detail therein as fact leaves the believer in a compromising position, because, as we have seen, there is so much obvious *disharmony* within the Bible that, again, over the centuries it has been necessary to develop an entire field of scholarship specifically designed to *harmonize* the texts. Some of this effort has been successful, while the rest will never be resolved to the satisfaction of those who demand greater evidence and practicality. As an example of needing to compromise integrity, honesty and rationality in order to adhere to the doctrines of inerrancy and literalism, while many Christian scholars over the centuries have admitted that "there *are* parallels between the Mysteries and Christianity"[1] and that "the miracle stories of the Gospels do in fact parallel literary forms found in pagan and Jewish miracle stories,"[2] they have also been compelled to come up with the most tortured and specious reasoning to separate out their own faith as "true" and "unique." Others simply deny the correspondences by waving them away.

In this manner, in a section called "The Gospels Are Vastly Different from Folklore and Myth," Christian apologist Dr. Norman Geisler argues against the idea that the gospels largely represent fictional accounts. Says he, "According to Form Criticism the Gospels are more like folklore and myth than historical fact." He then compares the canonical texts to the "apocryphal Gospels of the 2nd and third centuries," with their "fanciful tales of Jesus' alleged childhood miracles..."[3] In other words, unlike these other texts and stories, the gospels are not "fanciful." In consideration of the following aspects of the gospel story, it is difficult to see where Geisler and other apologists are able honestly to differentiate the story of Jesus from the myths and folklore of other cultures. *Which of the following implausibilities of the gospel tale do not fall into the "myth and folklore" category?*

- A virgin birth with an angel announcing it
- Astrologers following a star
- The heavens opening up, the Holy Spirit as a dove landing, and God's voice filling the air
- Battling with the Devil
- Changing water into wine
- Calming a storm

[1] Metzger, *HLS*, 8.
[2] Meier, II, 536.
[3] Geisler, *CA*, 320.

- Casting out demons into swine and causing the swine to drown themselves
- Raising a dead girl
- Instantly curing a 12-year hemorrhage through either touch or faith
- Walking on water
- Miraculously multiplying fish and loaves to feed multitudes
- Using spit to cure a blind man
- Transfiguring on the mount between Moses and Elijah
- Raising a dead man
- Destroying a fig tree by cursing it
- Dead saints rising out of their graves and wandering around town
- Jesus himself resurrecting from the dead
- Angels at Christ's empty tomb
- Ascending physically into heaven

As can be seen, there is plenty about the gospel tale that could be deemed "fanciful."

In a free society it is allowed that fundamentalist Christian preachers bring forth as fact that which cannot be conclusively proved and that which palpably stretches the credulity by bending natural laws and engaging in severe illogic, as well as adherence to repellant and disturbing notions. Unless such behavior constitutes willful fraud, it is protected under the First Amendment of the American Constitution, underscoring the freedom of speech so valued in civilized cultures. If, however, the educated elite know what is not true but present it as such in any event, are we not culpable of abusing the ignorance and gullibility of the innocents? Does such unethical behavior bode well for a society?

After discussing various churchmen who do not believe precisely as he does, in *The Gospel and the Greeks* conservative Christian scholar Ronald H. Nash writes:

> But how many serious blunders does a scholar have to make before his reputation is tarnished? If a scientist or even a historian made as many fanciful suggestions in his field that were as devoid of support as those of some of the theologians we have noticed,

or if he begged as many crucial questions, his reputation would surely suffer. But sometimes in theology, it appears, the reverse often holds. I am not sure that this speaks well for theology and biblical studies as intellectual disciplines.[1]

Although Nash's criticisms are ostensibly aimed at individuals who do not believe in the received history of the gospels and the inerrancy of the Bible, after conducting a scientific investigation, we must ask the same of those who *do* believe the received history of the gospel story and inerrancy of the Bible.

Terror in the Name of God

Even if the gospel story were true, the whole premise remains grotesque and irrational: Why would God need to take birth on Earth as his own son in order to give his life gruesomely as a ransom to himself so that he could remove magically and mystically the sins of his own creatures, which he created so badly in the first place that he needed to fix them? As we have seen, there are a number of other disturbing characteristics and repulsive doctrines in the Bible that should not be ignored or explained away, as they have been over the centuries.

For example, because of the gospel story, early Church fathers such as Tertullian and Origen asserted that Jesus's death at the hands of the Jews was the reason Jerusalem was destroyed by the Romans in 70 AD/CE. This sentiment towards Jews as "Christkillers," along with the attendant excuse of "punishment from God" for the catastrophes and persecutions suffered by Jews, has been pervasive throughout the history of Christianity, illustrating the need for honest and intense examination of Christian beliefs. No ideology with so much blood on its hands should be dealt with lightly, with kids' gloves, excused for anything so atrocious as the torture and deaths of millions. We of conscience are rightfully revolted by the evil and bloodthirsty behavior of Cambodia's Pol Pot in mercilessly slaughtering millions of people. Yet, if we attach a god of any sort to this bloodthirstiness, it becomes something "holy," as in "Holy

---

[1] Nash, 249.

Crusade," "Holy Jihad" or "Holy War." It is not a sane or healthy society that allows its hallowed spiritual institutions and ideologies to be soaked in blood and gore. It is equally unsound for those individuals who survive these bloody campaigns that have killed their own ancestors to turn around and support their perpetrators by being active and obedient members of their organizations, *especially* when they are no longer compelled by force to do so.

As concerns the quote in the Second Epistle of Peter with the author proclaiming not to follow "cleverly devised myths," we reply that we think he doth protest too much! This opinion becomes especially true considering that only conservative Christians believe 2 Peter to have been written by the apostle himself, the apostolic authorship having been contested even in ancient times, with the epistle deemed pseudepigraphical along with so many other writings from that era. This fact means that, in representing himself as an "eyewitness" to the events in the gospel story, the writer of 2 Peter is clearly being mendacious. Hence, his protest of not following "cleverly devised myths" ranks as disingenuous and, in reality, indicative of the opposite: To wit, they *were* following myths—otherwise, why even bring it up?

To reiterate, this issue is not to be taken lightly, as the threat of the global destruction of civilization by religious fanatics looms larger by the day. The devisers of clever fables have, in fact, established a bizarre and dangerous fairytale that is setting up the entire world for a decimating holocaust, apocalypse and Armageddon the likes of which we have never seen before. With its constant portrayal of "End Times" scenes of death and destruction, the fundamentalist Christian perception of reality, which incorporates the Muslim and Jewish paradigms as well, constitutes a deleterious delusion that teaches a variety of doctrines incompatible with the love for life but repeatedly calling for a cosmic battle that *ends* all life. With its eschatological doctrines of the Second Coming, Rapture and End Times, the Christian *myth* is, in the final analysis, unsustainable.

Vacuous Christianity?

In studying the gospel scenario in a manner as realistic and scientific as possible, we must factor in the entire environment into which it was placed, including both Jewish and Hellenistic milieus. The supernatural genesis of Christianity in a pristine vacuum untouched by the outside world ranks as simply ludicrous and utterly unsupportable by the facts of either the time or of human nature. The drama depicted by the Christian tale, as played out many times in the media over the millennia, plainly did not unfold in the manner in which it is believed. In other words, upon close inspection we remain left with a tale riddled with suspicious holes, indicating it did not happen as depicted.

The fact is that, when all the evidence is weighed, it would seem irresponsible and unscientific merely to assume the gospel tale as historical, either in part or as a whole. If we are to treat with disdain the myths of other cultures that possess a variety of similar themes and motifs as Christianity, are we not being hypocritical and arrogant, as well as culturally biased, to hold up the patent myths of the Judeo-Christian culture as "real" and "true?" In such an environment of multitudinous miracles, myths and fairytales, the most logical and honest perspective would be to approach the gospel story as if it is *not* historical until evidence is presented otherwise. This present book does not delve extensively into the extremely important field of comparative mythology in order to demonstrate other likely influences on the gospel tale.[1] Suffice it to say, however, that such material is highly germane to this subject. Regardless of how much we study the Bible, without placing the Christ story within its historical milieu, surrounded by the myths and traditions of other supernatural gods, sons of gods and legendary heroes, we will never know who Jesus really was.

Instead of a supernatural being from heaven, could Jesus actually be a fictional character created for political purposes? There is more than enough evidence to make such a suggestion, particularly in consideration of the Jewish environment of the time. The Jews were waiting—and *agitating*—for a messiah or messiahs, one peaceful and another warlike; yet, none powerful enough was forthcoming. Could it be that, as they had done in the past with certain

---

[1] For a more thorough study of the comparative religion and mythology concerning the gospel story, see *The Christ Conspiracy* and *Suns of God*.

biblical characters created for inspirational purposes, Jewish authorities took matters into their own hands in order to *create* a messiah of their own making? With the scriptures in front of them, as well as certain non-Jewish influences, it would be a simple matter of firstly cutting and pasting various "messianic prophecies" and assorted other appropriate pericopes in order to compete with the gods and heroes of other cultures. The next decades would be spent in a concerted effort that eventually included powerful Gentile leaders to place this fictional and created savior into history.

In discussing the scholarship that suggests Jesus to be as mythical as Hercules and other gods, many have expressed surprise at such an assertion, with some suggesting that the Christ of the New Testament possesses a personality "too definite and too coherent to be regarded as unreal."[1] This contention constitutes a logical fallacy, however, as the same argument could be applied to many *mythical* and *literary* figures, including Zeus, Gulliver, Tom Sawyer and Harry Potter, to name but a few.

It is because there appears to be so little honest admission—as well as, often, *civil response*—that many people feel put off and antagonistic toward biblical stories and doctrines. Instead of saying, "Well now, you're right— that doesn't sound too good," the rejoinder is all too often to attack the person making the observation. Judging by its "fruits," it seems to many people that Christianity teaches disrespect of human beings, such that its defenders feel they can personally attack those not convinced of the faith, addressing them with little respect and making offensive comments and insults. Among others, the Christian teaching that people are "born in sin" appears to make fervent believers hostile towards others. Other scriptures calling for the deaths and/or torture of "evildoers," as well as remarks concerning "anti-Christs" as at 1 John 4:3 or the condemnation of non-believers at Mark 16:16—categories consisting of *people who do not believe in Jesus*—have contributed to an atmosphere of hatred and prejudice against individuals who may be moral and ethical but who

---

[1] *UJE*, 83.

simply cannot believe in something that may in fact be spurious and thus go *against* their morality.

With so much of our global social structure based on holy writ of some sort or another, it is imperative that we examine thoroughly our sacred cows and not shirk from exposing them to the bright sunlight. In consideration of the current political climate, which includes an ardent movement to "fulfill prophecy" by bringing about Armageddon and all of the attendant "End Times" tribulations and horrors, the issue of who Jesus was is not to be taken lightly. We should not blindly follow mummified traditions and ancient texts that could very well prove to be misleading, misinterpreted and mythical. Leading our lives and creating—or destroying—our futures based on such texts is perilous and irresponsible. It is paramount, therefore, that we consider the possibility that, rather than being the omnipotent Son of God, Jesus Christ is a manmade, literary character devised for a variety of purposes that no longer serve the greater good of humanity.

Bibliography

"A Harmonized Chronology of the Resurrection,"
www.shoutingman.com/bible/harmony/resharmonyhandout.pdf

"An Unpublished Fragment of the Fourth Gospel," John
Rylands University Library of Manchester,
rylibweb.man.ac.uk/data1/dg/text/fragment.htm

"Christian Authors Database: Bible Reference Authors,"
faith.propadeutic.com/authors/bibleref.html

"Dominus Flevit—the site where 'The Lord Wept,'"
198.62.75.1/www1/ofm/san/TSflevitmn.html

"From Jesus to Christ: Primary Sources,"
www.pbs.org/wgbh/pages/frontline/shows/religion/maps/primary/
pliny.html

"From Jesus to Christ: The Story of the Storytellers,"
www.pbs.org/wgbh/pages/frontline/shows/religion/story/gospels.
html

"Jesus Outside the New Testament,"
www.mystae.com/restricted/reflections/messiah/sources.html

"Prophecies of the Old Testament fulfilled in Jesus Christ,"
www.biblia.com/jesusbible/prophecies.htm

"Provenance of Tacitus' *Annals*,"
answers.google.com/answers/threadview?id=31122

"Rylands Library Papyrus P52,"
en.wikipedia.org/wiki/Papyrus_52

"Testimonium Flavianum; in what languages where,"
www.iidb.org/vbb/archive/index.php/t-212054.html

"'The camel and the eye of the needle', Matthew 19:24, Mark
10:25, Luke 18:25,"
www.biblicalhebrew.com/nt/camelneedle.htm

"The Temptation of Buddha by Mara and his Daughters," The
Amica Library,
www.davidrumsey.com/amico/amico12101415-38449.html

Acharya S, *Suns of God: Krishna, Buddha and Christ
Unveiled*, AUP, IL, 2004.

— *The Christ Conspiracy: The Greatest Story Ever Sold*,
Adventures Unlimited Press, IL, 1999.

—"Bone Box No Proof of Jesus,"
www.truthbeknown.com/ossuary.htm

Alexander, Bishop, "The Gospels,"
www.fatheralexander.org/booklets/english/gospel.htm
Amirault, Gary, "The King James Bible is 'Inerrant?'"
www.tentmaker.org/Biblematters/KJV.htm
Anchor Bible Dictionary, The, Doubleday, 1992.
Ankerberg, John and Weldon, John, "The Historical Reliability
of the New Testament Text,"
www.johnankerberg.com/Articles/_PDFArchives/editors-
choice/EC2W1002.pdf
—"The Truth About the Founder of Christianity,"
www.ankerberg.com/Articles/_PDFArchives/historical-
Jesus/HJ2W0506.pdf
Arlandson, James, "Discovering and Classifying New
Testament Manuscripts,"
www.biblicalstudies.org.uk/pdf/jma/nts-mss_3_arlandson.pdf
Augustine, *Tractates on the Gospel of John,*
www.newadvent.org/fathers/1701034.htm
Barker, Dan, "Leave No Stone Unturned: An Easter
Challenge for Christians," frf.org/books/lfif/?t=stone
Bernhard, Andrew, tr., *The Infancy Gospel,*
www.gospels.net/translations/infancythomastranslation.html
Bible Encyclopedia, "Capernaum,"
www.christiananswers.net/dictionary/capernaum.html
Bible Study Guide,
www.mindprod.com/religion/biblestudy.html
Blank, Wayne, "Paul in Rome,"
www.keyway.ca/htm2000/20000203.htm
Blomberg, Craig L., "The Historical Reliability of the Gospels,"
www.4truth.net/site/apps/nl/content3.asp?c=hiKXLbPNLrF&b=78
4441&ct=981289
Blue Letter Bible, "Harmony of the Gospels,"
www.blueletterbible.org/tmp_dir/c/1158536290-8386.html
Blunt, John Henry, *Dictionary of Sects, Heresies,
Ecclesiastical Parties, and Schools of Religious Thought,*
Rivingtons, London, 1874
Botti, Joe; Dixon, Tom and Steinman, Alex, "The Problem of
Apparent Chronological Contradictions in the Synoptics,"
www.xenos.org/MINISTRIES/crossroads/OnlineJournal/issue1/
synoprob.htm
Bradlaugh, Charles, "Who Was Jesus Christ?"
www.infidels.org/library/historical/charles_bradlaugh/who
_was_jesus.html

Briggs, Charles A., "The Use of the Logia of Matthew in the Gospel of Mark," *Journal of Biblical Literature*, Vol. 23, No. 2 (1904), pp. 191-210.

Bruce, F.F., *New Testament History*, Doubleday, NY, 1971.
—*New Testament Documents: Are They Reliable?*
www.worldinvisible.com/library/ffbruce/ntdocrli/ntdocont.htm

Bucher, Richard, "Caesar Augustus, Quirinius, and the Census," www.orlutheran.com/html/census.html

Budge, E.A. Wallis, *The Egyptian Book of the Dead*, Dover, NY, 1967.

Carlson, Paul, "New Testament Contradictions,"
www.infidels.org/library/modern/paul_carlson/nt_contradictions.html

Carlson, Stephen C., "Brent Nongbri on P52,"
www.hypotyposeis.org/weblog/2005/08/brent-nongbri-on-p52.html

Carr, Steven, "Textual Reliability of the New Testament,"
www.bowness.demon.co.uk/reli2.htm

Carrier, Richard, "Luke and Josephus,"
www.infidels.org/library/modern/richard_carrier/lukeandjosephus.html
—"Thallus: An Analysis (1999),"
www.infidels.org/library/modern/richard_carrier/thallus.html

Cassels, Walter, *Supernatural Religion: an inquiry into the reality of divine revelation*, D.M. Bennett, NY, 1879.

Catholic Encyclopedia, "Brethren of the Lord,"
www.newadvent.org/cathen/02767a.htm
—"Desiderius Erasmus,"
www.newadvent.org/cathen/05510b.htm
—"Ecclesiastical Art,"
www.newadvent.org/cathen/05248a.htm
—"Gospel of St. Matthew,"
www.newadvent.org/cathen/10057a.htm
—"Gospel of St. Mark,"
www.newadvent.org/cathen/09674b.htm
—"Gospel of St. Luke,"
www.newadvent.org/cathen/09420a.htm
—"Gospel of St. John,"
www.newadvent.org/cathen/08438a.htm
—"Gospel and Gospels,"
www.newadvent.org/cathen/06655b.htm
—"Joseph," www.newadvent.org/cathen/08506a.htm

—"Julius Africanus,"
www.newadvent.org/cathen/08565a.htm
—"Mithraism," www.newadvent.org/cathen/10402a.htm
—"St. Papias," www.newadvent.org/cathen/11457c.htm
—"Tertullian," www.newadvent.org/cathen/14520c.htm
—"Theophilus," www.newadvent.org/cathen/14625a.htm
Clement of Alexandria, *Exhortation to the Heathen*,
www.newadvent.org/fathers/020804.htm
—*The Stromata*, tr. Rev. William Wilson,
www.mb-soft.com/believe/txv/clemena6.htm
Coats, Daryl, "The Two Lies,"
av1611.com/kjbp/articles/coats-twolies.html
Craig, William Lane, "The Evidence for Jesus,"
www.leaderu.com/offices/billcraig/docs/rediscover2.html
Crossan, John Dominic, *The Historical Jesus: The Life of a
Mediterranean Jewish Peasant*, Harper, San Francisco,
1991.
Crossan, John Dominic and Reed, Jonathan L., *Excavating
Jesus: Beneath the Stones, Behind the Texts*,
HarperCollins, 2001.
Crossan, John Dominic and Watts, Richard G., *Who Is
Jesus?: Answers to Your Questions about the Historical
Jesus*, Westminster John Knox Press, 1999.
Dods, Marcus, "Introductory Note to Theophilus of Antioch,"
www.ccel.org/ccel/schaff/anf02.iv.i.html
Doherty, Earl, *The Jesus Puzzle*, Canadian Humanist
Publications, 1999.
—"Dating Gospel Fragments,"
pages.ca.inter.net/~oblio/rfset5.htm
Doughty, Darrell J., "Rescript of Hadrian Regarding
Treatment of Christians,"
users.drew.edu/ddoughty/Christianorigins/persecutions/hadrian.
html
—"Tacitus' Account of Nero's Persecution of Christians,"
users.drew.edu/ddoughty/Christianorigins/persecutions/tacitus.html
Ehrman, Bart, *Misquoting Jesus*, Harper, San Francisco,
2005.
—"Lecture One: Text and Interpretation: The Exegetical
Significance of the 'Original' Text,"
rosetta.reltech.org/TC/vol05/Ehrman2000a.html
—"Text and Tradition: The Role of New Testament

Manuscripts in Early Christian Studies,"
rosetta.reltech.org/TC/vol05/Ehrman2000b.html
Elliot, Rich, "Evolution of the Uncial Script,"
www.skypoint.com/members/waltzmn/UncialScript.htm
—"The Textus Receptus,"
www.skypoint.com/members/waltzmn/TR.html
Encyclopedia Britannica, "Sacred Doves,"
www.britannica.com/eb/topic-407449/article-9055129
Epiphanius, *Panarion*, tr. J.P. Migne,
www.christianhospitality.org/texts/epiph-pan-08-pg41-0873-
0972.pdf
Eusebius, *The History of the Church*, Penguin, NY, 1989.
Felix, Minucuis, *Octavius*, newadvent.org/fathers/0410.htm
Friedlander, Gerald, *The Jewish Sources of the Sermon on
the Mount* (1911), KTAV Publishing, NY, 1969.
Geisler, Norman L., *Christian Apologetics*, OM Books,
Secunderabad, 1999.
Geisler, Norman and Rowe, Thomas, *When Critics Ask: A
Popular Handbook on Bible Difficulties*, Baker Books, MI,
1992.
Giles, J.A., *The Complete Works of Venerable Bede: In the
Original Latin*, vol. X, Whittaker and Co., London, 1844.
Gilman, Jean, "Jerusalem Burial Cave Reveals: Names,
Testimonies of First Christians," *Jerusalem Christian
Review*, www.leaderu.com/theology/burialcave.html
Gleghorn, Michael, "Ancient Evidence for Jesus from Non-
Christian Sources," www.probe.org/content/view/18/77/
Goldberg, G.J., "The Mystery of the Testimonium
Flavianum," members.aol.com/fljosephus/testhist.htm
Habermas, Gary, *The Historical Jesus: Ancient Evidence for
the Life of Christ*,
www.garyhabermas.com/books/historicaljesus/historicaljesus.htm
—"The Lost Tomb of Jesus: A Response to the Discovery-
Channel Documentary,"
www.garyhabermas.com/articles/The_Lost_Tomb_of_Jesus/
losttombofjesus_response.htm
—"Why I Believe the New Testament is Historically
Reliable," www.theapologiaproject.org/WHYIBE~1.pdf
Hamblin, William and Peterson, Daniel, "The Evangelical Is
Our Brother," www.tinyurl.com/2mwzwx

Head, Peter M., "New Testament Manuscripts on Papyrus" (2003),
www.tyndale.cam.ac.uk/Tyndale/staff/Head/NTPapyri.htm

Heath, Dunbar Isadore, *Phoenician Inscriptions*, Oxford University, 1873.

Henry, Matthew, "Commentary on John 2," *et al.*,
www.blueletterbible.org

Herodotus, *The History*,
classics.mit.edu/Herodotus/history.2.ii.html

Hesiod, Homeric Hymns, tr. Hugh G. Evelyn-White, Loeb Classical Library, 1914.

Hijmans, Steven, "In search of St. Peter's Tomb,"
www.expressnews.ualberta.ca/article.cfm?id=794

Hippolytus, *Refutation of All Heresies*,
www.newadvent.org/fathers/050110.htm

Homer, *The Iliad*, tr. Samuel Butler,
classics.mit.edu/Homer/iliad.5.v.html

Hooker, Richard, "Tacitus (c. 55 -117 CE): Nero's persecution of the Christians,"
www.wsu.edu:8080/~wldciv/world_civ_reader/world_civ_reader_1/tacitus.html

Humphreys, Kenneth, *Jesus Never Existed*, Historical Review Press, 2005.

Hurtado, Larry W., *The Earliest Christian Artifacts: Manuscripts and Christian Origins*, Wm. B. Eerdmans, 2006.

Interpreter's Dictionary of the Bible, The, vol. IV, R-Z, Abingdon Press, 1996.

Ireland, John D., "Padhana Sutta: The Great Struggle,"
myweb.ncku.edu.tw/~lausinan/AccessToInsight/html/canon/sutta/khuddaka/suttanipata/snp3-02a.html

Irenaeus, *Against Heresies*,
www.newadvent.org/fathers/0103311.htm

Jerome, *Against Jovinianus*,
www.newadvent.org/fathers/3009.htm
—*De Viris Illustribus*,
www.newadvent.org/fathers/2708.htm

Kirby, Peter, "The Gospel of Mark,"
www.earlychristianwritings.com/mark.html

Leidner, Harold, *The Fabrication of The Christ Myth*, Survey Press, 2000.

Kuchinsky, Yuri, "The Rylands Papyrus Fraud,"
www.trends.ca/~yuku/bbl/rylands.htm

Lindemans, Micha, "Balder," *Encyclopedia Mythica*,
www.pantheon.org/articles/b/balder.html

Lowder, Jeffrey, "Josh McDowell's 'Evidence for Jesus'—Is it
Reliable?,"
www.infidels.org/library/modern/jeff_lowder/jury/chap5.html
—"The Jury Is In: Luke and Quirinius,"
www.infidels.org/library/modern/jeff_lowder/jury/
luke_and_quirinius.html

MacMullen, Ramsay, *Paganism in the Roman Empire*, Yale
University, 1981.

Martyr, Justin, *Dialogue with Trypho*,
www.ccel.org/ccel/schaff/anf01.viii.iv.ciii.html
—*The First Apology*,
www.newadvent.org/fathers/0126.htm

McCallum, Dennis and DeLashmutt, Gary, "Principles
Involved in Harmonizing the Synoptic Gospels,"
www.xenos.org/essays/harmony.htm

McDowell, Josh, *New Evidence that Demands a Verdict*,
Thomas Nelson Publishers, Nashville, 1999.

Meier, John P., *A Marginal Jew: Rethinking the Historical
Jesus*, v. I & II, Doubleday, 1991 & 1994.

Metzger, Bruce M., "Historical and Literary Studies: Pagan,
Jewish and Christian," www.frontline-
apologetics.com/mystery_religions_early_christianity.htm

Moreland, James P., "The Rationality Of Belief In Inerrancy,"
www.biblicalstudies.org.uk/article_inerrancy_moreland.html
—"What Would Jesus Think or Do?"
www.trueu.org/Academics/LectureHall/A000000599.cfm

Murdock, D.M., see "Acharya S."

Murphy-O'Connor, Jerome, *The Holy Land: An Oxford
Archaeological Guide from Earliest Times to 1700*, Oxford
University Press, 1998.

Nash, Ronald H., *The Gospel and the Greeks*, P&R
Publishing, NJ, 2003.

Origen, *Contra Celsus*,
www.newadvent.org/fathers/0416.htm
—*Homily on Luke*, www.questia.com/read/88940831#

Ovid, *Metamorphoses*, tr. A.D. Melville, Oxford University
Press, 1987.

Pearse, Roger, "Josephus: the Main Manuscripts of 'Antiquities,'" www.tertullian.org/rpearse/manuscripts/josephus_antiquities.htm

Peterson, F. Paul, *Peter's Tomb Recently Discovered In Jerusalem*, biblelight.net/peters-jerusalem-tomb.htm

Philo, The Works of, tr. C.D. Yonge, Hendrickson Publishers, USA, 2000.

Plato, *Phaedrus*, tr. Benjamin Jowett, ccat.sas.upenn.edu/jod/texts/phaedrus.html

Pliny/Trajan Correspondence, tr. K.C. Hanson, www.kchanson.com/ANCDOCS/latin/pliny.html

Price, Robert M., *The Pre-Nicene New Testament: Fifty-Four Formative Texts*, Signature Books, Salt Lake City, 2006.

Reber, George, *Therapeutae: St. John Never in Asia Minor* (1872), Kessinger, 2003.

Reinhold Warttig Mattfeld y de la Torre, Walter, "Is the Bible 'Inerrant' or 'Errant'?", www.bibleorigins.net/BibleInerrancyOrErrancy.html

Renouf, Peter Le Page, *The Egyptian Book of the Dead*, The Society of Biblical Archaeology, London, 1904.

Scheidel, Walter, "Roman population size: the logic of the debate," www.princeton.edu/~pswpc/pdfs/scheidel/050705.pdf

Schneemelcher, Wilhelm and Wilson, R. MacLachlan, *New Testament Apocrypha*, Westminster John Knox Press, 2003.

Septuagint, The, www.septuagint.org/LXX/

Smith, Ben C., "Phlegon of Tralles on the passion phenomena," www.textexcavation.com/phlegontestimonium.html
—"Thallus on the passion phenomena," www.textexcavation.com/thallustestimonium.html
—"The Jewish-Christian gospels," www.textexcavation.com/jewishgospels.html

Sorenson, David, "Erasmus, King James, and His Translators," av1611.com/kjbp/articles/sorenson-ch10-1.html

Staggs, Brandon, "Aren't archaic words in the KJV in need of updating?", av1611.com/kjbp/faq/archaic.html
—"Aren't modern translations based on better manuscripts?", av1611.com/kjbp/faq/better-

manuscripts.html

—"If we have a perfect Bible in English, don't we need one in every other language?", av1611.com/kjbp/faq/language.html

—"King James Bible and other versions: why does it matter?", av1611.com/kjbp/

—"Shouldn't we value the original autographs above any mere translation?", av1611.com/kjbp/faq/originals.html

Strobel, Lee, *The Case for Christ*, Zondervan, 1998.

Strong's Biblical Concordance, www.blueletterbible.org/search.html#strongs

Suarez, Thomas, *Early Mapping of Southeast Asia*, Tuttle Publishing, 1999.

Suetonius, *The Lives of the Twelve Caesars*, tr. J.C. Rolfe, penelope.uchicago.edu/Thayer/E/Roman/Texts/Suetonius/12Caesars/home.html

—*Vita Divi Claudii*, penelope.uchicago.edu/Thayer/L/Roman/Texts/Suetonius/12Caesars/Claudius*.html

Tacitus: The Annals, www.sacred-texts.com/cla/tac/a15040.htm

Taylor, Joan E., *Christians and the Holy Places: The Myth of Jewish-Christian Origins*, Oxford University Press, 1993.

Tenney, Merrill C., *New Testament Survey*, Wm. B. Eerdmans Publishing Company, MI, 1985.

Tertullian, *Ad Nationes*, www.newadvent.org/fathers/03061.htm

—*Against Marcion*, www.newadvent.org/fathers/03124.htm

—*Apology*, www.newadvent.org/fathers/0301.htm

Theophilus, *Ad Autolychum*, www.ccel.org/ccel/schaff/anf02.iv.html

Theron, Daniel J., *Evidence of Tradition: selected source material for the study of the history of the early Church—introduction and canon of the New Testament*, Bowes & Bowes, London, 1957.

Thorgeirsson, Haukur, "Havamal," www.hi.is/~haukurth/norse/reader/runatal.html

Till, Farrell, "The Absence of Evidence," www.infidels.org/library/magazines/tsr/2002/2/022abs.html

Tyndale Bible Dictionary, "Bible, Manuscripts and Text of the (New Testament)," Tyndale House Publishers, 2001.

Universal Jewish Encyclopedia, The, v. 6, UJE, Co., Inc., NY, 1948.

van Minnen, Peter, "Dating the Oldest New Testament Manuscripts," scriptorium.lib.duke.edu/papyrus/texts/manuscripts.html

Van Voorst, Robert E., *Jesus Outside the New Testament: An Introduction to the Ancient Evidence,* Wm. B. Eerdmans, 2000.

Waite, Charles, *History of the Christian Religion to the Year Two Hundred,* Dr. Carroll Bierbower, OR, 1992.

Wharton, Edward C., "Jesus and History," web.archive.org/web/20060117074350/www.scripturessay.com/cev1.html

West, Jim, "The Tomb that Keeps on Giving," drjimwest.wordpress.com/2007/03/13/the-tomb-that-keeps-on-giving/

Whitson, William, *The Complete Works of Josephus,* Kregel Publications, MI, 1981.

Whittaker, Charles Richard, *Rome and Its Frontiers: The Dynamics of Empire,* Routledge, 2004.

Wilkins, Michael J. and Moreland, J.P., *Jesus Under Fire,* Zondervan, 1995.

Wilson, Horace Hayman, tr., *The Vishnu Purana* (1840), www.sacred-texts.com/hin/vp/vp121.htm

Witherington, Ben, *John's Wisdom: A Commentary on the Fourth Gospel,* Westminster John Knox, 1995.
—"Tomb of the (Still) Unknown Ancients," www.opinionjournal.com/taste/?id=110009735

Yamauchi, Edwin, *The Stones and the Scriptures (Evangelical Perspectives),* J.B. Lippincott Co., 1972.

Index

D.M. Murdock, also known as "Acharya S," majored in Classics, Greek Civilization, at Franklin & Marshall College in Lancaster, PA. She is also a Member of the American School of Classical Studies at Athens, Greece. Ms. Murdock is the author of the controversial books *The Christ Conspiracy: The Greatest Story Ever Sold* and *Suns of God: Krishna, Buddha and Christ Unveiled*. Many of Ms. Murdock's articles on the subjects of comparative religion, mythology and astrotheology may be found on her website TruthBeKnown.com.

Printed in the United States
104177LV00001B/45/A